CORE OF THE UNIVERSE

CORE

OF THE

UNIVERSE

GOD'S VISION FOR LOVE, SEX, AND INTIMACY

HIGH NOON

Print ISBN: 978-1-7366668-0-7
E-book ISBN: 978-1-7366668-1-4

Printed in the United States of America

Acknowledgments

This Hoon Dok Hwe study book is the first of its kind. It is based on the words of Reverend Sun Myung Moon and Dr. Hak Ja Han Moon, who are referred to in this book as True Father and True Mother respectively, and as True Parents together. Each chapter explores a theme True Father spoke about with great passion. His clear explanations about God's design and purpose for sexual love inspired us to have open, thought-provoking discussions in this book. Without his courage and leadership in life, this book could not have been written. True Father was a student of life from boyhood and had deep experiences with God in prayer as he sought to understand the core of our existence. What he discovered is that the sexual organs are at the center of God's ideal world. He taught us a new paradigm about the sexual organs of men and women.

This book is a collaboration of people from different backgrounds, each contributing something unique to the understanding of True Parents' words on this topic. I am very grateful to the writing team, which consisted of Poppy Paviour Richie, Robert Cunningham, and my beloved wife, Mitsue. Poppy, co-author of a popular character education curriculum for K-12, *Discovering the Real Me*, and other educational publications, saw this project through from beginning to end. Robert, a long-time supporter of High Noon's work, recently received the Marriage Blessing, offering a fresh perspective as a young husband, and supported this book as project manager. Even though English is Mitsue's second language, she always had much to contribute both in substance and, surprisingly, grammar.

I am also grateful to Sammy Uyama, director of High Noon, and Andrew Love, the leading content developer at High Noon, for bringing their wise opinions to the review team. Sammy helped in the writing of several chapters as well. Dr. Tyler Hendricks, professor emeritus at the Unification Theological Seminary, was always available when I had a theological question or when I was confused about True Parents' words, and often brought clarity.

Mai Thurston and Heather Thalheimer contributed as editors. Heather gave great advice about how to fine-tune the book. She helped us draw out the love and compassion embedded in True Father's words so that readers could feel the heart behind his often strong and challenging words. Mai played a key role in keeping the chapters consistent in tone and in organizing the citations.

I am thankful for all those who so openly shared life experiences with their personal testimonies and allowed us to include them in this book. I am grateful to the staff members of the Blessed Marriage Project and School of Love. I am indebted to everyone who attended High Noon programs in America, Europe, Korea, and Southeast Asia. Their sincere questions and desperate desires to create radiant marriages through the Marriage Blessing touched my soul and caused me to deep-dive for answers in True Parents' words. It was through speaking with participants all over the world that we at High Noon came to realize the urgent need for education on sexuality that is grounded in teachings of the *Divine Principle* and in True Parents' words. Mitsue and I were surprised at how many people approached us at our programs seeking advice about their relationships, pornography, and other intimate issues.

I am so grateful for Mitsue. As she searched for True Parents' quotes for the book, she'd often begin to cry, touched by True Father's words about the holiness and preciousness of the sexual organs. For Mitsue and I, this book has been the continuation of a life-long journey. We hope you will be moved when reading True Parents' words about God's ideal for sex. Our experience has been that when we read this content as a couple, we feel a joy beyond what we could ever have imagined. I am eternally grateful to True Parents. Their profound understanding and guidance about what sex was created for has the power to change the world.

David Wolfenberger
High Noon Founder

Preface

For many of us, the subject of sex brings up feelings of shame, embarrassment, and confusion. As a result, most people avoid talking about it even though we all share a longing to experience and understand love and sexuality. The purpose of this book is to share a clear and hopeful vision from the teachings of Reverend Sun Myung Moon and Dr. Hak Ja Han Moon, who we affectionately call True Parents. Their revolutionary insight is that the sexual relationship between a husband and wife *is* the very core of the universe. This resource can help young adults grow their sexual integrity in preparation for marriage and support blessed couples[1] to create heavenly intimacy.

We acknowledge that not everyone is in the place they may want to be in terms of their habits and attitudes regarding sex or their relationship with their spouse. We encourage you to start from wherever you are and to bravely take steps towards realizing God's beautiful ideal for His gift of sexuality.

Few people have had healthy conversations about sexual intimacy growing up in their family, and even fewer have had good role models. In today's culture, we see a lot of misinformation about sex coming out of schools, Hollywood, and the internet. Because sex can be an embarrassing subject, there has been little to no conversation about it in the home. As quiet as most families are about sex, churches are often more silent, which has led many to believe that God has nothing to say on the topic either. Conse-

---

1. Blessed couples refer to the men and women who participated in the Marriage Blessing Ceremony officiated by True Parents, thereby receiving the Marriage Blessing and becoming eternal husbands and wives.

quently, internet pornography has replaced the home and the church as a major source of sex education.

True Father was not silent on the subject of sex. He wanted people to understand that the sexual organs are God's most precious gift to us. Through them, a husband and wife can experience love in their marriage bed and experience God in a greater capacity than they ever could as individuals. In the *Divine Principle*, we learn how the misuse of sex caused the Fall of our first human ancestors, and from there, all the problems in the world. It's only through True Father's words on the holiness of the sexual organs that we understand why the misuse of this sacred act caused the greatest tragedy for God and for all humankind.

Even though there are volumes of speeches from True Father about the sexual organs and related topics, people are often unaware these speeches exist. When they do stumble upon them, they find it is uncomfortable to discuss the content and challenging to see how it applies to their lives. This leaves many confused about essential questions regarding sex.

This Hoon Dok Hwe[2] study book is the first to compile True Parents' quotes from hundreds of speeches to create a comprehensive understanding of God's vision for sex. It is organized into six sections: Core of the Universe, God's Design for Sex, Conjugal Love, Absolute Sex, The Fall, and Restoration.

Each chapter begins with True Parents' words. This is followed by Sharing Thoughts, in which we extract and explain the central theme. You may be surprised and challenged by some of True Parents' teachings on the subject of sex. We ask you to keep an open mind. There is a story in each chapter highlighting historical events, great people, or fables to support your understanding and discuss the main theme. Every chapter includes a segment on Making It Real, showing how to apply the theme to your lives, and ending with suggested discussion questions. If you are reading this together with your spouse, small group, or family members, these stories and questions can provide a path to a more free and open discussion about sex.

---

2. Hoon Dok Hwe is a tradition established by True Parents whereby we read the eight holy scriptures they have specified and learn God's Word together as a family.

We are confident that this book has something for you regardless of your stage in life. It can help you develop sexual integrity and prepare you for your future Marriage Blessing for those who are single. Married couples can find inspiration to create a more beautiful and enriching relationship. Parents can be empowered to guide their children toward healthy sexuality. When we understand the full measure of what Heavenly Parent[3] intended for us to experience as husband and wife, we can create blessed couples that radiate with joy and change the world with love.

---

3. In our faith community, we often refer to God as our Heavenly Parent, embodying all masculine and feminine nature. For simplicity, in this book, we will refer to God using masculine pronouns only.

Note on True Parents' Quotes

True Parents' quotes included in this book were pulled from various speeches and books, the original version and the 2nd edition of the *Cheon Seong Gyeong* being the primary resources. In the References for True Parents' Words section, these volumes of text are cited in italics followed by the book number, chapter, section and page number. Other book titles are italicized preceded by the author and followed by the publisher, year of publication, and relevant page numbers. Speech titles are cited in quotation marks preceded by the speaker and followed by the location and dates.

Each quote listed in each chapter has been numbered. Readers can refer to the Reference for True Parent's Words section at the back of the book for the full source citation. Following each quote listed in each chapter is a date found in parentheses indicating when the words were first spoken (year. month.day) or just the year the speech was first added to a publication.

Contents

Section I
Core of the Universe

Core of the Universe

If you asked people, what is the most important thing in the universe, you would get many different kinds of answers. It is a question that perhaps you have asked yourself. This is the very question that True Father sought to answer as a young man. Through years of anguished prayer and study, True Father came to a radical conclusion. He realized the success of God's plan for the cosmos was 100% dependent on the correct use of the sexual organs. That is not your typical religious answer! Nevertheless, the sexual organs of men and women are the place where love, life, and lineage meet. Therefore, True Father calls the sexual organs the core or the root of the universe.

From the very beginning, God's desire was to establish Himself as an eternal loving parent through the first man and woman, Adam and Eve. We have often heard True Father speak of the sexual organs as the original palace of love, the original palace of life, and the original palace of lineage. But what do each of these terms mean? In the following chapters, each of these palaces will be further explored to fully understand the preciousness of our sexual organs. These quotes provide insight into True Father's unique wisdom concerning the sexual organs and our responsibility to them. This is a completely novel way of thinking that can open up new possibilities for us.

True Father's Words

1. "In my strenuous efforts to find the answer to the fundamental problems of humankind, and the root of the universe, I realized it was the sexual organs. Once I realized it was them and thought the whole matter through, I found that the harmony of heaven and

earth was swirling around the sexual organs. It is an amazing fact."
(1990.1.7)

2. "How did man and woman come into existence? What makes
    them different? How do they become one? Centering on what
    do man and woman unite? Centering on the sexual organs. This
    is how they harmonize. Love is perfected in this place. True love
    is perfected for the first time there. That is also where the lives of
    man and woman are united, and their lineages are interchanged
    and planted. The sexual organs are the original palace of the ideal
    love and lineage. The absolute original place is called the original
    palace, and no one can change its value." (1992.3.3)

3. "What are the sexual organs? They are the palaces centered on true
    love, true life, and true lineage. They are the most precious things.
    If they disappeared, so would heaven and earth, and without them,
    God's ideal, God's family, and God's will could not be fulfilled.
    They are the origin, from which the perfection of everything can
    be achieved." (1991.4.1)

4. "'My sexual organ is the original palace of love, life, and lineage.'
    Only in this way can it become the palace in which God can
    reside. Since God is the King of kings, He needs to reside in His
    original palace. So if you want God to come and dwell within you,
    you need to become the original palace of love, life, lineage, and
    conscience." (1997.1.1)

5. "God based His work of creation on the male and female organs,
    which are incorporated and connected to all elements including
    those of the spirit, the body, and the blood. Didn't the elements
    that make up your eyes also come from there? Don't the elements
    of your teeth resemble those of your mother and father? Is there
    any part of you that doesn't take after them? Even your minds
    resemble those of your parents. On account of this, everything
    is concentrated on the sexual organs, and every nerve and blood

vessel stems from them. The genitals are the roots. The root of a human being is not the head; our roots lie at the genitals." (1989.10.17)

6. "Adam and Eve were in the position of the original palace, and their descendants were meant to become palaces naturally; however, the site for the original palace was lost. The male and female sexual organs are that amazing. You need to realize that they are the three great palaces of love, life, and lineage, and at the same time, the starting base for God's Kingdom on earth and in heaven. It is truly astonishing." (1995.1.8)

7. "Everybody in history pursued this. It is incredibly powerful. It transcends culture and economics, even in the fallen world. Yet what would it have been like in the original world? If you think about it, it is most precious. It is the original palace of all palaces. It is the palace of life as well as the palace of lineage. The foundations of these three palaces are the genitals. They are the most important place. Even God seeks it. If He had occupied these three palaces, all of the people of this world would have become His kindred." (1993.1.28)

8. "God wishes to live at the center. The ideal family, nation, and world all desire to be connected to that root. Yet everything was lost due to the Fall. We are in a piteous plight. What is the male organ? It is the palace of eternal love. Is this true just for your generation? It is not! It's for eternity. It's the place of the eternal palace. It is the palace of eternal life. From then, the life of man and woman are bound together as one for the first time based on love. What are the sexual organs? They are first, the palace of love, second, the palace of life, and third, the palace of God's lineage. This is the most precious thing. Wouldn't you all be happy about that?" (1993.8.1)

9. "Conjugal and parental love settle eternally when we are married

and making love. Through which part of the body do we make love? Is it the mouth, the eyes, or the ears? I don't know, but I believe you all know the answer very well! What is it? Until now, people have regarded the sexual organs as something bad, but now I'm teaching that it is the holy original palace. How amazing are the male and female sexual organs? Without them, true love, life, lineage, and conscience cannot be connected. Can God's Kingdom begin without them? It cannot! Only through that organ is the world of freedom, happiness, peace, and unity possible." (1996.5.5)

Sharing Thoughts on True Father's Words

After years of agonizing and prayerful searching, True Father discovered the *Core of the Universe*: the precious and holy sexual organs. It is from this place that the harmony of all of heaven and earth unfolds. No one in history had been able to truly understand and explain the meaning of God's beautiful plan for the sexual organ, and because of this, the world has been trapped in confusion. True Father was the first to uncover the truth. He explains that the sexual organs are not to be regarded as something shameful.

The exciting truth is that the male and female sexual organs are the original palaces of love, life, and lineage and the origin for *everything* God desired. They are called palaces because they are the holiest and most beautiful dwelling place in all of God's creation. Only through their correct use can the ideal family, nation, and world evolve, where all people can enjoy freedom, peace, unity, and happiness. God has longed for the day when He can dwell in these palaces together with His children forever.

Making It Real

The Eagle Has Landed

NASA scientists launched Apollo 11 on July 16, 1969. Four days later, the lunar module, manned by Astronauts Neil Armstrong and Buzz Aldrin, separated from the command module and touched down near the Sea of Tranquility. It was a dramatic descent that was almost aborted. Upon arrival, Armstrong transmitted the now-famous message "The Eagle has landed." The iconic photo of the first footprint on the moon created a huge sensation. What is less known is that Aldrin celebrated holy communion there with the traditional wafer and wine, as he read from John 15:5: "I am the vine, you are the branches. Whoever remains in me, and I in him, will bear much fruit, for you can do nothing without me."

The dream of landing on the moon was at first just a noble idea. U.S. President John F. Kennedy inspired the nation to pursue this monumental goal in a famous speech he gave in 1961: "We choose to go to the moon in this decade and do the other things, not because they are easy, but because they are hard, because that goal will serve to organize and measure the best of our energies and skills, because that challenge is one that we are willing to accept, one we are unwilling to postpone, and one which we intend to win, and the others, too." Kennedy inspired his country to get involved in the space race because there was concern that the conflicts on earth would continue in outer space without America's leadership to ensure peaceful exploration and international cooperation.

Landing on the moon was a grandiose project. It required $25 billion with an estimated 400,000 people working for eight years to launch Armstrong and his team off the ground! What only existed in our collective imagination eventually took form, and only then could the rocket be launched and the dream come true.

The command module could be considered the core of NASA's lunar program. Its thrusters were responsible for slingshotting the module out of the earth's orbit and propelling it to the moon. If the thrusters had been engaged too early or too late, the trajectory would have carried the rocket into deep space and doomed the mission. The success of the entire project was dependent upon the exact timing and perfect performance of the command module.

The Apollo story is a dramatic example of the number of people required and the precise calculations needed to make an awesome dream come true.

It can help us understand something about the heart of God. Our Creator had a longing to realize His ideal. For billions of years, God invested 100% of His heart and energy to create the universe and, at its core, the incredibly beautiful and intricate sexual organs. With the union of Adam and Eve's sexual organs at the appropriate time, everything God had been working towards would have been successfully launched. As the palaces of love, life, and lineage, the sexual organs have this significance.

True Father emphasizes this because the sexual organs are the Core of the Universe. There is a special season for sexual love, and it must be in accordance with God's plan and timing. There was an ordered sequence of events that were necessary for the creation of this complex, wonderful, and eternal world that was meant to begin with Adam and Eve at the center. God's plan required a time of growth and a commitment to follow the strict guidelines of the commandment. Adam and Eve would have been given permission to experience conjugal love and become one after their marriage ceremony. Just as the fate of the lunar landing depended entirely on the precise timing of the rocket launch, the fate of successfully launching God's plan depended on Adam and Eve's patience, self-control, and obedience to God's words. The sexual organs are the core of the universe, as True Father exclaims, "It is truly astonishing!"

Points for Consideration/Activities

- What does True Father's revelation of the sexual organs as the core of the universe make you think or feel?

- Share an important event or moment in your life that was a great success because your timing was perfect.

- In a world where the sexual organs are honored and valued as they should be, what would family life, schools, entertainment, marriages, and so on look like?

The Original Palace of Love

When you were a kid, did you and your best friend visit somewhere really special that was known only by the two of you? A secret hangout just for you and your friend and no one else? Reading True Father's words may bring us to the conclusion that this was God's thinking when He created the sexual organs. He wanted to create an exclusive place where only husband and wife could meet together and connect with God as a couple. The sexual organs are that special place, the original palace of love, where husband and wife share only with each other.

True Father's Words

10. "The sexual organs of Adam and Eve are places of greatness. That is why they are termed the original palace of love. This is an amazing term. The palace wherein all creation can be perfected and even God Himself can be perfected and dwell, is in the original palace." (1996.5.24)

11. "You'll hear it said that the founder of the Unification Church is a religious leader of sex. Were it not for the Fall, the sexual relationship would be the original palace of love. It would have been the original palace wherein the King can always come in and reside. You should know that it is the original palace of love. The sexual organs are the headquarters, the palace of love." (1996.5.24)

12. "The genitals through which a loving couple has intercourse are the palace of love. Love begins from that place. They are the

palace of true love and the place where life first begins. Think about whether this is true or not. The sexual organs are the palace of love. In the original state without the Fall, the genitals are the palace of love, life, and lineage. Where man and woman are joined together centering on love, there, life and lineage are perpetuated." (1994.2.15)

13. "After Adam's creation, his sexual organ—as originally intended and idealized by God, and untainted by the Fall—should become a base and original palace that is united with God. It is to connect the lineage and life centering on true love. They are the original palace of love." (1998.2.2)

14. "It is ideal to have the two palaces meet and make them into the queen and king of the ideal. That is referred to as loving. Those who have shown such love can become God's sons and daughters, and together with Him, participate equally in the one ideal sphere of life. People were created to be of such value." (1983.10.2)

15. "The female sexual organ is the universal origin. The place where one forms the connection of love is the original palace of love. It is the original palace. Love begins there. Lovemaking on the wedding night is the beginning of the original palace of love. It is the place where the life of man and woman unite for the first time. Thus, this place is the original palace of ideal life, and it is also the original palace of lineage since lineage begins there. Furthermore, since the Kingdom of Heaven also begins there, that place is the original palace of God's Kingdom on earth and in heaven, the original palace of perfection of humankind and of God." (1994.3.16)

16. "You should attend and love the sexual organs more than you do God, for only then would He rejoice. Where on earth would you hear such words? If religious people heard them, they would jump and fall down in shock, but this is the plain truth. Only when you attend the love organs more than you do God can the foundation

on which God can settle be laid. It is more precious than life, and you cannot exchange it for the world, the universe, and even God. Only when you worship, love, and recognize the value of your spouse's sexual organ more than you do all God's creation put together will God come to reside in your homes." (2000.7.1)

17. "Where is the palace of love? You should not think it strange if I speak of such things. If our thinking of the sexual organs is not aligned with God's thinking, then the whole world will go awry. When the first step goes wrong, then the whole universe will be filled with wickedness. In my strenuous efforts to find the answer to the fundamental problems of humankind and the root of the universe, I realized it was the sexual organs. Once I realized it was them and thought the whole matter through, I found that the harmony of heaven and earth was swirling around the sexual organs. It is an amazing fact." (1990.1.7)

18. "In conclusion, into which part would God have invested the greatest effort when He was creating human beings? Would it have been the eyes, the mouth, the nose, or the hands? People have not given the slightest thought to this. That part would be the stronghold of love. Where would the stronghold of love be? It would be the male and female sexual organs. The sexual organs are the original palace of love. It is through them that the love of man and the love of woman can be learned. Without them, we would remain ignorant of love, for the owners of love could not appear. The owner of man's love is woman, and the owner of woman's love is man, and it is the love organs that qualify us as the owners of love." (1999.6.14)

19. "You are bound to be punished if you use your love organs recklessly. They are the palace of love and the ancestral garden of love. Love began there. The origin of God's Kingdom on earth and in heaven and the origin of the beginning of God's happiness are

molded there. God's laughter begins from there. That is where God can find love at last and dance for joy. We must seek this place." (1994.3.13)

Sharing Thoughts on True Father's Words

True Father calls our sexual organs a palace of love because it is where a husband and wife connect in the most intimate way, creating a bond of eternal love. Furthermore, he teaches us to honor our sexual organs and our spouse's even more than we attend God! When a young person saves their sexual organ for their future spouse, they protect the original palace of love. In this way, they learn to discipline themselves to keep their sexuality aligned with God's values. After they are mature and blessed, they care for each other as husband and wife and experience the fullness of sexual love. New life emerges from their growing love and perpetuates God's lineage. God settles in their couple and family, and it is there that He can truly rejoice. This is why the sexual organs are called the palace of love, life, and lineage.

Making It Real

The Secret Garden by Frances Hodgson Burnett

This is a story about happiness and healing in a secret garden. Mary is an unfortunate and sickly child sent to a relative's home in England after her family is killed by cholera in India. She lives with her uncle, Archibald Craven, in a sprawling, old estate with over one hundred rooms. The uncle has been unfriendly and grief-stricken ever since the death of his beloved wife ten years ago. He and his wife had made beautiful memories in their garden, walking the paths and enjoying the flowers. Now the garden only reminds him that she is gone, so it remains locked so no one can enter.

Mary's health improves, especially when she finds the key to the garden and starts secretly working there to bring it back to life. But when she starts hearing strange noises from inside the house, Mary becomes increasingly curious and decides to investigate. She quietly trespasses into a forbidden section of the house and makes an amazing discovery. The cries are coming from Archibald's invalid son, Colin, who has been hidden away in a private room because his grief-stricken father can't stand to be near him. Archibald lost his wife during childbirth and blames his son for her death. Mary uncovers the boy's story as they develop a secret friendship. Colin has been sick in bed all his life and feels he is doomed to become a hunchback like his father. Servants have tended to Colin, and consequently, he is very self-centered. Mary, sensitive because of her own personal tragedy when she lost her parents, sympathizes with Colin and eventually brings him out of isolation and into the garden.

The secret garden becomes a protected place for the two children. It is where they find happiness, healing, and hope. There is more to this heartwarming story. One day, Archibald receives a dream in which his wife tells him that she will meet him in the garden. When he enters, expecting to see his wife, he is met by Colin, who is now on the road to recovery and able to walk. As Archibald and Colin embrace, the father's heart heals. The happy reconciliation of father and son brings back memories of the love that husband and wife enjoyed so much while she was alive.

The secret garden became a place where everyone found hope. The children could find that which they desired most deeply—happiness, hope, and friendship. Archibald found what he needed there as well, a reunion with his wife through embracing and loving their son. The couple had created this beautiful place out of their love for each other. Now he could enjoy it once again and savor fond remembrances of their walks together. The secret garden became a treasure for those who entered, a place where dreams come true.

As True Father teaches us, God created the original palace of love as a hidden place reserved exclusively for two people, a husband and wife, where love and hope are meant to thrive. It becomes a haven of refuge where a couple goes to recharge and encourage each other to face the challenges of life. When a couple who has received the Marriage Blessing goes to their secret garden, the place where their sexual organs meet, God experiences joy, and His broken heart is healed through their love and union.

Points for Consideration/Activities

- Why do you think True Father calls the sexual organs a palace of love?

- What are the benefits of "entering the garden" with only your spouse?

- How does making love with your spouse benefit your life?

The Original Palace of Life

One of the most spectacular events in life is the birth of a new child. According to UNICEF, this happens about 353,000 times every day! How wonderful is that? When mothers and fathers everywhere experience this miracle, it also brings immense joy to our Heavenly Parent. The investment and heart that went into our Creator's design for reproduction, pregnancy, and birth are astounding. We would like to reflect on this incredible origin of life and inspire you with the words of True Parents, followed by a personal story from proud, new parents.

True Parents' Words

20. "The male and female sexual organs are the palace of love, the royal palace of love. Which is more precious: the womb or the male and female sexual organs? Answer me. Did they come into being because of the womb or vice versa? These are serious words and not for you to laugh at. The womb came into being because of the existence of man. The female sexual organ was made for man. Without the sexual organs, there cannot be love. Love could not be found. Without passing through them, life cannot continue. What good would be the existence of man and woman? Life could not continue. Without passing through them, the lineage that links history could not continue." —True Father (1993.2.28)

21. "If human beings had not fallen, the male organ would be the palace of love. Therefore, it cannot be used recklessly. It is also the palace

of life. Isn't life generated from it? Where does life come from? The palace of life. The sexual organs are also the palace of lineage. From them, our life is born, inheriting lineage. They are the source of our life, lineage, and love. As such, our ancestors should have valued and esteemed them." —True Father (1990.10.3)

22. "Our sexual organs are palaces of true love, true life, and true lineage. They are the most precious place. If these organs were to disappear, heaven and earth would disappear. Without these organs, God's ideal, His family, and His will could not be fulfilled. These organs are an origin from which everything can be perfected." —True Father (1991.4.1)

23. "We started out in our mother's womb. The womb was the first world in which we were nurtured. When we were born, we separated from that world and entered a new world. Likewise, in death, the spirit self cuts off and flies away from the physical body, which is like its womb. Human beings pass through a world of water and a world of land and air until they come to live in the eternal world of love." —True Mother (1999)

24. "Reflect on yourself and ask, where does my life begin? It starts from your parents. Our life begins in our mother's womb. When a fetus is in its mother's womb, it absorbs elements from the mother in order to grow. If there is anything a baby wants while in the womb, it is that his mother be joyful, happy, and singing all the time. That might be the most important wish of the fetus. That is why prenatal education consists of the pregnant woman listening to beautiful music, looking at beautiful scenes, and thinking beautiful thoughts. That is good for the baby as well." —True Father (1974.11.10)

25. "In the term *saeng shik gi* (sexual organs), the Chinese character for *saeng* (生), meaning life, can be used with either *shik* (食), meaning food, or *shik* (殖), meaning to plant. These organs are called the vessels that plant life. *Shik* can also be represented by the character

meaning to multiply. In other words, the organs for planting life are also the organs for multiplying life. That is how we can interpret the word. The organs are the vessels for the planting of life."
—True Father (1999.6.13)

26. "How much would God have delighted in making them? Think about which parts of the male and female bodies He would have created with the utmost pleasure and care. It is the sexual organs that were thus created. They are not receptacles for storing uncooked rice. They are receptacles that generate life. They are the sexual organs of life that initiate life. Without them, no life would emerge, even after the passing of eons. Then there would be no nations, and heaven and earth would become one vast expanse of darkness and desert." —True Father (1997.4.13)

Sharing Thoughts on True Parents' Words

True Parents taught us that the sexual organs are the original palace of life, love, and lineage. In this chapter, we are talking about the Palace of Life. The sexual organs were designed to plant and generate new life making them the most precious part of our body. Our nerves and blood vessels are all connected to this root.

We spend the first stage of our lives growing inside of our mother's womb. This is where new life is nourished, protected, and cared for both physically and spiritually. For this reason, True Parents encourage expectant couples, especially the mother, to be aware of their environment as it has a paramount impact on the developing child. When a pregnant woman thinks peaceful thoughts and listens to beautiful music, it creates a healthy, loving atmosphere that contributes to the child's emotional and spiritual wellbeing in the womb. There is no greater happiness than welcoming a new life. True Parents encourage couples to live joyfully in this special time.

Making It Real

Miracle of New Life

When we look at the universe, we are in awe of its design. As a child, True Father explored the hills and fields around his family home in the countryside of North Korea, marveling at all the plants and animals, mountains, and rivers that taught him about God's character. In contemplating nature, the question naturally arises, did God create anything without considering how it would interact with everything else in its environment? There are countless examples of how elements in nature complement and support each other in various ways testifying to an ingenious Creator who designed the universe to go on forever. When we look at creation, we might conclude that God's greatest achievement was the plan for human life, the creation of His children. The act of love and reproductive organs were the means through which God could have an infinite number of children to love.

True Parents teach that there are three phases of life. The first stage of life is the world of water, which begins in the womb. The second stage is our life on earth, and the third is our life in the spirit world. The first phase of life begins when the man's sperm successfully unites with a woman's egg. Through special imaging, scientists recently discovered that there's a visible spark when this happens!

Life starts out so small. At four weeks old, the embryo is the size of a grain of rice and only an inch and a half at 12 weeks. The first features that appear are the nose, eyelids, and ears, but no mouth. The embryo has arms and legs with webbed toes like a frog, and its brain and spinal cord are developing as well as the heart and other organs. At this point, the embryo looks a little less alien. Genitals show up in pictures around this time, so the sex is known. At the end of the first trimester, the embryo becomes a fetus.

The little developing human is constantly being nourished through the umbilical cord. When the mother eats a salad or banana, the nutrients are absorbed into her bloodstream and flow through the umbilical cord into the baby's bloodstream.

At roughly 17 weeks, bone structures harden, enabling the fetus to flip and roll around. The size is still very small, only four and a half inches long from crown to rump. From 25 to 27 weeks old, the lungs are formed, and newly developed ears enable the baby to hear sounds outside the womb.

At around 37 weeks, it's departure time, as the baby leaves its mother's womb into the second phase of life. When the newborn inhales its first breath of air, its spirit enters the tiny body, all set to grow in the love of the family. This is God's brilliant plan for creation.

Michael and Nicole La Hogue, Proud New Parents

This beautiful couple from America and Germany received the Marriage Blessing in 2018 and shared this story weeks after giving birth to their first child.

Nicole La Hogue:
"In 2019, Elijah La Hogue was conceived in North Carolina, at a time when my husband, Mickey, and I were both relaxed and happy. Since then, our journey of understanding, adaptation, and changes began. My pregnancy was a beautiful time for me. I loved to see my belly grow as my body prepared for the final moment of birth.

Because of True Parents' teachings about the value of creating a new life, I knew that pregnancy was an important period for the baby. I wanted to be as happy and joyful as I could be. It did not always work as I thought because life is life, but there were moments when I consciously decided to stay positive, to forgive, and continue to love for the sake of my baby. I always had the wish to go to Cheon Bo (Cheongpyeong Heaven and Earth Training Center in South Korea) because I knew that this was where I would definitely find peace with God, myself, and the nature around me. Unfortunately, due to the global outbreak of the Coronavirus, I wasn't able to leave Germany.

There was one upside of the whole pandemic situation—my husband was able to work at home until the end of my pregnancy. I prepared physically and mentally for the birth. I only focused on positive things. I really enjoyed this time with Mickey because we both did a prayer condition and sang songs for Elijah every day, and read God's Words. The warmth and love of my husband played a crucial role during that time.

Giving birth was an unforgettable experience for me. I am sure for every mother, it is a special and unique moment. Something that came to my mind was that giving birth is pure self-denial and sacrifice for a higher purpose. Even though it was one of the most painful experiences I had so far, I refused to take any medications. I did not want to harm my baby and wanted to be there for him when he arrived. In the time after birth, I suddenly felt very close to my own mother and could only feel gratitude towards her. I also reflected on True Mother giving birth fourteen times. I can only have respect and admiration for such superwomen who delivered more than once."

Mickey La Hogue:
"As Nicole wrote above, we did a prayer condition, daily Hoon Dok Hwe study, and sang every day for about two months before our son was born. During that time, I really felt that the investment and sincerity that I was putting into creating a holy environment would help our son. We were very peaceful and happy at home, especially for the last two months, and I am convinced that that was one of the reasons Elijah is such a patient and calm baby.

One of the most amazing parts of being a dad is realizing that I am 100 percent responsible for another human being who is completely help-less and ungrateful! I found myself in the unique situation where I had to learn to give unconditional love since it seemed like it would be months and even years before Elijah would be able to reciprocate. Becoming a parent has helped me understand my parents and God better since I'm now going through what they went through. Seeing childbirth and becoming a father is such a surreal experience. I can't think of any moment in my life where I felt as much of a change in who I am and what my responsibilities are in life. Even two weeks after being a dad, it is still hard to fathom that this is a permanent change. It still sometimes feels like we're going to return him to the hospital and get back to a 'normal' life at some point!

The birth was amazing. Nicole showed so much determination and focus (and became kind of scary, too, haha). Seeing Elijah actually come out of Nicole was completely strange but beautiful, and the way that Nicole instinctively grabbed for him was so wonderful! I could really see the way God designed a mother to want to protect her baby. It was so hard to fathom that I had become a father and that this little human being had been with us this whole time, just inside mommy's belly. Elijah was now with us, and his birth was definitely one of the best moments of my life."

Points for Consideration/Activities

- Why do you think God designed three stages of life for humans?

- How did you learn about reproduction and life in the womb? How would you like your children to learn about it?

- Take time to watch a video about fetal development: Nova video, "Life's Greatest Miracle" (55 minutes).

The Original Palace of Lineage

If you could go back in time and meet any person, who would you choose? Many famous figures may come to mind, such as Mother Teresa, Martin Luther King Jr., Abraham Lincoln, or even Jesus. Out of all the interesting people who have ever lived, wouldn't it be amazing to meet your own ancestors? Imagine a conversation with your great-great-great-grandparents! You may find you share something in common, like similar mannerisms or physical features. Wouldn't it be interesting to know how their choices impacted your family? Through their lineage, our ancestors have forever left their mark on this world in each one of us.

True Father's Words

27. "Remember, all ancestors are waiting in your blood, lined up there. We always need to be reminded that hundreds of generations of ancestors are waiting in line and they are at the tip of your sexual organ expecting the best possible descendant." (2001.2.18)

28. "The reproductive organs, with which a man and woman make love, are the original palace of lineage. Your grandfather and grandmother live holding onto this place; your mother and father live holding on to it; your couple lives holding on to it, and your sons and daughters to come in the future also will live holding on to it. Then why have we turned this into something base and vulgar? The name of this original palace is actually something that is very holy. We must uphold it with holiness. It is because of it that eter-

nal life and eternal lineage appear. It is the most precious thing."
(1990.12.1)

29. "Your organ of love is more important than your brain. The origin
of true love is not in your brain. The origin of true lineage is not
in your brain. Where is that origin? It is in the reproductive organ.
Everything is in the reproductive organ. In there is life, in there
is love, and in there is lineage. It is the original palace of love. We
find also the root of life and of lineage residing there. This is the
most precious place, not only in the human body but also in the
world and throughout history. Without it, the multiplication of
humankind would be impossible." (1990.6.17)

30. "We should be eternal and unchanging like God. Love is absolutely
unique, eternal, and unchanging, like God, and the place it settles is the sexual organs. No one knew this until now. That's how
precious the genitals are. A family of happiness is formed when
the sexual organs of the grandparents, parents, husband and wife,
and also your sons and daughters in the future, are in union. If
that is broken, the whole family falls apart. The grandmother has
taken hold of the grandfather's sexual part and will try never to
let it go, and the grandfather has occupied the grandmother's and
will try never to lose it. Everything—love, happiness, freedom,
and so on—begins from the sexual organs. That is undeniable."
(1996.5.24)

31. "They were created by God with the utmost care. The core marrow
of all created beings were extracted and connected to them. The
sexual organs are connected one hundred percent to the essence of
love and life, and the essence of history springs from them. Hope,
happiness, and the beginning of the realm of freedom based on
love all stem from these organs." (1994.7.23)

32. "The sexual organs of human beings are the place of true love. Isn't that where man and woman are connected in the act of love? It is not anywhere else. That is the palace where the lives of man and woman are connected and made one. When man and woman are unified, their sons and daughters are born from that lineage. Therefore, it is the palace of the lineage. The sexual organs are that important." (1992.6.7)

33. "The final, ideal destination of the assimilation of all creation is the male and female organs. That is a fact. Why is that so? It is where the love of God, humankind, and the universe combine. It is where love and life become one. It is also where descendants are connected vertically through lineage, and through this vertical connection, countless peoples are connected horizontally. This is how God's Kingdom on earth is established. That's how valuable the sexual organs are. How important they are!" (1995.4.9)

34. "What are absolute faith, absolute love, and absolute obedience? These are all terms concerned with the genitals. The Fall refers to the failure of God and human genitals to become one; they failed to attain oneness. You must believe this absolutely. They are the pillars of the history of our family, clan, and lineage." (1999.10.10)

35. "Where do God's love and the love of humankind meet? At the point where love, life, and lineage settle. If it were not for that place, there would be no way for love, life, and lineage to connect. What is that place, that sexual organ, and what is it used for? It is the place where the lives of man and woman connect and where their lineage and blood intersect. God's life, love, and lineage, and those of man and woman are connected through this one point of settlement. Based on it, their descendants come forth." (1990.7.7)

Sharing Thoughts on True Father's Words

True Father discovered that God made the whole creation for the purpose of establishing His unending lineage substantially on earth through His children. It is through the sexual organs that God's Kingdom is established. The sexual organs are the original palace of lineage. It is the part of the body that connects our life with our ancestors and descendants, linking us to both the past and the future. God intended for generations of grandparents, parents, and children to be connected through the sexual organs.

This is why God created the genitals with more care and attention than the eyes, nose, heart, and brain. These organs are in the position of the most precious place, not only in the human body but throughout history. Life, love, and lineage would be impossible without the ingenious design of the sexual organs. Happiness, freedom and everything important begins there. Without these vessels, all human life would end. Thus, the sexual organs were created by God to be the wellspring of endless generations to fill God's Kingdom.

Making It Real

DNA: God's Plan for Uniqueness and Similarity

"For you created my inmost being; you knit me together in my mother's womb. I praise you because I am fearfully and wonderfully made; your works are wonderful, I know that full well." (Psalm 139:13-14 New International Version)

Science has finally supported religion in its assertion that each person is unique. They just haven't agreed yet that God made us that way. Recent research, helped by 23andMe and other similar companies, has pioneered new discoveries about DNA. The science of genetics has made startling discoveries about the building blocks of human life, our DNA, the molecule that contains the blueprint for making us who we are.

DNA is the hereditary material in humans and almost all other organisms. Scientists have learned that DNA reflects each individual's unique identity, but not only that, it also shows how closely related we are to one another. The genetic difference in humans is usually about 0.1%—not much of a variation. It's noteworthy that each person's genome is unique, and a copy of that genome, organized into 46 chromosomes in 23 pairs, is found in almost every cell of our body. We are both wholly and uniquely a creation of God, and at the same time, related to one another as members of the same human family.

Now here's the really interesting part: no matter how many billions of people are born, there will never be two that are exactly the same. From the *Divine Principle* we learn that each person is a distinct manifestation of God. A baby's genome is formed when the mother's egg forms a union with the father's sperm. They are both made of specialized cells called gametes. These cells are different from all other cells in our bodies in one significant way. They contain only half the usual number of chromosomes. Why? When fertilization occurs as the sperm unites with the egg, half of the father's genome is mixed with half of the mother's genome and forms the complete genome of the next generation.

"Before creating, God had in His mind an Individual Image for each being to be created… In order to receive infinite joy, God creates innumerable individuals, each one resembling the specific attributes of one of His Individual Images. The individuality, or specific attributes, of a person is quite distinguishable from that of another… We need to understand that God has given us unique individuality (individual image) in order to derive unique joy from each one of us."[4]

These complex processes designed by God ensure that life and lineage will go on forever, that babies will continue to be born, and each one will be uniquely different from the next. True Father helped us to learn that this kind of diversity brings great joy to our Heavenly Parent, who wants to bask in the love of an infinite number of children. That's how big God's heart is! As we learn more about the science of lineage, we are in awe of God's design

---

4. Sang Hun Lee, *Explaining Unification Thought* (Bridgeport: Unification Thought Institute, 1981), 103.

to pass on His infinite, divine traits through unending generations of individuals who are both unique yet very similar.

Inheritance: More Than Physical

Inheritance involves more than bequeathing our possessions or physical traits. Our unique personality and behaviors, which shape our destiny, are also a product of our lineage.

The study of epigenetics has been gaining much attention in recent years, revealing something remarkable about heritability. It explores the ways our gene expression is impacted by our environment, thoughts, and experiences. Not only that, it has shown the way our actions and habits can influence and even change the traits we pass on to future generations.

To illustrate the effect our lives can have on future generations, we can look at an interesting comparison of two very different genealogies. Here is an account comparing descendants of Jonathan Edwards (1703-1758), a renowned preacher and theologian, to those of a contemporary, Max Jukes (Born around 1720), who had a notorious reputation and legacy. Their descendants are described in an article, "Multigenerational Legacies — The Story of Jonathan Edwards," by Larry Ballard.

Jonathan Edwards and his wife, Sarah, enjoyed a wonderful marriage and family life. They gave birth to eleven children. He was known to be exceptionally attentive to his wife and children, which was unusual in the mid-1700s. The good qualities of this husband and wife pair were passed down to future generations. A genealogical study identified the occupations of this couple's descendants. The list includes a U.S. vice president, three senators, three governors, three mayors, 13 college presidents, 30 judges, 65 professors, 80 public office-holders, 100 lawyers, 62 physicians, 75 Army or Navy officers, 100 clergymen, missionaries, and theological professors. There were practically no lawbreakers.[5]

---

5. Larry Ballard, "Multigenerational Legacies — The Story of Jonathan Edwards," July 1, 2017, https://www.ywam-fmi.org/news/multigenerational-legacies-the-story-of-jonathan-edwards/.

Max Jukes (not his real name) lived during the same period as Jonathan Edwards. He and other family members lived and survived by fishing and hunting in the woods of New York State. He attracted the attention of genealogists when it was discovered that the family trees of 42 different men in the New York prison system were traced back to him. Jukes' descendants included seven murderers, 60 thieves, 128 prostitutes, 140 other convicts, and 440 people whose lives were adversely affected by alcohol addiction. It was found that 300 out of 1,200 descendants studied died prematurely, and 67 were reported to have contracted syphilis.[6] Moreover, it was estimated that Jukes' descendants cost the state more than a million dollars.

The stories of Jonathan Edwards and Max Jukes illustrate the significance of a person's life regarding its impact on future descendants. One life multiplies goodness, while the other produces pain and suffering. True Father calls the sacred sexual organs the palace of lineage and explains how their treatment can lead one to either heaven or hell. When the sexual organs are treated carelessly, they become vulgar and base and may cause the whole family to fall apart for generations. True Father says that when their owners regard their sexual organs as holy, they will become the pillars of history as they generate love, happiness, and freedom.

A Vision from God

Mark Hernandez, a former pastor of the Dallas Family Church, had an unexpected and unforgettable moment at the time of his spiritual rebirth when he saw a vision of many people carrying luminous objects as they walked toward a large basket. The container was empty until each person, one at a time, placed rubies, emeralds, and precious gems into the basket. Eventually, it became full of the most beautiful, sparkling treasures!

Mark understood that these were his ancestors and that each item symbolized the good deeds and sacrifices they had made during their lives. He intuited that all of these offerings were lovingly made as blessings to him and

---

6. ibid

his descendants. Then it hit him that it was his ancestors' efforts that allowed him to be able to meet True Parents.

DNA contains the blueprint of our entire lineage, past and future, our ancestors, and descendants. It's not just our physical blueprint, but our spiritual blueprint as well. We inherit the spiritual treasures from all our ancestors. We benefit from every good deed and all the sacrifices they have made during their lifetimes. Likewise, our children and descendants receive blessings that we accumulate during our lifetime.

We were given the means by which to transfer both our physical traits and spiritual merit through our sexual organs. When a blessed couple makes love, they begin a completely new lineage, never before seen in history, where God can dwell. This is why each person's sexual organ is an original palace of lineage.

Points for Consideration/Activities

- Share any stories that have been passed down in your family about your parents, grandparents, or ancestors. How has that impacted you?

- What characteristics did you receive from your parents or grandparents?

- What would you like your descendants to inherit from you?

Section II
God's Design for Sex

God's Purpose for the Sexual Organs

We all know the headache of trying to assemble a new bike, bookshelf, or bed on our own. When all else fails, we inevitably have to look at the instructions. But what if there isn't an instruction manual? This has been the case for the sexual organs. No one has known their purpose throughout history, so we have all been left to figure it out for ourselves. Sex can give us great pleasure and create new life; however, it can also lead to confusion and heartbreak. Why is that, and what is the true purpose of our sexual organs? True Father wrestled with these questions. The key to finding the answers is to know what God was thinking when He designed the sexual organs. This chapter and section will delve into God's design, and purpose for sex revealed to us in True Father's words.

True Father's Words

36. "Aren't the genitals magical organs? The organs connecting the love and life of man and woman, that blend and bring together their blood, are placed at the center of our bodies. These are the sexual organs. Am I right? If you were to delve into this origin, you would fathom the reason for God's act of creation. Why did He create? What did He base His creation on? Today, there is no one who ponders such questions. Even if you were to visit all the world's libraries, you would find that I was the first to advocate this point. That is so precious. It became clear that this is the conclusion for everything. Why did He create? The fact that man and woman become one through the sexual organs proves

that He created with love. It is the source of His ideal love."
(1989.10.15)

37. "What was God's standard in creating human beings? If one were
to ask what the standard for creating the man was, would it be
right to say, 'God created him based upon his face'? With regard
to the creation of women, is it right to claim, 'He created her to
be distinguished by having less facial hair, smoother skin, and a
smaller stature'? Of course not. You need to understand the fact
that He created them based on the sexual organs. The man is the
way he is today in correspondence to his genitals, and the woman
is the way she is in correspondence to her genitals. I was the first
to make this statement. No one else ever uttered such words."
(1989.10.3)

38. "Why were the sexual organs created? Certainly not just for one
individual person or another. They were given to you for the great
Way of heaven and earth and the great providential governance of
heaven and earth. How will the ideal world come upon the earth
in the future?... Until now, because of Satan, we were ignorant
regarding the owners of the sexual organs and how they came to
be created. In order to disclose this truth, and to clean away the
evil and foul tumult and turmoil of Satan, both on earth and in
heaven, I came forth and hoisted my banner." (1989.10.3)

39. "When do the blood and flesh of a man and a woman join in harmony? This takes place when they make love. The lifeblood of a
man and a woman cannot mingle just by their looking into each
other's eyes. It mingles through their living as husband and wife,
that is, by making love. The place where they make love is the
source of life. The lifeblood of the man and the woman does not
intermingle anywhere else. There is only one place for it: the place
where they connect in love-making. That is also the place where
lineages are connected. It is the place where lives attach and adhere

together. It is where lineage begins and where love settles. And it is the only point where love engenders oneness." (1994.3.13)

40. "If a man insisted on absolute ownership over his reproductive organ, and a woman did the same with hers, both would remain exactly where they are without moving for all eternity. This is not right. In order to have the other come to my side and for me to go to the other's side, ownership should be exchanged. Marital love is this kind of action. The value of the action of giving and receiving appears only when the ownership of the reproductive organs has been exchanged through marriage. When a wife faces her husband, is her reproductive organ her own? The owner of the wife's organ of love is her husband. The owner of the husband's organ of love is his wife. Since we haven't realized this until now, the world became licentious. This law is absolute. This is why marital love is great because, in it, ownership is exchanged absolutely." (1986.2.12)

41. "God wants a love partner. Thus, centering on the place where husband and wife become one through their sexual organs, God wants to appear and meet us. Why is that the place where man and woman become one centering on God? It is because love is absolute, and that place is where man and woman have the absolute desire to become one. Looking horizontally, man, who is plus, approaches that center, and woman, who is minus, also approaches that center. In God also, the masculine characteristic and the feminine characteristic become one as plus and minus. That union in God, as a bigger plus, becomes one with a bigger minus, namely, the union of man and woman." (1996.8.1)

42. "The original palace of love, life, and lineage are the sexual organs. The origin and the destination of true love most sought after by God are the male and female sexual organs. From there, the life of man and woman fuse together. From there, their lineages are interwoven, and human beings, who, embodying history, are connected

by a kinship of blood, which is why they are most precious."
(1991.1.8)

Sharing Thoughts on True Father's Words

Why did God create the sexual organs? This question has been central to True Father's efforts to uncover the truth, hidden for thousands of years by Satan. The sexual organs are the only place where the lifeblood of a man and a woman mingle together, and their lineages are connected. The place where this fusion and interweaving between God and human beings occur is where love, life, and lineage flourish. God created everything based on the sexual organs of man and woman. Thus, this is the place where God can fully and joyfully meet with husband and wife. The fact that man and woman become one and experience unparalleled joy through their sexual organs proves the sexual organs were given to us for the sake of love.

Making It Real

Young children are unaware of sex and the full function of their sexual organs. They only know this is where pee comes out. Some little boys with big imaginations might think of another use, "That was a smart idea. God gave me a hose to direct my pee so I can put out fires!" Inevitably, most children eventually start asking questions about their sexual organs and where babies come from. Curiosity about sex is natural, but most parents find it difficult to talk freely and openly with their children about it.

With unanswered questions about sex, young people have felt lost and are left to figure it out on their own, often going to the internet for information. Misunderstanding surrounding the purpose of the sexual organs has led to confusion. Instead of practicing sex in the way God intended, people often use it solely for self-centered pleasure. It has become a commodity that can be bought and sold. Sex has lost its precious value because no one has ever fully explained why God created it.

Religion should give us answers about sex, but even Jesus made no mention of it. Churches give us moral guidance on the sanctity of marriage, but they are mostly silent on the topic of sex. Historically, religion has considered the act of sex a distraction to a holy lifestyle, which has led to celibacy among monks, priests, and nuns.

True Father explains that love, life, and lineage are all connected to the sexual organ. When we understand God's intention for sex between husband and wife, this clears up all the confusion and shows us how to use our divine gift. God's purpose for creating the sexual organs was for couples to become deeply intimate with each other, physically, emotionally, and sexually.

The Gods Must Be Crazy

When the purpose of something is misunderstood, the resultant confusion can lead to misuse and other consequences. The following story illustrates the various problems that occur when this happens.

In the film, *The Gods Must Be Crazy*, a pilot flying over the Kalahari desert drops a glass coke bottle which is discovered by a tribe of Bushmen who have no connection to the world outside of their desert home. Because it falls out of the sky, the tribe welcomes the object as a gift from the gods. It's beautiful to look at and possibly useful. The tribe members are intrigued by the bottle and use it in various ways, not knowing its original purpose. They discover that the bottle is ideal for curing snakeskin and is harder and smoother than anything else in their environment. It's excellent for pounding grain and can also make music.

At first, the tribe members take turns using it in different ways. The Bushmen are normally peaceful and community-minded, but the coke bottle starts to stimulate greed, envy, and selfishness, and arguments about ownership ensue. To whom does it belong? What is the best way to use it? Eventually, they conclude the gods must be crazy for sending this thing because it is causing so much trouble. The elders decide that they must get rid of this "evil" thing that's disrupting their once-peaceful community. They bury it, but then a warthog digs it up, a child finds it and brings the bottle back to camp. Throwing it up in the sky in an effort to give it back to the gods also ends in failure. After a bushman gets hit on the head by the bottle, they give up. Finally, the tribe elders decide that it needs to be taken to the "edge of the world" and dropped off the cliff.

What is the lesson from *The Gods Must Be Crazy*? This light-hearted story provides an analogy to a much more serious problem of misunderstanding and misuse. Humanity has suffered from not knowing God's purpose for creating the sexual organs. When we understand the purpose of our sexual organs, we can live with sexual integrity and stand before God as His divine sons and daughters.

Points for Consideration/Activities

- Have you ever tried to assemble something you purchased without the instructions? What was the outcome?

- What do you think your friends would say is the purpose of their sexual organs?

- Watch "The Gods Must Be Crazy" by Jamie Uys.

The Chemistry of Love

What does chemistry have to do with love? Many of us are inspired by the magic in chemistry. Do you remember being surprised when you learned that two hydrogen molecules and one molecule of oxygen, both gases, can make water an entirely different state of matter? True Father paints the picture of God as the supreme chemist who intentionally created us to experience the greatest love in all of heaven and earth in every cell of our body. We have specific chemical and neurological aspects intended to support eternal, monogamous love between husband and wife. Scientists now call the sexual pleasure cycle a biological reward system that stimulates a powerful bonding action when a couple engages in sex. All the body's senses work together with these sex hormones to create a formidable energetic force for attraction and pleasure.

True Father's Words

43. "Why do men and women like love? The human body consists of as many as 100 trillion cells, and the time when these cells move as a whole is when they make love. The time when all the cells of the human body can move as one is none other than the time when a man and woman make love." (1982.4.26)

44. "The electricity of love that arises in the original world is the lightning of the love of the universe. It surpasses the former in strength several thousand times; moreover, the sound of the movement of the cells of each human organ is like the sound of thunder. The

principle view of love is that the man and woman engaged in the true love of the original world cannot meet God unless they concentrate with all their might towards the contact point where the lightning of love meets." (1997)

45. "A man and a woman embracing and kissing light up like two poles with opposite charges touching and sending out sparks. If that light is white, we must add heat to create five brilliant colors. When this colorful display is mixed with the vertical love of God, it is transformed into a world of ideal, brilliant hope, like the colors of the rainbow. Since human love is on a horizontal plane, it is simple. People of original love want to combine colors, to see perfectly combined colors through the love of a man and a woman. When that occurs, vertical love will come down. Like a rainbow, God's love will descend to this horizontal love." (1985.4.7)

46. "So there were man and woman, and then there had to be a union. Why? Because both man and woman become excited, and just as positive and negative electricity creates a spark, when man and woman are fully charged, they create a spark. That's the union. The spark between man and woman should be stronger than that of electricity, so strong that they cannot be separated." (1999.12.26)

47. "That ideal loving couple wouldn't have to think about getting into their bed because God Himself would be right there to form a perfect cushion for their lovemaking. God will be participating in their love so that they can experience the most harmonious unity. God will be like the nucleus, and surrounding Him will be the man and woman—all three united into one. At this time, the faster and more fierce the crashing together, the better it is. They are traveling so fast and with such an impact that God as the buffer will feel pain, but He doesn't mind. He wants to participate in their love. After the man and woman come together by the force of their love, what happens? By the law of physics, that energy will

diffuse and return to a slower state. Then the next time they engage in love, the force between them will have grown a little more. Every time they repeat their lovemaking, the energy between them becomes broader and broader. Ultimately everything feels their love—the individual, the family, the nation, and even the whole earth. When the man and woman are loving in this fashion and with this force and magnitude, they will have sons and daughters who can embrace the universe as a result of the universal love of the parents." (1984.1.8)

48. "The cells of the love organs of man and woman are the most minute. To have the feelings of all the cells of that part through which runs all paths of love that unites mind and body, to enter that world as one of its elements: this is the aim of all beings in the created world. Then where do man and woman unite? Through the sexual organs. That is where man and woman directly unite and become one with God. Through the Fall, the organs came to be the worst thing, but originally, they are extremely holy. When man and woman open that door, the world is opened, and when the door is closed, the world is closed; when they are happy, the world and the entire universe are happy." (1993.6.20)

49. "When plus and minus become one, the result is light, new strength, and energy. This is the principle of heaven and earth. Taking the example of a magnet, it has plus and minus poles. Likewise, when our mind and body become completely one, we become like a magnet. Even a man's body and a woman's body can be like magnets with plus and minus poles. That is why a man and woman are attracted to each other to become one in body." (1976.2.1)

Sharing Thoughts on True Father's Words

The sexual organs are where man and woman unite and become one with God. True Father uses many colorful metaphors to explain the energy of love that is created. God participates in each couple's sexual love so that they can experience the greatest harmony and joy. They become inseparable. All the cells of their body move together as one. This ripple of love and happiness eventually becomes a tsunami that engulfs the family, the nation, and the entire world.

Making It Real

God created us for love and wired our brains to be interested in sex. Powerful chemicals, namely dopamine, and oxytocin, nicknamed the "cuddle hormone," are released during orgasm to produce feelings of excitement and joy. The euphoric high from sex is so intense the body remembers vivid details of one's first sexual experience. Over time, repeated sexual activity carves deep neural pathways in the brain that create a sexual template. Eventually, the sexual response becomes second nature. Whatever person, image, sound, or smell we associate with sex can act as a trigger that sets into motion our sex drive, which is very difficult to ignore once stimulated. Scientists refer to this as the "sexual pleasure cycle."

These dynamic chemical and neurological processes act as a heavenly bonding agent to attract husband and wife in an exclusive connection of love. God designed us in this way so that husbands and wives would be naturally attracted to each other without the need for conscious thought. God's plan was for us to experience a jolt of electricity every time we see our spouse so that they would be our one and only trigger to awaken this chemistry of love flowing through our veins.

Southern Rockhopper Penguins

True Parents often describe how they learned about love from nature. Here's a story about the chemistry of love in Rockhopper penguins.

On a rocky shoreline in the Falkland Islands, a female, spiky-haired penguin with red plumage and a single yellow eyebrow, steps onto land. She's one of thousands in this group of newly arrived Rockhopper penguins, ready to breed, looking for their mates. The males are gathered among the high grasses, where the nest will be built soon after the reunion. This particular female penguin had selected a mate years ago and now is tasked with searching for her one and only true love in the sea of white and black bodies and feathery heads. How will she ever find him?

Additionally, she's been separated from her companion for about six months, as far away as hundreds and sometimes thousands of kilometers. How will the couple recognize each other when there are so many lookalikes? Suddenly the air is filled with loud braying calls, all sounding about the same to anyone but these penguins. The two long-distance lovers find each other by recognizing the unique sounds they make. Now reunited, their next task is to locate the nest they used the previous year, mate, and give birth to one or two chicks.

This is an example from the animal kingdom of God's magical chemistry. The Rockhopper penguins are designed to be monogamous like us, and they have this amazing memory of and attraction to their mate. How much more would God have invested into the chemistry of love for His own children?

The Upside of Monogamy

True Parents teach that God created sexual love to be experienced exclusively between one man and one woman after receiving the Marriage Blessing. We were not designed to have relationships outside of marriage, including imaginary sexual partners. Scientific studies that address the effects of pornography on the brain provide evidence that this is an unhealthy, habit-forming activity. Pornography can easily become an addiction because it acts as a super stimulus that triggers an unnatural surge of chemicals in the brain. This level of stimulus is several times greater than anything that can be experienced in a real-life relationship. The more one consumes pornography, the more is required to achieve the same high, and the less one becomes satisfied having sex with a real person. This hijacks the pleasure reward cycle that God created to enable us to be attracted to our spouse.

Contrary to popular belief, married people have more satisfying sex-lives than single people. An article in the *HuffPost*, by Linda and Charlie Bloom, addresses the findings of one of the most comprehensive studies on the subject, released in 2010 by the Center for Sexual Health Promotion at Indiana University. In this study, researchers found that married couples have *more* sex than single people. In other words, single life is falsely glamorized, while married couples are having fun in the bedroom. The article continues its argument for committed sex in marriage, citing studies that demonstrate how a good sex life is instrumental in promoting happiness and quality of life. It has to do with feeling safe and satisfied in the area of emotional intimacy.[7]

Not only are married couples having more sex, but they are also healthier as a result. Michael Roizen, MD, is a gerontologist at the University of Chicago. In his best-selling book, *RealAge: Are You as Young as You Can Be?* (1999) he claims that married couples who have sex twice a week are biologically two years younger than their chronological age. That's because committed sex has a positive impact on the efficiency of the heart, respiration, muscle strength, and other organs in the body. Talk about a fountain of youth!

As researchers explore the science of sex, their findings uncover the amazing power of sexual love and its inerasable effect on us. This scientific knowledge gives us even more reasons to believe that God's plan was for one woman and one man to be together forever. He equipped us with loads of sex hormones to help us out. The chemical bonding that takes place during sexual intercourse is like a kind of super glue that provides a deep feeling of connection. This helps create an emotional memory that lasts forever.

Points for Consideration/Activities:

- For married couples, share what attracts you to your spouse, physically, emotionally, and/or mentally? For single people, what can you do to grow your heart and become your best self for your

---

7. Linda Bloom and Charlie Bloom, "Want More and Better Sex? Get Married and Stay Married," *HuffPost*, July 13, 2017, https://www.huffpost.com/entry/want-more-and-better-sex-get-married-and-stay-married _b_5967b618e4b022bb9372aff2.

future spouse?

- What is it that makes you feel loved, by your spouse, and/or family members? Is it physical touch, words of affirmation, quality time, or something else?

- Read *The Five Love Languages by* Gary Chapman and identify yours and your spouse's love language if you're married.

The Chemistry of First Love

Romeo and Juliet is a play about two young, star-crossed lovers. They become obsessed with one another and incapable of thinking about anything else. Their infatuation is so overwhelming that they choose death rather than be separated. How could they experience such intense feelings so quickly? What makes first love so powerful and intoxicating?

True Father's Words

50. "The first spark of true love is so important, and it should not be misused. Once that intense first spark is misused, it is impossible to completely unwind that mistake. Each person has the duty to preserve his pure first love until the time when it can spark for the sake of the universe and for God. Therefore, you cannot behave in a casual way toward your love; that is the way an animal behaves. Love is noble and sacred; it is not vulgar or dirty, although the sacredness of love can be defiled into dirty love." (1983.1.30)

51. "One's first love is very, very important. Your first contact with love should be done with great care because that meeting is like 100% gold wires connecting with each other. A person's first love is one of 100% conductance—it doesn't matter whether the beloved is black, white, or yellow—once you make contact with each other, you make a spark of great power. Therefore, first love should be experienced very carefully. Intense first love, done in a rightful and honorable way, comes together and creates a beautiful and

powerful spark. The love of God will spark with that love, and it becomes the best, most extraordinary spark in Heaven. The impact of that spark is so strong that it flattens you to the ground. Yet still, you feel joyful, even knocked out on the ground, because of the impact of love. First love should be experienced very carefully." (1983.1.30)

52. "When lightning is created, thunder booms through the air. When Adam and Eve's love would collide, not only lightning would spark, but thunder would resound throughout the universe. With this kind of love, do you think negative articles in the media would matter to them? Would persecution perturb the lightning of their love? No, their love would penetrate all that and ignite it. First love is the most intense; that is the true love. First love has the power of dynamite." (1979.2.4)

53. "You might try to tell your eyes to go the wrong way, but they know better. All five of your senses know what is right. When the power of love, particularly first love, is working, nothing under the sun can stop it. The formula of original love cannot be stopped." (1987.8.20)

54. "You have to realize the importance of the love organs of men and women. God comes down through them... The gate of the first love relationship of the kingdom of heaven on earth and in the spirit world opens in that place." (1994.5.15)

Sharing Thoughts on True Father's Words

True Parents have shown us the beautiful truth that God's heart is big enough to embrace and forgive all mistakes. He longs for all of His children to happily receive the Marriage Blessing and will help each one of us to reach that place and to raise our children to experience that same real love.

When True Father cautions us about the importance of first love, it is because he knows God created it as an extremely powerful force to be unleashed at the right moment. Mistakes made prior to receiving the Marriage Blessing can have painful consequences, difficult to resolve. Therefore, young people must approach this seriously and prayerfully. True Parents' sincere desire is to help us avoid hurting our hearts and the hearts of others.

As we read True Father's words, we should understand that his primary task was to teach God's Ideal. In the realm of first love, God intended for a person's first sexual experience to be with their eternal partner. It's the way we are wired. Joyful sparks fly in the sexual union between a husband and wife who save their first love for each other. This is the ideal way to start an eternal, absolute marriage."

Making It Real

What Is the Science behind the Chemistry of First Love?

True Parents teach us that God created His children to develop an attraction to the opposite sex spiritually, emotionally, and sexually. It was part of His greater design for all of us to grow deeply in love with our spouse. We are wired with chemical support mechanisms that strengthen this force of attraction. Studies show that sexual activity has a powerful impact on the brain and its neural pathways. Certain chemicals such as testosterone and estrogen, the neurotransmitter dopamine, and the "cuddle hormone," oxytocin, work together to create a behavior and reward cycle that reinforces sexual activity.

Sex and novelty trigger our brain to release the highest dosage of dopamine, which is why most people can recall with perfect clarity their first exposure to a sexual stimulus. God created us in this way so that we would "imprint" upon our first love. His intention was for us to be sexually aroused only by our eternal spouse.

A Movie about Imprinting: *Fly Away Home*

It's so cute when we see a line of ducks waddling obediently in a perfect row behind their mother. The interesting thing is that when ducklings hatch and their mother is not around, they will imprint on the first person or animal they see. The 1999 movie, *Fly Away Home*, was inspired by Bill Lishman's experiments with geese. He successfully trained them to imprint on the sound of his airplane's engine, then fly with him, following the flight path of the plane.

In the movie, a teenage girl, Amy, finds an abandoned nest of goose eggs and hides them in her drawer. When the eggs hatch, the goslings see Amy first and follow her as if she was their mother. The girl learns from a local wildlife officer that the geese have imprinted on her. Baby geese are totally dependent on their parents, who teach them everything about survival, including migratory routes. The officer advises Amy to clip their wings, which is required if they are to be kept as pets. Refusing to do this, Amy and her dad train the geese to fly using a very light aircraft. But they will only fly if Amy is the pilot! So she learns to fly, and the geese follow her miles from home to a bird sanctuary, their new migratory home.

In the case of humans, True Parents teach us that God created a man and woman to "imprint" upon each other during their first lovemaking as a blessed couple. The intensity of this unique and intoxicating experience makes a beautiful memory that will never be forgotten. The intimacy they share will forever be a source of strength as they deepen their love and face the challenges of life together.

One Love versus Many Loves

When a society supports casual sex, this results in a great deal of "chemical confusion," especially among young people. When a person's body and heart is glued to many others, the bonding hormones get thrown into disarray. With casual sex, the body, including thoughts, emotions, and spirit, is being used in ways that were never intended. When people misuse sexual love, they become confused and disrupt God's original plan for happiness.

What are the psychological impacts of premarital sex? Thomas Lickona, a developmental psychologist and author of *Sex, Love, and You: Making the Right Decision* (2003), describes how casual sex can affect the emotional well-being of young people and put them at risk for future difficulties in their adult years. He describes the possible psychological outcomes of teenage and young adult premarital sex in a 2007 article for his online newsletter, *The Fourth and Fifth R's: Respect and Responsibility.* The list includes the following: guilt, regret, loss of self-esteem and self-confidence, corruption of character, fear of commitment, depression, and suicide, damaged relationships, stunted personal development, and negative effects on marriage.[8] It is obvious that the dangers of premarital sex are far greater than unwanted pregnancy and disease.

There is a growing concern about the "hook up" culture among young people. *Hooked: New Science on How Casual Sex is Affecting Our Children*, written by Joe S. McIlhaney Jr., MD and Freda McKissic Bush, MD (2008), is a powerful resource that uses research data from studies about premarital sex as well as the authors' own clinical experiences. Their findings show that young people who make this choice suffer negative psychological consequences that can last a lifetime.

McIlhaney and Bush emphasize that the "neurochemical imprints" of premature sexual activity can interfere in one's ability to be fully, emotionally invested in future relationships. This is because an immature person who isn't fully emotionally developed and lacks relationship skills isn't ready for sex. He or she experiences only the dopamine high, without the mature emotional connection that is part of a committed relationship. This sets in motion a chemical pattern that can negatively affect their ability to have healthy relationships in the future. "The inability to bond after multiple liaisons is almost like tape that loses its stickiness after being applied and removed multiple times."[9]

The authors explain that one's first experience of casual sex can easily lead to bad decision-making regarding sexual activity. This is because the brain

---

8. Thomas Lickona, "Ten Emotional Dangers of Premature Sexual Involvement," *Center for the 4th and 5th Rs*, 2007, https://www2.cortland.edu/centers/character/images/sex_character/2007-Fall-red.pdf.

9. Joe S. McIlhaney and Freda McKissic Bush, *Hooked: New Science on How Casual Sex is Affecting Our Children* (Chicago: Northfield Publishing, 2008), 43.

synapses that govern sexual self-restraint become weaker. A person's ability to weigh the consequences of their actions is diminished, making it easier to say "yes" to sex. This can become a self-destructive cycle, which continues into a person's marriage.

Additionally, an unhealthy craving arises because the dopamine rush increases one's sexual appetite. Thus, a person who has casual sex the first time is more likely to quickly jump into sex the next time around. In this way sex no longer becomes a big deal.

Clearly, science and True Father agree that the chemistry of first love releases an array of powerful biological and emotional forces that can be either wonderfully beneficial or destructive. These chemical forces work to our advantage as bonding agents when we are in a committed God-centered marriage. When there's no commitment, these same forces can severely damage a person's ability to develop healthy intimacy in marriage. One's first sexual experience affects one's arousal template so powerfully that it is never forgotten. This may be the most important reason why we should save our first love for the person with whom we will spend our whole life.

Points for Consideration/Activities

- Why do you think God designed us so that our first exposure to sex would have such a profound and lasting effect?

- What do you imagine God's purpose was when He gave teenagers powerful sexual desires before they were ready for the Marriage Blessing?

- Watch *Fly Away Home,* directed by Carroll Ballard.

First Night

A baby takes its first steps, falls down, but gets back up again smiling and so excited! Years later, that little baby becomes an Olympic athlete, a gold medalist, the fastest runner in the world! The thrill of reaching one's highest potential in anything begins in a very humble way and is achieved over a period of time.

Just as a future athlete needs to grow up in order to participate in races, young people must develop physically, spiritually, and emotionally before they are ready for first love. Furthermore, getting married and having sex for the first time isn't that different from the example of the athlete starting out with baby steps. It may be awkward at first, but, at the same time, stimulating and fun. In sports, practice yields results, and the same can be said about learning how to make love. Success in love begins with proper preparation, knowing the sacredness of one's sexual organ, and safeguarding it in anticipation of that first night.

True Father's Words

55. "The best relationship is the one that is formed during first love. It is the best, no matter what others say. This cannot be bought at any price. If you can have such a world for eternity, how splendid this is! Everyone should at least reach that level." (1969.5.11)

56. "The place of conjugal love is the flower of the universe. A wife is a composite of all people in the museum of human history. She is the flower of her entire lineage. God is present on her wedding

night. After waiting throughout history, finally, God can settle in the joyful place of a man and woman's love. How awesome is this place! She must think, 'I have the role to open the way, to reconnect the broken path, and to explode in love as a perfect minus, where this has never been done before.' From here, the bright sun of love rises above heaven and earth. When a man enters his wife's room, he should do so as the embodiment of love and of the ideal." (1988.7.22)

57. "A woman on her way to find her man should be thinking: 'I am seeking the one who is more precious than God. I am on my way to meet you with what is most precious. With great care, I have treasured and saved this my whole life. I love you.' When women yearn for their men in such a manner, their sexual area throbs." (1990.10.3)

58. "Where do God's absolute love and the absolute love of humankind meet? Only at one point. Where would that be? It is where the sexual organs unite on the wedding night. Well, did you ever think about meeting God there? The question is: where would you unite with Him?" (1997.4.7)

59. "Therefore, if you use your reproductive organs however you want, you will be in serious trouble... This was true for Adam and Eve; they were supposed to have treasured their first love. God guides the first love." (1976.1.25)

60. "Great is the love of the first night of marriage. That is first love. This is the moment a woman offers her body, which she has safeguarded all her life, to her man. This is also the case for the man. On that night, a man offers his chaste body one hundred percent to his woman. The lives they led before marriage were all in preparation for that night." (1993.10.12)

61. "Once you experience the first love with your God-given spouse,

your challenge is to maintain it and share it freely with the rest of humankind. This way of life serves as the foundation for the heavenly life on earth." (1983.11.20)

62. "Once Adam and Eve realized the explosion of their love, the entire universe would have been like one beautiful, fragrant flower garden. They would feel everything echoing their love. When that electrifying sensation came to God, then He would be pulled to them, and His entire creation would have been activated with love. God was supposed to be the matchmaker bringing Adam and Eve together in the explosion of love... In the ensuing explosion of love, all three of them would be consumed! The important thing is that there be no foreign element there, that men and women be pure when they consummate their first love." (1983.6.5)

63. "At this meeting point, your mind, body, and all forty billion cells are focused, pulled in, and poured in there. That is what is known as first love. Based upon first love, all your forty billion cells begin dancing. If you reach that level through your love, then all your forty billion cells, your blood, and body will become harmonized into one. This is total unification. The husband's body belongs to the wife, and the wife's body belongs to the husband. God would come to that place of His absolute partnership and become one. Absolute man and absolute woman combine into an absolute couple and then combine with God and make one body. After they become one body with God, then everything belongs to that one body place forever. Forever yours." (1997.5.4)

64. "Filial love is perfected at the moment a married man and woman make love, that is, have sexual intercourse, for the first time. Here, the perfection of fraternal heart and conjugal heart takes place. This moment is also the starting point for the perfection of the heart of future parents. Thus, the woman's sexual part is the orig-

inal palace of love, the origin of love. From there, love begins; it does not begin in midair." (1994.3.13)

65. "After marrying, the moment when a couple first experiences conjugal love is the moment of their perfection as a man and a woman. They reign supreme. The man is the antenna that represents God's entire plus world, all male characteristics and right-sided things. The woman is the antenna that represents God's entire minus world, all female characteristics and left-sided things. Their union is like the point at which a negative charge and a positive charge meet at the top of the antenna. The place where a man and a woman make love is where they achieve perfection as a man and as a woman. The royal palace of love that can settle on earth as the center of heaven and earth begins from that point. Then the origin of love can finally emerge and connect to our life. Our lineage is connected to that place. At the same time, a nation comes forth from that place. The kingdom of heaven on earth and in heaven begins from the place where the gates of the first love are opened." (1994.05.15)

Sharing Thoughts on True Father's Words

True Father talks about a couple's first night with lots of enthusiasm, using words like "electrifying" and phrases like "explosion of love." He describes how a man and woman who save their sexual organs for the first night experience this explosion in which God can fully participate. Now the husband's body belongs to the wife, and the wife's body belongs to the husband.

In reality, the first night may not be all that great. It could even be disappointing and not meet the couple's expectations. It's important to keep in mind that this is just the start of a process, leading to experiences in which this wonderful new partnership will eventually feel like an explosion of love. For couples who have received the Marriage Blessing, the real preciousness of their first night has to do with God, who has been waiting for thousands of years to experience Adam and Eve's first love. Maybe it's just God that explodes with joy that first night and perhaps that is the real value of a blessed couple's first love.

The time leading up to marriage is the best opportunity to prepare well for this first night. It's important to seek God's guidance through our parents and prayer and not let ourselves just be led by our emotions. When the marriage bond is nurtured over time, and their love consistently grows, the couple will ultimately have electrifying experiences physically, emotionally, and sexually. Through sharing joy and giving comfort and strength to one another in both good and bad times, they build unity and eternal love both as a couple and with God. Their example of a marriage filled with love will inspire their children and others around them. That's an electrifying thought!

Making It Real

My First Night

"Growing up in a world where sex is plastered everywhere, I felt like I had developed some unhealthy concepts of what lovemaking would be like after I received the Marriage Blessing. I had waited my whole life to give my purity to my wife, so I had no real experience of what sex was like, only what I saw from the world. I thought that sex would be easy; it seems simple, right? However, my first experience showed that the reality of sex is soooo different from what the world shows you. I always thought that right before the first time, I would be so aroused that I would not be able to control myself at all. However, right before our first experience, I was the most nervous I have ever been in my entire life, literally shaking. Once we got started, that went away, but the actual act was also nothing like what I expected. It was not the crazy, intense, pleasure-filled, passionate experience with lots of moaning and odd noises that I was expecting. Rather than that, it was fun, curious, kind of icky, and filled with a lot of laughter. I realized that sex is like anything else in life, it takes time and practice to master, and the real deal is not what you expect.

For me, I feel that more than the physical pleasure that it offers, sex is an act of coming closer to each other in heart, trusting one another, and understanding your spouse's needs so you can make her happy. I feel so much more satisfied when my wife has a good experience than when I do, and that is not an easy thing to do. It takes a lot of time and effort! It is tough to explain just how different the reality of sex is from what I expected, but I have to say that it's much more fun and exciting than the intense stuff you see on TV. I think that it is probably different for every person, but in the end, it is super beautiful to jump into your sexual relationship and just figure it all out with the person that you love and have committed your life to. It is a special thing that is just for you two. Totally worth waiting for and worth knowing; it's something that takes time to make great."

A Beautiful Family Celebration

Dr. Chung Sik Yong, Regional President of Family Fed North America, shared the guidance he gave to his son and daughter-in-law after they received the Marriage Blessing and were ready to consummate their marriage. His couple had been praying in preparation for this special occasion. Dr. Yong and his wife performed a beautiful ceremony in their home with the whole family present.

First, the young couple bowed to their father and mother, and then to each other. Dr. Yong then said, "My beloved son and my beloved daughter-in-law, please do well and always put God as the top priority."

Dr. and Mrs. Yong then placed their hands on the heads of the newly blessed couple, who stood between them, and Dr. Yong offered a benediction:

"Heavenly Parent, today my son and his wife are starting their family. How long You have waited for this day. I came from a fallen blood lineage, but because of Your grace, my child came directly from heaven. How long You have waited for this day. Today is an incredible day. How much joy our Heavenly Father must feel!"

After the ceremony, Dr. Yong exclaimed: "Wow! Today is an amazing day for both of you and our Heavenly Parent. We are creating a new tradition."

Dr. Yong went on to describe the rest of the day, sharing how "The whole family enjoyed a lively celebration with cake, and we gave flowers to the new couple. My son's father-in-law shared beautiful words for the occasion, and my wife and I also offered congratulatory remarks.

"The new couple's younger brothers and sisters have a strong determination to want to be like them someday. After our second child received the Marriage Blessing, she asked, 'Father, we are ready to start our family. When are you going to give us a benediction?' Our third child made the same request. I said, with a smile, 'OK, wait, wait.'

"The first night is so precious; really, really precious. I think this should be one of the most important traditions of our blessed families. This is the way families can become rooted in the tradition of filial piety."

Planning the First Night

Most young couples, before their first night together, are curious about what to expect. Some may turn to pornography for information. It's normal to be curious. God created us to be interested in sex, but viewing pornography isn't the way to prepare for an awesome sex life with your future spouse. That choice will inevitably lead to unrealistic expectations and could turn into a serious addiction.

If you want to know more about lovemaking, you could talk with your parents or a married older brother or sister who can share about what to expect and how to prepare for what is meant to be a very beautiful and natural experience. A pastor may be able to recommend a good book for newlyweds as well. Expect to have a wonderful time exploring this glorious new world together with your spouse.

The first night doesn't have to be electrifying. A priority for this unique experience is to not worry, have fun, and create beautiful memories that can be recalled years later. Your inexperience and mistakes may make the first night even more memorable, especially if you were both laughing about them in the moment. As a couple, you will learn and grow and become more and more intimate. Practice makes perfect! Families may want to consider adopting Dr. Yong's tradition with their own children. This is a wonderful way to invite Heavenly Parent into their children's future lives.

Points for Consideration/Activities

- How does the first night tradition in Dr. Yong's family differ from the way most couples begin their sexual relationship?

- How would you like to prepare for your child's first night? If you are single, how would you like to prepare for the first night with your spouse?

- If you're single, what expectations do you have for your first night? If you have already received the Marriage Blessing, what were your expectations for your first night, and were they met?

God's Wedding

Parents, at the wedding of their adult children, have a glow in their eyes, and they feel like they're floating on clouds! When we see their joy or experience it ourselves, we catch a glimpse of God's desire to participate in the marriage of His own children. God may be invisible, but that doesn't mean He can't be fully present when His children get married. We can imagine our Heavenly Father dancing with His newly blessed daughter and Heavenly Mother dancing with Her newly blessed son on their wedding day!

True Father's Words

66. "Should not Adam and Eve's wedding also be God's wedding? Where will you go to meet God, who created the object partner of His love to be superior to Him? Where will you go to unite with Him? Through the nose? Where would it be? This is a weighty matter. As such, the sexual organs, found in both men and women, are the original garden wherein God can reside. That is where His love is perfected for the first time. That is the place where concave and convex come together as one. That is where the perfection of human beings, that is, the perfection of woman, man, and God, takes place centering on love." (1994.6.19)

67. "God's wedding is Adam and Eve's wedding, which is why His kingdom on earth and in heaven come into existence simultaneously. It starts with the love nest. The moment the male and female sexual organs come together without falling is the point where God's King-

dom on earth and in heaven originate. That is also the base where the three great kingships should be established. A love nest cannot be built anywhere else except in that place." (1994.8.16)

68. "Whose wedding is the marriage ceremony of Adam and Eve? It is God's wedding. If that had been the case, what would have been the result? The sexual organs would have become first of all the palace of God's love, the original palace of love. That is why the family is said to be the palace because the organs are the original palace of love. The family generally is the palace, and the organs are the vertical original palace of love. How precious they are!" (1994.11.23)

69. "We seek to return to the original homeland—the place where the love of God and humankind are connected—the male and female organs. Where does the love of God and humankind begin to unite? God, who is the root of the life, love, conscience, and lineage of Adam and Eve, will, from the vertical position, inevitably enter the center of the union of the external form and internal nature of Adam and Eve, who are in the horizontal position. Therefore, Adam and Eve's marriage is also God's marriage. The male and female organs are the instruments that will liberate and perfect God. Hence, God is the Father, the vertical Father, while perfected Adam is the horizontal father." (1994.3.16)

70. "For the sake of love, God divided Himself into man and woman. The invisible God, as one united being, cannot experience the stimulation of love. It was to feel this stimulation that He divided Himself into man and woman, manifesting His incorporeal substance into corporeal substance… These must become one if they are to return stimulation to the realm of incorporeal substance… So when a man and a woman become substantial object partners by becoming one with each other, they finally become the partners of God's love." (1994.1.30)

71. "Is that not the place where our existence began? Men and women are born there. They did not come into being through kissing, did they? Therefore, would it not be desirable for the male and female sexual organs to unite absolutely? Do husbands and wives long to unite absolutely or moderately? To receive love through that organ, a woman needs to stand in the position where she attends not only her husband but also God spiritually. Externally, Adam's sexual organ is his own, but internally, it is God's. Externally, the woman's sexual organ is also Eve's, but it is His internally. What is invisible is vertical, and what is visible is horizontal. That is how the vertical Parent and the horizontal parents attain oneness." (1997.4.7)

72. "God's wedding takes place on Adam and Eve's wedding day. There would be one vertical wedding and one horizontal wedding. Through their sexual organs, man and woman would attain God's absolute love and, at the same time, reach the center of that love and be united centered on His love. Had this come about, they would have been united centering on their minds, like God." (1997.4.15)

73. "Internally, Adam and Eve's marriage ceremony is God's marriage: in other words, it is a dual wedding. What unites the two are the male and female organs. Without those, one's life would not have come into being. Through the organs, the lineages and history of humanity have been perpetuated. Even God's ideal world will be established by the children, the beloved children, who have passed through those gates. That is how His kingdom will be built." (1998.2.3)

74. "Adam's wedding is also God's wedding. This is His greatest secret. By finding this out, I became a specialist in the anatomy of the sexual organs. Everything unites centered on the sexual organs. If not for them, man and woman would not know love, and there would be no place for their lives to come together." (1995.11.3)

75. "Even the wall is looking forward to seeing you without falling asleep, wondering, 'Tonight what time is my master couple going

to hold a banquet for the celebration of love where God will come down and participate?'" (2000.9.22)

Sharing Thoughts on True Father's Words

True Father discovered God's greatest secret: Adam and Eve's wedding was to be God's wedding! Adam's masculine nature and Eve's feminine nature both came from God. Had Adam and Eve waited until God gave them permission to marry and then become one, through their sexual organs, those two parts of God also would have united. God would have become complete when Adam and Eve made love. That was to be God's wedding. What does this mean for each of us?

The Marriage Blessing is core to our faith because it is through our spouse that we can love and attend God in a new and profound way. True Father teaches that both the husband and wife's sexual organs are God's sexual organs. Therefore, married couples should love each other as God's representatives. When a husband and wife strive to give love, care, and attention to each other, they express the love God intended for each spouse to receive.

The more a couple can be aware of God's presence during lovemaking, the more they can experience divine love. Our Marriage Blessing has the potential to create this kind of inseparable connection, where husband and wife can share their joy with God. True Father refers to this as the union of the vertical and horizontal. The wedding of a true man and true woman is God's wedding. This has always been God's ideal since before He created the cosmos, with the Marriage Blessing as the culmination of His creation.

Making It Real

God's Dwelling Place

"Do you not know that you are God's temple and that God's Spirit dwells in you?" (1 Corinthians 3:16 English Standard Version)

Jesus came with a new teaching at a time when the Jewish people believed that the holiest place was the temple of Jerusalem. He stated that this Old Testament belief was being replaced by a new truth proclaiming that we, as God's children, are meant to be His temples. There was so much more for Jesus to reveal, but his crucifixion made it impossible. Sadly, God had to wait until He could send the True Parents in the Completed Testament Age so that the whole truth could be proclaimed.

True Parents revealed that God created Heaven as a place we enter as husband and wife, not as individuals and that complete salvation can only be accomplished through the Marriage Blessing. A crucial part of True Parent's mission is to model the lifestyle of a heavenly couple. As we look back on when they were together on this earth, we observed a beautiful, affectionate couple, holding hands, hugging, kissing, singing, and dancing with one another, praying and doing God's Will together every single day. It was clear that they were continuously inviting God into their marriage, both publicly and privately. The lesson we've learned from their example is that our Heavenly Parent wishes to be fully present in the hearts, minds, and bodies of blessed couples at all times. The time in which God can manifest Himself most completely is when a blessed couple is making love. This is where God, husband, and wife, all three, can experience unparalleled everlasting love.

Blessed couples need to develop the sensitivity that their spouse's body is God's body and that their sexual organ is God's sexual organ. When we make love with our husband or wife with this awareness, we are loving and honoring God as well as our husband or wife, and inviting Him into our marriage. True Father teaches us that God is present and stimulated in a way He could never experience by Himself. Likewise, the couple comes to know God in a more intimate way than they could as individuals. This is the place where couples develop their deepest love and become the most powerful manifestations of our Heavenly Parent, and it is also the place where God rejoices.

God could not experience love all by Himself, and neither can we. Thus, He designed us with the desire to experience love with a partner of the opposite sex. All of creation was to revel in the beauty of a blessed couple making love.

"For the creation waits with eager longing for the revealing of the songs of God." (Romans 8:19 English Standard Version)

How amazing and beautiful is this truth, that God and all of creation are eager to celebrate the love of a husband and wife. A blessed couple in Scandinavia illustrates this in a delightful story:

"In the early days of our marriage, we were up in the Laplands making love outside in nature when suddenly we looked up and there standing over us was an enormous moose. We froze. Then I looked at my husband, and I said, 'I think he's waiting for us to finish.' So we did, and the moose turned and walked away!"

The Radical Marriage of a Runaway Nun and a Renegade Monk

This is the true story of the marriage between the great reformer, Martin Luther (1483-1546) and Katharina von Bora (1499-1552). Before marrying, they had both dedicated their lives in service to God. Martin Luther had been a monk when he broke his vow of celibacy to marry and have a family with Katharina von Bora, a nun.

In a daring act in 1517, Martin Luther published his *Ninety-five Theses,* a list of protests against the Catholic Church's corrupt sale of indulgences.[10] What most people don't know about this famous religious man is that he had a remarkable marriage. It all started when, in 1523, Martin Luther became a matchmaker for twelve nuns who were rumored to have escaped in smelly pickle barrels from a Roman Catholic nunnery near Wittenberg, Germany. These women were there against their will, and that is why they escaped. Apparently, he found husbands for all of the women but one, Katharina von Bora, whom he eventually married himself.

The attraction between this husband and wife didn't start out as a physical attraction. He was drawn to her spiritual devotion and grew to love her deeply as his chosen wife. Martin Luther disagreed that sex was merely for procreation. He promoted the novel idea (novel in the 1500s) that sex in

---

10. Items that were purchased to buy one's way out of trouble with God

Christian marriage is meant to glorify God and is a gift intended by the Creator for our pleasure. According to this famous reformer, "The greatest good in married life, that which makes all suffering and labor worthwhile, is that God grants offspring and commands that they be brought up to worship and serve Him."

How do we know so much about their marriage? Martin Luther shared about his marriage and family in his sermon, "The Estate of Marriage." He was a husband and father with a modern view of family life. He and Katharina had six children, so that meant lots of diaper washing. His comment on that was witty, "God, with all his angels and creatures, is smiling—not because that father is washing diapers, but because he is doing so in Christian faith."

Martin and Katharina were both devoted to their faith, but after they married and had children, their collaboration to do God's Will accomplished a great deal more than they could have achieved on their own. Katharina discovered she had a talent for business, and through her efforts, the family property was expanded to provide a financial base and venue for their work. Fellow reformers gathered at their home to discuss ideas and make plans, and this became the epicenter of the Reformation movement. Martin was able to devote himself fully to teaching and promoting needed reforms while Katharina managed their estate. She also joined in their discussions and was said to have made significant contributions to the reform movement's progress. God's energy had multiplied exponentially through their marriage.

Teamwork Makes the Dream Work

Worshipping God as a single person is deeply fulfilling and uplifting. When a husband and wife have a common faith and shared passions, they can achieve a lot more together than they could as individuals. True Parents' lifestyle of serious but joyful teamwork inspires us to dedicate our marriages to God and to the promotion of world peace. When husband and wife collaborate to make God happy, they experience a special feeling of divine presence in their relationship.

Imagine sitting alone watching a magnificent sunset over the ocean on a warm, sandy beach. It's inspiring and peaceful and fills you with serenity. But wouldn't it be even better watching that same glowing array of intense orange, pink, and blue with a beloved spouse, arms wrapped around each other, whispering tender words of love?

Points for Consideration/Activities

- Name a couple that you look up to? What is it about them that inspires you?

- Do you think it's important for a couple to share values and a common faith in their marriage? Why or why not?

- Share your thoughts about how marriage helps people grow.

Guardians of the Universe

Soccer fans enjoy watching goalies make extraordinary saves to defend the net. Goalies practice many different strategies so they can prevent the offense from scoring. Just as a goalie has the job of guarding the net, we have something very special to protect, our sexual organs. True Father has said the sexual organs are the core of the universe. When we protect our purity, we are doing much more than saving ourselves for marriage. We are guarding the future God has envisioned for this world.

True Father's Words

76. "Because of the Fall, we have misperceived, mistreated, and abused the word 'love' to this day. In truth, love is the original, holy palace. The original place of love is the holy palace, the most precious place. The palace door cannot be opened just as you please. Only when you become the king and queen of love can you open that palace door. This is the original tradition of love for all people. The king and queen who have True Parents can open that palace door. From that palace, that original palace, God's beloved sons and daughters are born." (1983.10.2)

77. "Protecting and guarding the chastity of men and women is the same as protecting the universe. This is because the order of love between men and women is the basis of the universe. The sexual organ is more important than the head. You cannot find the origin of true love in your head. You cannot find the origin of true life in

your head. You cannot find the origin of true lineage in your head. Where is this origin, then? It is in the sexual organs. Isn't that only too true? Everything can be found in the sexual organs—life, love, and lineage. It is the main palace of love. You can find the root of life there. It is the same in the case of the lineage. The sexual organ is the most precious part of the human body as well as the human world and history of humanity." (1990.6.17)

78. "The sexual organs are the palace of love, the palace in which eternal life is born, the palace that inherits the future descendants and lineage which will succeed to the eternally unchanging traditions of heaven. It is the palace of true life, true love, and true lineage. It is the most precious place of all. You cannot do anything you like with it. You cannot use it without permission from God. It is a place that cannot be touched by anyone other than your husband or wife, who has gained the approval of God and the universe." (1991.3.31)

79. "Sexual organs are the palace of love. What is the current state of that palace of love? The sexual organs of human beings are the most precious in the world: they are the palace of love, life, and lineage. They are the most sacred in the world. Through the Fall, however, they became defiled. From the original viewpoint of God, the sexual organ is not unclean but sacred. It is most precious. Life, love, and lineage are connected to it. This sacred organ was defiled by Satan." *(1991.7.28)*

80. "If this world became one that absolutely valued the sexual organs, would that world be a good world or a bad one? Would it be a thriving world or a perishing world? When God created human beings, which part of the body do you think he put the most effort into making? Would it have been the eyes, nose, heart, or brain? None of these organs are capable of reproducing new life and die out in the end. Isn't that true?" (1996.9.15)

81. "Women need to become sovereigns over their ears and mouths. The Chinese characters for these three words (ear, mouth, and king) combine to form the character for *seong* (聖), meaning saint. When asked, 'Would you like to be a holy woman or a wicked woman?,' every woman will answer that she wants to be the former. That is what is referred to here by *seong* (聖), not the *seong* (性), meaning sexual desire between man and woman. Though the same Korean word is used, the *seong* I am talking about is the combination of ear, mouth, and king. You would do well to think of it as the female genitals. This is true. Isn't it the king? By safeguarding them, you will become saints. Isn't that something worthwhile to learn? You cannot find this in any dictionary or anywhere else. You've never seen such teachings even in Japanese textbooks, have you?" (1997.4.8)

82. "Which is better: the fingers or the head? Which is best in man? Which part of the body is the most precious in men and women? Is it not the sexual organ? How precious it is that it was created so as to be protected against unwelcome intrusions from all directions! That would not be the case if it were located where it could be touched just in passing. So it is thoroughly protected. This is the case for men as well as women. Even if I were God, I could not have found anywhere else to put it. In creating and installing that organ, where would you have placed it in the body? Would you have put it somewhere else? If you had done that, what would happen when a man and a woman are walking together?" (1990.2.21)

Sharing Thoughts on True Father's Words

There are many global issues that concern us all, such as protecting vulnerable people, keeping our children safe, and preserving our planet for future generations. True Father emphasizes another responsibility, which is to protect our purity. Our sexual organ is a sacred treasure that we save exclusively for our spouse. When we safeguard our purity, we build God-centered families, communities, nations, and a God-centered world. In this way, we become guardians of the universe.

Making It Real

The Virgin Saints

Saint Agatha, Saint Lucy, Saint Agnes, and Saint Maria Goretti are called virgin saints by the Catholic Church because they sacrificed their lives to preserve their virginity. Each of these women faced situations in which men tried to force them to enter into sexual relationships even though the women had devoted themselves to be chaste. These very special women understood that the sexual organ is holy and not to be misused, even if it meant enduring suffering. They all were submitted to horrible torture and eventually death to be faithful to their beliefs.

Saint Maria Goretti (1890-1902) was born to an Italian farming family. Her family was poor, and things got even more difficult when her father died of malaria, leaving behind his wife and children. Maria took care of her siblings and worked in the fields to support the family. One day, she was approached by a young man who wanted to force her into a sexual relationship. She cried out, protesting his advances, "No, it is a sin! God does not want it!" In his rage, her attacker stabbed her 14 times. The doctors tried to save her life, but her injuries were too severe. Those who were with her in the hospital observed that as she lay dying, she meditated on the Passion of Christ and saw clearly that Our Lord forgave all sinners. In the last few moments of her earthly life, she was able to forgive her attacker. On her deathbed, she told her mother, "I too, pardon him, and I wish that he could come someday and join me in heaven." The next day, she died peacefully. She was not yet 12 years of age.

The story doesn't end there. St. Maria Goretti's attacker was sentenced to 30 years in prison. He continued to angrily justify his actions, blaming Maria for defending herself and wanting to safeguard her purity. Then he had a life-changing dream in which Maria appeared, looking radiant. She was picking lilies in a field. Then she turned to him and handed him fourteen flowers. He received a message that each lily represented a wound that she had suffered from his dagger and that by giving him the flowers, she forgave him for hurting and killing her. He heard her repeat the wish she made as she was dying, that he could join her in heaven someday.

This event transformed him, and he asked her mother to forgive him. He dedicated the next 40 years of his life to God and did penance for his sin at a Capuchin monastery. His testimony about how Maria died and what he experienced in the dream provided the evidence needed by the Catholic Church to canonize Maria as a saint in 1950.

Even though Maria was only 12 years old, she had the wisdom, faith, and courage to protect her purity with her life. She trusted that God's words were to be taken seriously, so much that she didn't hesitate to courageously abide by what she believed was true.

Heaven's Most Holy Place

Life is precious and must be protected. We are not saying it's better to die than to lose one's purity. We are emphasizing the power that comes with understanding the value of purity. In today's world, a person is less likely to come at you with a knife or a gun and more likely to use flattery and charm. When faced with such deception, we can learn from Saint Maria Goretti's example and inherit her clarity and conviction to protect our sexual organs for our future spouse.

Why is it such a big deal to protect the sexual organs? True Father teaches that God made the sexual organs with the greatest concern and devotion as the source of love, life, and lineage. The cause of the human fall was due to unprincipled sexual love. Adam and Eve misused their sexual organs, breaking the heart of God and destroying His ideal of creation. Since then, God has been working tirelessly throughout history to restore the sexual organs to their original value. Through the Marriage Blessing, True Parents have given men and women the means to restore the failure of our first ancestors and create radiantly happy families and a peaceful world.

Points for Consideration/Activities

- What makes the sexual organ unique from all other parts of the body?

- Why is protecting your sexual organ important to you?

- What would the world look like if everyone valued the sexual organs the way God does?

Sexual Purity in Mind and Body

Have you ever considered what the highest love is? Our greatest desire in life is to share our deepest thoughts and feelings with someone we trust completely. Developing and protecting our purity is foundational for achieving this aspiration. True Father urges us to be wary of sexual relationships and habits based on self-centered desire. He encourages us to build a life of honesty and integrity, where our body is united with the higher vision of the mind and heart. As we develop a life of purity, we learn to value ourselves and others as children of God. Then we are ready to receive our lifelong partner with whom we will experience God's great gift of sexual love.

True Father's Words

83. "Before you try to master the universe, you must first master yourself. This was my motto at the time I was pioneering the path of truth. I told everyone, 'Before you try to gain dominion over the universe or connect with everything in the world, you must gain dominion over yourself.' Our mind can become the true owner, true teacher, and true parent... Our mind wants to live for the sake of our body, but our body doesn't want to serve our mind. That is the problem." (1990.3.30)

84. "Religions teach us to live a sexually abstinent life as a shield against immoral love. The flesh can be an enemy, and this enemy has three great weapons: eating, sleeping, and sexual desire. I have faced all of these. You have no idea how much I struggled,

how many tears I shed to overcome them. In order to make the indemnity conditions to conquer these, you have to do whatever it takes." (1977.10.9)

85. "When young men and women meet as young adults, their hearts leap. When these feelings arise, their hearts go through a change. However, if their minds are not fixed on God, and they stand on the opposite side, they fall into evil. Our mind must be fixed on God. Love is what allows our mind and heart, when focused on God, to rise to the position of oneness with God's heart. Since people have to go through their lives in that position, they absolutely must have dreams and hopes with love as their center." (1969.10.25)

86. "Body and mind need to unite through the sexual organs. There should be only one starting place: if there were two, there would be two different directions. The final destination where the love of humankind and God's love come into contact and settle is the sexual organs." (1994.11.20)

87. "God created the universe with love. Therefore, Adam and Eve should have made the created world a community of love centering on God's love and connecting it to Him. Since this was their responsibility, Adam and Eve should have thought about how and with what attitude they would share the love permitted by God. As matters of love are extremely serious, this determined whether they would live or die." (1997)

88. "If you go to a certain point, you can't trust yourself not to go farther. So don't start. On this matter, the outlook is very strict. We are all human beings, and we know how tempting love can be. We do not even like to have men and women going somewhere together because we know that humans are not strong... Never trust yourself too much. My dispensation is to establish a new lineage of pure blood." (1965)

89. "When a woman is walking on a road and meets a handsome man, she thinks she wants to see him again. This is the nature of the fall. If you are sons and daughters of God, you should not show even the slightest interest in anyone except the spouse that God selected for you. Looking at someone directly itself is not a sin. But when you look with interest, the powerful force of the fall can take effect and can lead to an unexpected accident. That is why when you are walking on a road and come face to face with a handsome man or a beautiful woman, you should not look with interest. I have this worry and anxiety for your sake. God also said, 'Do not eat,' out of His love for Adam and Eve." (1997)

90. "Our mind accompanies us for eternity, while our body accompanies us for a lifespan. Our mind regulates our life, while our body regulates our everyday routine... When we examine this, we can see that the mind's outlook is far broader than the body's." (1970.10.4)

91. "Religion is the training ground where we learn to control our body and its physical desires with the mind. It is the training ground where we cultivate ourselves to become original people in accordance with the ideal of creation. No one, though, can conquer the body without welcoming God into him or herself. Only with the power of God's true love and truth can the mind become the subject partner, take command of the body as its object partner, and realize the ideal of oneness with God. The result is the human perfection that all religions speak of." (1991.8.27)

92. "Life starts from a pure being... Even the heart of a young man, who can smell the fragrance of spring in his puberty, is born pure. Body and mind all are born innocent and spotless. But if a person has self-centered and licentious thinking, can that person be pure?" (1997)

93. "You should not sully your innocence during adolescence. It is the precious period when you can overcome and indemnify the resentment of Adam and Eve, who lost their innocence during their youth. You should preserve your innocence, precious and clean. You should have the integrity and determination that, 'Even if I have to live alone for a thousand years or ten thousand years, I will not allow anyone to trample my love.'" (1997)

Sharing Thoughts on True Father's Words

True Father teaches that sexual purity is about mastering oneself through training the mind and body to resist temptation, especially sexual temptations. He knew this struggle and fought vigorously to be victorious in his mind and body unity. With a parent's heart, he warns us to avoid scenarios where we can be tempted and encourages us to strengthen our mind through a life of faith. True Father says that the power of sexual desire equals the power of desire to meet God; that's why this is such a challenge.

We can maintain purity when we are fixed on God. What does that mean? As we follow the way of our conscience, learn to live for the sake of others, and cultivate our relationship with God, we gain needed skills and experiences that prepare us for marriage. With God at the center of all our love, we strive to become the best person we can be for our future spouse. When we have gained mastery of ourselves by developing our mind and body unity, we can be ready to offer our sexuality as a gift to our future spouse and God. Our sexual organs are the place where God's love and the love of humankind come together.

Making It Real

Religion places a strong emphasis on the importance of purity. In the Bible, God told Adam and Eve not to eat or even touch the fruit of the Tree of the Knowledge of Good and Evil, which True Father teaches symbolized their sexual organs. While True Father cautions us about being attracted to someone of the opposite sex, isn't that the way God created us? Although we may be drawn to someone with a desire to be more than just friends, it's what we do with that desire that matters. Having these feelings is not a mistake in itself. It's best to notice them and allow the sensations to pass, ending our give and take with them. We can adjust our focus to something else so the feelings won't grow into something more.

For many, to remain sexually pure merely means to refrain from having sexual intercourse prior to marriage. But is that all there is to it? What about other forms of sexual activity outside of marriage, such as oral sex and pornography? These are important questions.

God created us to fully experience the joy of sex and doesn't want us to settle for anything less. Purity is about refraining from sexual activities outside of the Marriage Blessing. What we see, think, feel, and do will impact our sexual integrity. Provocative images and words can affect our thoughts and feelings and possibly lead to behavior that we will later regret.

Honest communication allows us to have the experience of accountability and grace. When people, especially parents and children, have open conversations about the ideal for sex and can be honest and forgiving about mistakes, trust deepens. This can help rekindle hope and create a clear vision for the Marriage Blessing. Proverbs 29:18 advises us to plan for a wonderful future: "Where there is no vision, people run wild, but blessed are those who follow God's teachings."

Living with purity involves setting goals to build good character and create healthy ways to cope with life's challenges. When we cast off bad habits, we need to backfill the void with good ones; otherwise, we will be constantly drawn into our old ways. There are many great routines we can develop to protect and strengthen our purity.

Clubs and youth groups can be a healthy way to explore friendships with the opposite sex without being tied to the commitments of an exclusive dating relationship. Getting to know what characteristics we like and are drawn to without becoming sexual is an important skill for everybody. Participating in sports, creative hobbies, and small groups gives us the means to invest ourselves, and, in return, we receive energy, inspiration, and fulfillment. Getting in touch with our hearts through meditation, prayer, and reading True Parents' words will guide us to make the best decisions and take advantage of all of life's possibilities. Remember, this is a marathon, not a sprint. Building new habits in our lives will require patience and consistency.

The Karate Kid

Most of us have seen the movie, *The Karate Kid,* in which a teenager, Daniel, is strongly motivated to protect himself from being beaten up by bullies of the Cobra Kai Karate dojo. To accomplish his goal, he needs both a vision for his future and skills training. The wise Mr. Miyagi becomes his teacher and prepares Daniel for a future karate contest.

It's quite funny when Mr. Miyagi begins the training by having Daniel wax a car, and Daniel follows his instructions to "wax on, wax off" over and over again. The training continues as Mr. Miyagi gives Daniel tasks seemingly unrelated to karate, like sanding a floor and painting a fence, in which he repeats specific motions thousands of times.

The Karate Kid is initially confused about this, but eventually, he learns to trust Mr. Miyagi when he realizes he's not only learning valuable skills, he's learning self-discipline and the value of hard work. He comes to understand that with relentless practice, offensive and defensive strategies become second nature and automatic. As he practices, he becomes more confident that he can win, and the vision for success is more solid and promising.

How does the Karate Kid's story relate to living a life of purity? To prepare for the challenges of living with pure thoughts, feelings, and behaviors, first, one has to have a vision for a wonderful marriage, similar to Daniel's vision to win the contest. Just as Daniel practiced offensive and defensive moves, we have to learn and acquire healthy habits that empower us to make purity a lifestyle.

Purity Is Not an Egg

There is a common misconception that purity is like an egg, and if it gets cracked, it remains broken forever and can never be restored. This way of looking at purity has left many in despair of no longer attaining the "ideal" standard. Disheartened and ashamed, they walk away from the beautiful Marriage Blessing God has prepared for them in their life. God's heart is big enough to forgive and provide a way for purity to be restored. No matter what is in our past, we are all worthy of God's love.

It is helpful to consider our purity like a garden. To take care of the growing plants, we prepare the soil, water and tend to them daily, ensuring they receive all the proper nutrients. If we notice our plants are wilting, it only takes time and investment to nurse them back to health so that they can bloom and express their true beauty once again. What was broken can be restored.

Points for Consideration/Activities

- Share some good habits that you can use to keep your thoughts, feelings, and actions pure.

- Why would sexual purity be considered a gift to your spouse? How is it a gift to God?

- Watch *The Karate Kid*. Talk about any similarities you see between Daniel's training and your own training to live a life of purity.

Why Do We Marry?

If you were to ask ten friends why they think people marry, you would likely get ten different answers. One person may say that marriage is for love and security. Another believes it's for a better lifestyle. Some may say it's to make their parents happy, or because they don't want to be lonely. Oftentimes, people who are divorced say they married for the wrong reasons. Jackie Kennedy, the wife of former U.S. President John F. Kennedy, said, "The first time you marry for love, the second for money, and the third for companionship." This perspective causes many to wonder why they should even get married.

True Father's Words

94. "God is the source of love, life, and lineage. Where would the love, life, and lineage of man and woman come together? It would be the secret place of man and woman, namely their sexual organs. Thus, of all great enterprises in life, the greatest is marriage." (1990.12.30)

95. "Through marriage, a new future is created: Societies are formed; nations are built. God's world of peace is realized with married families at the center. It is in the family that God's Kingdom of Heaven is brought about." (2010)

96. "We should sing about the supreme sacredness of marriage. Married life is the path along which a man and a woman can love each other. Whom do they come to resemble through their unity? They resemble God Himself. A man and a woman must become one in

order to resemble God, who created them in His image. Only then will God dwell with them." (1974.2.8)

97. "Why get married? We marry to resemble God. He has dual characteristics and is a unified being in which both characteristics are harmonized. Man and woman were created to resemble each of His characteristics. Thus, man and woman should come together in complete unity and harmony and become like a seed, returning to the position of God's original character. Marriage signifies attaining the position in which the couple can become one with God." (1998.2.2)

98. "People marry to give love to God. We love God because we need to become one with God. When we become one with God based on the eternal love of the absolute God, we can realize eternal life. This is not all. The world created by God through love belongs to Him, of course, but that world can become mine through the right of inheritance. At the place where we come to meet with God, He bequeaths us the right to inherit the entire universe." (1985.12.20)

99. "Who is the owner of the male and female organs? It is the vertical God. Where do the ideal love of God and human beings come together? In the sexual organs. We marry to meet God. These are amazing words. God does not reside in some other separate place. When we have attained that position, we will find Him dwelling there. Where does the teaching concerning the three great subjects come together and take root? It is in love. The love of God and human beings come together through the sexual organs. Marriage is for us to be engrafted to God's vertical love." (1990.6.26)

100. "The time of marriage is the time when one inherits the love of God. It is also the time when we inherit the authority of re-creation. The joy God felt after He created Adam and Eve appears

through marriage. After that, the right of dominion commences."
(1975.1.26)

101. "What is marriage? Through marriage, the woman, who is only half-complete, is made whole by the fulfillment of love with a man. The same is true of man, in that he is perfected through marriage by becoming one in love with a woman. Thus, the male and female organs are absolutely necessary. The male organ was made for the woman, and the female sexual organ for the man. Their sexual organs were not made for themselves." (1994.11.20)

102. "What is marriage? Why is marriage important? Marriage is important because it is the road to finding love. It is the road to creating life. It is the road where the life of a man and a woman unite into one. It is the place where a man's lineage combines with a woman's lineage. History emerges through marriage, and from marriage, nations appear, and an ideal world begins. Without marriage, there is no meaning to the existence of individuals, nations, and an ideal world. This is the formula. Man and woman must become absolutely one. Parents and children must become absolutely one with God, love God, and live and die with God. And when they die and go to the spirit world, that is the place called Heaven." (1996.8.1)

103. "The purpose of marriage is self-perfection and dominion over the universe. When one perfects himself, he seizes control of the universe and embraces the world of the future. Marrying is a statement that we will perfect ourselves and come to possess God. Thus we will eternally remain as a counterpart of God, one who has assisted Him in realizing His ideal of creation." (1993.4.18)

104. "Mutual perfection is achieved through marriage and by the union of man and woman, who are two halves, through their sexual organs. Man becomes perfected through woman's love. He perfects her, and she, him. This perfection, and union of true life, takes

place centering on true love. Man and woman are unified in true love." (1997.1.1)

105. "Marriage is intended to perfect the ideal of the sexual organs. Marriage is to satisfy that ideal. Is that wrong or right? This may sound like a coarse conclusion, but it is not coarse at all. It seems coarse because it is expressed in the words of coarse people in a secular world, but it is holy in God's original world. Where is the most holy place desired by God? It's the place wherein love can dwell forever." (1996.7.24)

Sharing Thoughts on True Father's Words

What was God's hope for Adam and Eve in their marriage? True Father explains that God, as the original source of masculinity and femininity, divided Himself into man and woman. The marriage of Adam and Eve would have been God's marriage, too, planting a seed for the future world of heavenly families. True Father brings this larger perspective to marriage with this important discovery. Adam and Eve, and all their descendants following in their example, could have inherited God's love and co-creatorship through marriage. How magnificent is that!

Man and woman are incomplete halves who can only become complete and perfected through exchanging their sexual organs in marriage. To this end, God made something that man wants and placed it in woman, and He made something that woman wants and placed it in man. True Father says that when husband and wife are rooted in true love for the sake of the other, they become owners and can begin their journey of embracing each other's worlds. Ultimately, the answer to the question about why we marry is very simple. We marry to resemble God.

Making It Real

What is it about being married that makes a person happy? One new husband said, "I am really happy to have someone to share new life experiences with." A wife fondly recalls the way her husband treats her like a queen opening all the doors for her. Martin Luther, well known for his belief in conjugal love, stated, "There is no more lovely, friendly, and charming a relationship, communion or company than a good marriage."

Given the joy and fulfillment many married couples feel, why are there fewer young people today willing to make a lifelong commitment to one another? There are several answers to this question.

Historically, marriage agreements were entered into for a variety of reasons, most of them having nothing to do with God. If you were part of a royal family, marriages were arranged in order to best preserve a country's well-being, expand its territory, or avoid war. In farming communities, parents wanted their adult children to marry someone who would help out on the farm and have many sons to provide labor. In some cultures, it was common for a man to have several wives in order to have lots of progeny to carry on the lineage. There were societies where women were not allowed to own anything, so they depended on marriage to provide them with property and security. Many of these situations still exist today, depending on the laws and customs of the region.

Modern marriages often begin with physical attraction or a feeling of good chemistry. These marriages may not last long because they are based on conditional qualities that may not last. A successful lifelong union depends on the mature character of both spouses and their shared values.

Today, many young people choose to live together without the commitment of marriage. From the world's view, it seems a very pragmatic approach, like taking a car for a test drive before buying it. Still, others avoid romantic partnerships altogether, preferring a computer screen over a real person. In Japan, a study found that 42 percent of 18-34-year-olds had never been in a sexual relationship and never intended to be.[11] Real relationships are just too complicated, and so people become satisfied with fake sex instead.

---

11. Victoriano Izquierdo, "How Porn & Technology Might Be Replacing Sex for Japanese Millennials," *Fight the New Drug*, April 17, 2019, https://fightthenewdrug. org/how-porn-sex-technology-is-contributing-to-japans-sexless-population/.

Today we face a relentless attack on the sanctity of marriage due to a vast misunderstanding about the purpose of the sexual organs. We live in a society where people get a distorted view of sex through advertising, entertainment, and in schools that encourage sexual experimentation. There are so many options, now acceptable and available, in the free sex world that falsely promise happiness and satisfaction. These activities substitute real intimacy in favor of fake arousal and short term highs from viewing pornography or other self-serving, sexual activities. People now question the value of marriage and the need to commit to one person for the rest of their lives.

It's no wonder people are confused about marriage and sexuality. Young people lack healthy role models to show them the importance of maintaining purity. Where can they find valuable education about the purpose of their sexual organs and the sanctity of marriage? Who prepares engaged couples for a God-centered marriage and family in the future? True Father said that we must create a Pure Love movement to educate everyone about the importance of keeping their purity in preparation for a wonderful marriage. This is the mission of High Noon and other educational programs that evolved through the teachings and activities of True Parents.

A True Love Story

An elderly couple, Margaret and Don, were both hospitalized for different reasons. They were at the same hospital but on different floors. Their daughter, Pattie, tried for months to get them placed together in the same room. Finally, the devoted daughter's persuasion worked, and the couple, nearing their final days on earth, were placed in the same room. It was here that the couple could reach across the space between their beds and hold hands, a habit they had enjoyed for 59 years of marriage. Margaret and Don spent their last few days this way and finally passed away within hours of each other. The daughter remembers her parents sharing during that time about the future. Her dad said to his wife, "When we get to heaven, we can walk in together, just like we're getting married again. Another honeymoon!"[12]

Points for Consideration/Activities

- Before you married, what were your reasons for marrying? Be specific.

- If you're not married, why would you choose to get married?

- What is one thing you could do to improve your marriage or prepare for a great marriage in the future?

---

12. Megan Bailey, "7 Godly Love Stories that Inspire," *Beliefnet*, 2019, https://www.beliefnet.com/love-family/relationships/marriage/7-godly-love-stories-that-inspire.aspx.

Section III
Conjugal Love

The Sacred Value of Sex

What do you consider sacred? Perhaps your family treats the dinner table as a sacred place without phones and distractions, just a place to connect and share delicious food and personal stories. Maybe your family starts the meal with grace, inviting God to enjoy this time with you all. Sacred may not be the first word you'd use to describe this time, but as it is a moment your family connects in heart and invites God, He is certainly present. True Father teaches that sex is also meant to be a special and holy time when husband and wife come together in mind, body, and heart, inviting God into this deeply intimate experience. His teaching about the sacred value of sex is not common in society or churches, but it is with this understanding that we truly bring joy to God and ourselves.

True Father's Words

106. "The sexual organs are sacred entities. Is that right or not? Why do you look at me so strangely? Why are you looking at me as if to say, 'The founder of the Unification Church is talking about sexual organs?' Can pastors speak of such sexual organs? They would all be spat upon. Are there men and women who spit on the sexual organs? Do men spit on the female organs, and do women spit on the male? Sexual organs are sacred things. Sacred, sacred, sacred is the sexual organs. They are sacred. They are the place of the perfected Adam who has not fallen. They are the sacred place, the sacred palace. They are the highest palace. The sexual organs are the original palace of life and love." (1997.6.5)

107. "Your organ of love is more important than your brain. The origin of true love is not in your brain. The origin of true lineage is not in your brain. Where is that origin? It is the reproductive organ. Everything is in the reproductive organ. In there is life, and in there is love, and in there is lineage. It is the original palace of love. We find also the root of life and lineage residing there. This is the most precious place, not only in the human body but also in the world and throughout history. Without it, the multiplication of humankind would be impossible." (1990.6.17)

108. "In the Old Testament, we find terms such as 'holy place" and 'holy of holies.' The holy place symbolizes a person, and the holy of holies symbolizes the house of love, the house in which you can love. Every person has his or her own holy place and holy of holies. In other words, the holy place is a house where you can attend God... The holy of holies is the place where you connect to Heaven. It is where you create a direct relationship with God. If you wonder where that place is, it is your reproductive organ. No one can touch this. There are surely not two high priests serving the holy of holies. There is only one. Long ago, the one who had the key to Eve's holy of holies was Adam, and the one who had the key to Adam's holy of holies was Eve." (1984.6.20)

109. "Where were Adam and Eve supposed to meet each other? They were to meet on a vertical line. They were supposed to become one in love. What is love adjusted to? It is adjusted to the center. This center is the sexual organs of a man and a woman. This is where love is adjusted to. The genitals of a man and a woman are so precious. Therefore, men and women must treat them with respect like they do God throughout their lives. This organ is the most holy place." (1989.1.17)

110. "The sexual organs are the palace of love. What is the current state of that palace of love? The human sexual organs are the most pre-

cious in the world: they are the palace of love, life, and lineage. They are the most sacred, the most precious, in the world. Life, love, and lineage are connected to them. These sacred organs were defiled by Satan." (1991.7.28)

111. "If a beautiful man and a beautiful woman, each created as God's greatest work of art, were to make love centering on God, this would be a sublime expression of the highest, most transcendental love, rather than worldly love. This love is the most beautiful and representative love, the kind of love that will shine for all of eternity." (1969.10.25)

112. "The human sexual organs are sacred. They are the palace of life, where the seed of life is sown, the palace of love, where the flower of love is made to bloom, and the palace of lineage, where the fruit of lineage is borne. Through this absolute sexual organ, the absolute lineage, absolute love, and absolute life is brought forth; and absolute harmony, absolute unity, absolute liberation, and absolute Sabbath brought about." (2006.4.10)

Sharing Thoughts on True Father's Words

Christian ministers rarely talk about sex in their sermons, and when they do, they usually talk about its misuse. This is understandable since they do not fully know the sacred value of sex. Now with True Parents' revelation of the true significance of the sexual organs as God's most holy palace on Earth, we can experience a love that was meant to shine for all eternity.

God created the sexual organs as His greatest work of art, where He could manifest most fully when a husband and wife make love. Because love, life, and lineage are connected to the sexual organs, it is the most sacred part of our body. Without them, humankind would soon become extinct. True Father teaches that husbands and wives come to know God and build a relationship with Him through their sexual organs. This is why we must treat them with the same respect as we do God. It is through sexual relations that we perfect our character and spirit to become God's temples.

Making It Real

Why should we treat sex as sacred? Many young people are growing up believing that we should all be able to do whatever we want with our bodies as long as we're not hurting anyone else. Movies, TV, social media, locker room talk, Sex Ed classes in public schools all validate and encourage casual self-centered sexual activities. In today's world, the emphasis is on freedom of choice, immediate gratification, and doing whatever feels right to you. Meanwhile, intimacy is lost, and social problems are increasing. Unwanted pregnancies, human trafficking, prostitution, and pornography addiction are all on the rise because of society's acceptance of self-centered sex.

Many problems of humanity can be traced back to what religion refers to as sexual sin. True Father teaches that God has been separated from all His children because our first ancestors failed to regard their sexual organs as sacred. Although prayer and study help us come closer to God, we cannot fully connect with Him as single people. When we receive the Marriage Blessing and engage in sexual relations with our spouse, we come to experience God's love most completely. Even though most major religions don't talk openly about sex, they do believe that marriage is a holy sacrament between one man and one woman that God intended from the beginning. The sexual organs are sacred, and the act of love is holy.

God established various religions in different cultures to guide us on the journey of restoring our relationship with Him. The role of sex in marriage is emphasized in most major religious sacred texts.

Catholics believe that a married couple forms "the intimate partnership of life and love established by the Creator and governed by his laws; it is rooted in the conjugal covenant, that is, in their irrevocable personal consent... Both give themselves definitively and totally to one another. They are no longer two; from now on they form one flesh. The covenant they freely contracted imposes on the spouses the obligation to preserve it as unique and indissoluble... What therefore God has joined together, let not man put asunder." (Libreria Editrice Vaticana, *Catechism of the Catholic Church*, 2nd ed. Washington, D.C.: United States Conference of Catholic Bishops, 2019, 568)

The Prophet Muhammad stated in the Quran that Allah designed the relationship between husband and wife: "O' mankind! Have consciousness of your Lord who has created you from a single soul. From it He created your spouse and through them He populated the land with many men and women. Have spiritual awareness of the One by whose Name you swear to settle your differences and have respect for the wombs that bore you. Without doubt, Allah (SwT) keeps watch over you all." (Qur'an 4:1)

Judaism and Christianity regard marriage and sexual love as God's plan for human life: "Therefore a man shall leave his father and his mother and hold fast to his wife, and they shall become one flesh." (Genesis 2:24 English Standard Version)

The Nightingale by Hans Christian Andersen

A Story about Valuing a Treasure

In Ancient China, there was an Emperor whose kingdom was known for its natural beauty. Writers, poets, and artists often visited there for inspiration. One of the subjects of their work was a sweet singing Nightingale, and when the Emperor heard about this, he demanded its capture so he could listen to the bird sing. The Nightingale was captured and given to the Emperor as a gift on his birthday. She happily entertained the Emperor day and night. The ruler had never known such comfort and joy.

One day, he was given a man-made nightingale, all decked out in diamonds, rubies, and other jewels, and it had a music box inside. The Emperor turned the crank, and out came delightful songs. The real Nightingale had a loyal, generous heart, and she sang sweetly, but she was a dull grey color and not sparkly and beautiful. The Emperor chose to spend all his time with the mechanical toy, so his once-beloved friend left the palace, forgotten and no longer useful.

Years passed, and the Emperor was sick and dying. There was no music to cheer him up, for the toy nightingale was broken now and unfixable. As he lay in bed, he remembered how the real Nightingale had comforted him, and now he longed to hear her music again. He felt sorry he had neglected her, realizing that he hadn't appreciated her loyalty and love. Then, one morning, as he was close to death, he heard the perfect notes of his old friend, singing joyfully just outside his window. This was a happy reunion that rejuvenated and healed the Emperor.

The real Nightingale could not be replaced by an imitation. Likewise, "fake" sex cannot replace authentic sexual intimacy in marriage. God created our sexual organs to ensure that conjugal love would last forever. But like the Emperor, we sometimes fail to recognize the preciousness of the real thing. When we give in to cheap versions of love, like pornography and masturbation, we lose our connection with our spouse and with God, and eventually, we become as alone and isolated as the Emperor found himself at the end of his life.

True Father brought a unique and profound understanding of the sacred value of sex. Because of his foundation, blessed couples can be educated to honor their sexual organs and create successful marriages in the pursuit of bringing great joy to God.

Points for Consideration/Activities

- What impact has losing the sacredness of sex had on the world? Has it impacted your personal life?

- What does the word "sacred" mean to you as applied to marriage and sex? Can you give specific examples?

- Why would people choose imitation over something real?

Heaven's Gift Exchange

Have you ever participated in a Christmas Gift Exchange? There are many fun ways to exchange presents. In *White Elephant*, you swap gifts numerous times and can never be sure what you'll end up with. *Secret Santa*, on the other hand, is about getting assigned a random person, and you have to find the perfect gift specifically for them. Heaven prepared the ultimate gift exchange for each of us, one that is a little like both of these examples. Like *White Elephant*, it's impossible to know early on who we'll be giving our gift to. But, like *Secret Santa*, we've given thought to and prepared a special gift exclusively for a specific person. What gift did we prepare and how much thought did we put into it?

True Father's Words

113. "Woman absolutely wants what is man's and vice versa. You did not know that the female organ absolutely belongs to man, and the male organ absolutely belongs to woman. By occupying each other's sexual organs, man and woman come to know love. Only through the experience of the two attaining perfect oneness can we know the highest level of love. Nobody can ever deny these facts. Everyone must acknowledge them. An ideal couple comes into being in the place where the two achieve complete unity. Absolute love exists in that very place. God will come and dwell in such a place where love is absolutely unchanging." (1997.12.10)

114. "If all men and women acknowledge that their sexual organ

belongs to their spouse, we will all bow our heads and be humble when receiving our spouse's love. You should receive love only from your partner. There is no real love other than love for the sake of others. Remember that we can find absolute love when we absolutely live for the sake of others." (1996.8.1)

115. "Man's treasure is not owned by him. It is owned by the woman, and her treasure belongs to him. In short, ownership has been exchanged. The woman does not own her sexual organ. She needs to know that it belongs to her man; it is not hers. The same is true for the man. Therefore, one cannot do as one likes with one's sexual organs. American women think of their organs as belonging to them. As a result, they act freely and do whatever they want with them. This is also the case for the men. But you are only the caretaker of your sexual organ. In other words, the caretakers are passing themselves off as the owners." (1987.3.22)

116. "For what purpose were human beings born? To seek the path of love. So the sexual organs men and women have do not belong to them. The organ dangling from man's body is not his. However, he regarded it as his possession. Woman is not the owner of her sexual organ; it is the man's. The owner of the sexual organ on man's body is woman. You must understand this amazing fact that, in this way, the love organs and their owners were interchanged." (1986.3.15)

117. "Man is there for the object partner before him, woman. Since God is the King of wisdom, to prevent them from fighting and staying apart, He placed the most precious parts of each on the other's body; that is, He interchanged the owners. Those precious parts are the male and female organs. It is the most holy place. Wasn't the place built to store the Ark of the Covenant called the most holy place? Anyone who touched it was struck down by lightning, and destruction was wrought for his generation and myriads

of generations to come. The sole owner, the chief priest, is the husband." (1989.6.18)

118. "Present with us today are presidents from more than ten nations; I would like to ask them: try broadcasting this message on the air. Ask whether man's sexual organ is for himself or for woman. Those who claim theirs belongs to them are thieves. Those who think that they own what they have are thieves. This is not a laughing matter. It is a historical declaration. If everyone lived in accordance with this, the world of peace would unfold right before our eyes. As far as God's will is concerned, the most important things are those related to love. To instruct human beings about His will concerning love, God created the most precious organ, that is, the sexual organ and the male organ belongs to woman, and the woman's organ to man! Amen! Do you think this is not true? Do you think this is wrong?" (1996.4.15)

119. "Through the sexual organs, man and woman make love. Yet, God wisely interchanged these love organs, one with the other, so that they could not be apart even if they wanted to. Even when they are separated, one needs to return to the other, having nowhere else to go and no place else to rest. Only by taking one's counterpart along can one harmonize and be welcomed wherever one goes in heaven and earth." (1986.10.25)

120. "Who owns the male and female organs? The owner of the husband's sexual organ is his wife, and the owner of the wife's sexual organ is her husband. We did not know that a person's sexual organ is owned by someone of the opposite sex. This is a simple truth, which is undeniable. Even after history progresses for thousands of years, this truth will not change." (1996.9.15)

121. "Typically, a man thinks his sexual organ belongs to himself, and a woman thinks her sexual organ is her own. That is why the world is perishing. Everyone has been mistaken concerning the

ownership of the sexual organs. People have been thinking that love is absolute, eternal, and dreamlike, but had they known that the ownership of eternal love lies with the opposite sex, the world would not have become like it is today." (1996.9.15)

122. "In fact, the Fall of Adam and Eve originated in the violation of this law. Each of them erroneously thought that their sexual organ was their own. Due to this mistaken view, they were driven out and could not be acknowledged anywhere in the universe. In the mineral, plant, and animal kingdoms, masculinity and femininity—that is, the sexual organs—are reserved for the sake of one's partner of love. Adam and Eve did not know this. Then why do the sexual organs exist? For love. Thus male and female exist in order to find love." (1996.9.15)

Sharing Thoughts on True Father's Words

True Father teaches us that God created a man to value that which his wife holds most dear, her sexual organ. It has a natural power of attraction for him, and he cares for it as he would his own. The same is true for his wife. The transfer of ownership means that they take care of each other's needs. God's intention for exchanging ownership of the sexual organs was to enable husband and wife to become forever bonded in deep intimacy. By each fulfilling the other's desires, they experience more joy than they ever could on their own. When couples honor each other in this way and live according to this truth, they create faithful marriages and healthy families that become the cornerstone of their communities and a peaceful world

Making It Real

Exchange of Ownership

All of God's creation emerges based on the law of attraction. Parts meant to go together naturally enter into a give and take action, like the stamen and pistil of a flower. The pistil is made for the stamen and vice versa. There is an exchange of energy. When you cut open a tulip vertically along the stem's length, you will see the male part of the flower, the stamen, that consists of long tubes with pollen at the tips. In the center is a longer tube, the pistil, or female part of the flower that is usually sticky at the end. At the base of this is a bulge, the flower's ovary, and inside, it looks like there are little eggs. Bees pollinate flowers by transferring pollen from the stamen to the pistil as they collect nectar.

The stamen claims ownership of the pistil and delivers the pollen, and the pistil responds by receiving and taking possession of the stamen's delivery. They share a bond based on the exchange of ownership that is necessary for life to continue. This enables the flower to produce seeds for the next generation.

In his childhood, True Father lived in the countryside, where he spent a lot of time roaming around, exploring the natural world. He said it was there that he learned about love from the animals and plants. He concluded that in God's creation, everything exists for the sake of its partner. When the two parts become one through the exchange of ownership, God's energy multiplies and supplies the force needed for new creation.

Marriage is the place where true love between husband and wife begins and lasts for eternity. It is the place where God can bequeath His lineage. God designed us to come together to exchange ownership of our sexual organs to preserve and expand true love forever with our eternal partner.

The Gift of the Magi by O. Henry

Here is a story about a husband and wife who sacrifices that which they hold most dear for their spouse.

Della has only $1.87, and the very next day will be Christmas. She wants to buy something special for her husband, and this isn't going to be enough. She has an idea. She takes out an old pin that holds her hair back in a bun. Her beautiful locks of hair tumble down to her knees. She runs out the door and goes to a shop that buys human hair. Out the door with short hair and $20 to add to her purse, Della goes shopping at a jewelry store. Everything is too expensive until she finds a gold watch chain that would go with Jim's watch. With just eighty-seven cents left in her pocket, she goes home and tries to disguise her short hair before her husband comes home. When he opens the door and looks at his wife, his expression becomes unreadable and strange. Della thinks it's because of her new haircut, and she begs him not to get upset, explaining why she did it. Jim hugs her and takes something out of his pocket wrapped in paper. She unfolds the wrapping, and inside are the combs for her hair that she had admired in a shop window for months. She asks him how he could afford this? He explains that he sold his watch! She shows him the watch chain, and they decide to put the gifts aside and enjoy them later on in life.

The title of this story is taken from the Biblical story about the magi, the wise men who brought gifts to the baby Jesus. O. Henry compares Della and Jim to the magi at the end of his short story, saying that they are the wisest: "Each sold the most valuable thing he owned to buy a gift for the other." It is a wise choice when we decide to consider another's benefit over our own, and this is the way that love grows.

Heaven's Gift Exchange

True Father's revelatory paradigm about conjugal love is this in a nutshell: spouses exchange ownership of their sexual organs. Once a husband receives ownership of his wife's sexual organ, he begins to learn how to take care of his new treasure. He is asked to delay his own gratification in order to please his wife first. The same applies to the wife. She is tasked with understanding her husband's needs. They each devote themselves to fulfilling the happiness of the other. The exchange of the sexual organs between husband and wife is the foundation for an eternal relationship of true love. God prepared this gift exchange so that husband and wife can grow their love for each other each and every day, forever.

Points for Consideration/Activities

- Were you ever given the responsibility to take care of something very valuable? What did you do to take care of it?

- How might a couple's marriage be affected if they each believed the purpose of their sexual organ is to please their spouse?

- How do you feel when you give somebody a gift that they really love?

Two Become One

If you tasted the ingredients for making a chocolate cake before they were mixed, the butter, flour, chocolate, and sugar would not be delicious. After that cake is baked, it smells so good you can't wait to eat it. God as a creator also likes to combine very different elements to make something much greater than the sum of its parts. The best example of this is His plan for a man and woman to combine their masculinity and femininity to create a thriving marriage and beautiful family. Single people may wonder why they experience a feeling of loneliness at times, and those who are happily married can't imagine living without their spouse for the rest of their lives. Why do we feel incomplete until we come together as one with our spouse?

True Parents' Words

123. "Separately, God's spiritual dual characteristics were manifested in the form of Adam and Eve. Through marriage, the two can reunite vertically. The moment they are united in marriage, the incomplete halves are completed, achieve perfection, and embrace each other's worlds. Only the power of love can bring this about. Not only that, but through marriage, they occupy God and their spouse. That is exactly what marriage is. It cannot be done casually." —True Father (1994.3.11)

124. "Through marriage and the meeting of their reproductive organs, two beings become complete. Man becomes complete through woman's love. Woman becomes complete through man's love. Man

perfects woman, woman perfects man. They become one through true love. In that place, two lives come together as one, with love at the center. That place is the crucible where man's blood and woman's blood become one. From this place come sons and daughters."
—True Father (1997.1.1)

125. "In the Unification Church, we call marriage the 'Blessing.' The life of a married person is such that a man and woman who had been alone on their path to seek love abandon that path and stand as complements to each other—comforting each other when they feel lonely, sharing joy together when they feel joy and giving each other strength during difficulties. In this way, one becomes the right foot and the other the left; one becomes the right hand and the other the left. Together they praise God, saying they are moving forward with God's love superimposed on the theater of their lives." —True Father (1978.10.28)

126. "For humankind, love is an eternal thing—it is one, not two. When a man and a woman become joined through love, they are to grow old together for a hundred years on earth and live together eternally after death. Although the bodies are two, they join as one and rotate, thereby becoming one body. When the two bodies become one, God comes to rotate together with them, thus forming a four-position foundation of love. This is love's ideal setting. False love cannot invade it, and only true love comes to dwell in it." —True Father (1997)

127. "Unlike the relationship between parent and child or between brothers and sisters, the conjugal relationship is not an absolute one from the beginning, as it is not bonded through the blood relation. It involves truly revolutionary determination and resolution, where a man and a woman, who has lived under different environments and circumstances of growing up, meet with each other and create a new life together. Nonetheless, the conjugal

relationship will change into a stronger, more absolute one than the blood relations if a couple unites into one heart and one body through true love. Everlasting and inexhaustible treasures are hidden in the conjugal relationship. If the bond of marriage is once made centering on Heaven, it will grow into an absolute relationship that is eternally inseparable." —True Father (2004.12.2)

128. "At the place where a true man, a true woman, and God unite completely, based on true love, we can find the key to resolving all our problems, including our view of life, view of the universe, and view of God. God's true love invests and invests again, gives and gives again, and forgets having given." —True Mother (1992.5.11)

129. "When a husband and wife live together, they are happier if they experience hurricanes, rainstorms, and thunder as part of the ups and downs of life, and pursue the ideal of love while experiencing such diverse feelings, rather than living comfortably throughout their whole life." —True Father (1987.7.19)

130. "Mutual perfection is achieved through marriage and by the union of man and woman, who are two halves, through their sexual organs. Man becomes perfected through woman's love. He perfects her, and she, him. This perfection, and union of true life, takes place centering on true love. Man and woman are unified in true love." —True Father (1997.1.1)

131. "Where can human perfection be found? There is no way for a man to be perfected by himself any more than a woman by herself. This is all because they are only half-complete; they, therefore, can be perfected only through a complete union of love. In being perfected, whom would Adam absolutely need? He absolutely needs God vertically. To be perfected, Adam needs both vertical and horizontal connections. Without them, he could not generate the circular and spherical motion of love. For this reason, what he

absolutely needs horizontally is Eve. Likewise, Eve also absolutely needs Adam." —True Father (1986.6.1)

132. "Only through the experience of two becoming one can we know the highest level of love. No one can absolutely deny these facts. Everyone should recognize this. At the place where a husband and wife become completely one, the ideal couple will be created. In that very place, absolute love exists. That place of love, which is absolutely unchanging, is the dwelling place of God." —True Father (1997.8.10)

133. "Men and women are each only half of a whole entity. Therefore, women must conquer the world of men, and men must conquer the world of women. That is how they are perfected. They come to resemble God by joining their separate manifestations of God's dual characteristics back together through love." —True Father (1994.5.19)

Sharing Thoughts on True Parents' Words

We may wonder if we could ever become perfect. If we could, is it possible to reach perfection as an individual or is this an impossible dream? True Father teaches that our Creator manifested his dual characteristics in the form of Adam and Eve so that they could reunite substantially on earth as a blessed couple and grow in oneness to become the dwelling place of God. He explains that each of us is only one half of a whole, so it is impossible to reach perfection as an individual. Once we are joined together with our spouse, we begin the lifelong process of perfecting our love as a couple to live together eternally in the spiritual world. Wouldn't it be wonderful to know that when we marry, we give love to God and the world?

Making It Real

In chemistry, we learn about powerful reactions when two substances are put together. Two totally different elements can be combined to create a new substance with far superior qualities. For example, when you combine sodium with chloride, you get table salt.

Men and women are each incomplete until their two lives come together as one. When husband and wife support, comfort, and encourage each other, they become a much more powerful force than they were as individuals. They can digest even the most difficult circumstances and live extraordinary lives. Although we connect with people in various situations, marriage is the only place God created for two unrelated people to enter into a lifelong partnership. In the beginning, it may require lots of work to keep the relationship together. After years of investment, there's nothing that can tear them apart.

God designed sex as a beautiful and unique dimension where husband and wife become absolutely, unchangeably, and eternally one. The best part is that we are no longer alone in the universe, and neither is our spouse. We have connected with our soulmate in a deeply intimate and profound way.

Founding the Salvation Army

In 1865, William and Catherine Booth co-founded the Salvation Army in Great Britain. They shared the ministry, preaching the Gospel in unorthodox ways to the vulnerable and destitute. They chose to serve people with difficult lifestyles, like prostitutes and thieves who were not welcomed in traditional churches.

William and Catherine were devoted to each other as they raised eight children and developed the Salvation Army. At that time, it was unusual for a woman to share responsibility with her husband for church leadership, but God needed a faithful husband and wife team to carry out His plan. The Salvation Army has grown exponentially and is now active in 131 countries, running charity shops, operating shelters for the homeless, and providing humanitarian aid in times of natural disasters. The Booths are a testament to the power of God-centered marriage. When two become one with God, the outcome is one of everlasting and inexhaustible treasures.

True Parents' Holy Wedding

Even the mission of the Messiah could only be accomplished as a couple. True Parents' Holy Wedding Ceremony was held on April 11, 1960. During the marriage ceremony, True Father told True Mother:

"'I think you are already aware that marrying me will not be like any other marriage. We are becoming husband and wife to complete the mission given to us by God to become True Parents, and not to pursue the happiness of two individuals, as is the case with other people in this world. God wants to bring about the Kingdom of Heaven on earth through a true family. You and I will travel a different path to become True Parents who will open the gates to the Kingdom of Heaven for others. It is a path that no one else in history has traveled, so even I don't know all that it will involve.' She responded, 'My heart is already set. Please do not worry.'... I am sure her suffering was great. It took us seven years to conform ourselves to each other. I relate these things because the most important thing in a marriage relationship is trust. It is what makes it possible for two people to become as one." (*As a Peace-Loving Global Citizen*, p. 192-193)

True Parents shared a love for each other and a common vision that inspired them to embrace all the people of the world. It is a wonderful thing that our Heavenly Parent created us so that we would not have to go through life alone. God made the world of men and the world of women totally opposite and, at the same time, totally complementary. Through marriage, we have a partner to laugh and cry with as we help each other through both good times and bad. We can only imagine the possibilities when husband and wife come together in the way God planned.

Points for Consideration/Activities

- Have you ever worked on a project with your spouse that allowed you to accomplish something far greater than you would have on your own?

- Can you think of ways to improve your husband and wife teamwork? If you're single, what teamwork skills can you build to help your future marriage?

Fidelity in Marriage

If you ever walk across the Pont des Arts bridge in Paris, you will see thousands of locks placed there by couples in love. At the bottom of the river are the keys thrown from the bridge, making it impossible to reopen the locks. This beautiful tradition symbolizes lasting love that is unbreakable, locked in place by sacred vows. Locks and keys have often been a symbol of unwavering love and fidelity, from ancient China to modern-day Paris, and now, in the precious words of our True Parents!

True Parents' Words

134. "Who is the owner of that concave female organ? Is it the woman or the man who needs it? Does woman need it absolutely, or man? Man. Also, his is absolutely necessary to her. In terms of who holds the keys to them, he has hers, and she has his. Thus, there is only one person who can open it. Since true love is one, only true men and women can be in charge of it." —True Father (1990.12.1)

135. "More precious than life itself, this is the heavenly law of absolute fidelity. Husband and wife are eternal partners given to each other by Heaven. Through having children, they become the co-creators of true love, true life, and true lineage, and the origin of that which is absolute, unique, unchanging, and eternal." —True Father (2007.2.23)

136. "To whom is a man's sexual organ absolutely necessary? It exists for his wife. Each lives for the sake of the other. At the place where

husband and wife become completely one, the ideal couple will be created. In that very place, absolute love exists. That place of love, which is absolutely unchanging, is the dwelling place of God. Fidelity in marriage, which we can call absolute sex, is centered on God, and free sex is centered on Satan." —True Mother (1997.11.17)

137. "Only your partner can stand eternally in the position of the owner of your love. A woman is the one who perfects a man. Only a woman makes a man an owner of love, and only a man makes a woman an owner of love. Any other kind of owner is false. There is only one key—one partner—to unlock a person's love; not two." —True Father (2004.6.13)

138. "The sexual organ is the point at which two people become one as a unified body of life with love at the center and is the place where the blood of a man and the blood of a woman blend into one, in one melting pot. You should know that this place is more precious than your sons and daughters, more precious than your husband, and more precious even than God. They will call me a heretic for saying things like this... What is that place like? It is a place that is more precious than your children, more precious than your husband, and more precious than your parents. Without it, your parents would have no value, your couple would have no value, and your sons and daughters would have no value. Because it is so precious, it is kept under lock and key as the most precious treasure of your whole life, in order to keep it from being seen by anyone in the world. The key to the man's organ is held by the woman, and the key to the woman's organ is held by the man, and there is only one key each. There must be one key only." —True Father (1997.1.1)

139. "By nature, human beings do not like to share their spouses' love with others. The horizontal relationship of love between hus-

band and wife is different from the vertical relationship of love between parents and children in that once it is shared with others, it becomes ruined. This is because, by virtue of the principle of creation, it becomes necessary for husband and wife to form an absolute unity in love. Human beings have the responsibility to live for the sake of their spouses absolutely." —True Father (1996.4.16)

140. "In loving a woman with God's love, a man should be able to say, 'I love her completely. We share a love that will not change from beginning to end.' Also, a woman should keep her body tightly sealed in order to share such a love. She should close it tightly like a peony flower as if it were wrapped up in many layers. This way, the couple should see the harmony of heaven and earth in spring and start a new life in unity with this. They should do this well." —True Father (1969.10.25)

Sharing Thoughts on True Parents' Words

Fidelity in marriage is sharing that which is most precious with only one person, your eternal spouse. Real intimacy is in direct relation to exclusivity, and that's part of what makes it so special. This is why True Father says there should only be one key for your sexual organ. In a world of free sex, where there are many keys, the ideals of love and family are lost. God's main strategy for building ideal families is fidelity in marriage. According to heaven's beautiful design, a husband and wife are sacred partners given to each other by Heaven. A husband's sexual organ belongs exclusively to his wife and vice-versa. We must always resist free sex so that we can experience resplendent true love.

Chun Hyang

This is a traditional Korean folktale that takes place in the 18th century. Korean culture, highly influenced by Confucianism's guidelines for morality, has praised virtuous behavior in women for thousands of years, thus preparing a heavenly culture of sexual purity for the messiah to be born into.

The protagonists in the story are Mong Ryong Lee, a governor's son, and the woman he falls in love with and marries, Chun Hyang Sung, the daughter of a commoner. Knowing that the governor would immediately disown Mong Ryong if he found that his son married beneath him, the young couple keeps their marriage a secret. When the governor gets a new assignment, he moves the family to Seoul. Mong Ryong is forced to leave his faithful wife behind and promises to return for her when he passes the official exam.

The new governor, Hakdo Byun, replaces Mong Ryong's father, and when he meets Chun Hyang, he wants her for himself. When she refuses, stating that she already has a husband and will forever remain faithful to her beloved, the new governor punishes her by flogging her. Meanwhile, back in Seoul, Mong Ryong becomes an officer, and after three years of separation from his secret wife, he is assigned to return to the city of Naju. There, he finds out the shocking news that his wife is to be beaten to death on the governor's birthday as a punishment for denying his lust. Mong Ryong arrests the greedy and corrupt governor, and the happy husband and wife are reunited.

This story is a lesson in heavenly morality. We may never have to risk our lives to uphold our marriage vows, but our commitment should be as absolute and unwavering as Chun Hyang's.

141. "We advocate the ideals of purity and absolute sexual fidelity. To promote these ideals we have created a pure love movement and a true family movement based on true love. Without true love, there can be neither sexual purity nor true families. Also, a true family cannot be established without absolute fidelity between husband and wife. You must honor relationships to the same degree as Chun Hyang, a chaste wife who remained faithful to her husband, Lee Mong-Ryong, even while facing threats of death from a corrupt court official. In this way, we can realize the true family."
—True Father (1997.8.9)

What Is Infidelity?

In the United States, 50 percent of marriages end in divorce, with infidelity being a major impetus for the breakup. In fact, at least one out of four marriages experience an affair. Infidelity is a violation of the marriage contract regarding both emotional and sexual exclusivity. The starting point of most extramarital relationships begins with an unmet emotional need. When a husband or wife seeks out someone other than each other to satisfy their needs, they devalue their partner and jeopardize the relationship. Having an affair destroys trust and severely damages the marriage. Many couples give up after this, but some marriages can survive when one spouse is willing to fight to resolve the problems and recommit to vows of fidelity.

Making It Real

Fidelity in Practice

Social scientists and marriage experts have been unable to reduce the disturbing trend of extramarital affairs. What could they be missing? To understand the ultimate solution, we need to know God's intention for the sexual organs. True Father teaches us that our sexual organ is most holy and precious and that God designed it to be shared with one person only, our eternal spouse. This is what is meant by one key. When a man and woman enter into marriage and share their sexual organs exclusively with each other, they can experience healthy intimacy and love that can last forever.

True Father teaches that fidelity in marriage is about a husband and wife honoring the promise they made to each other on the day they received the Marriage Blessing and every day after that. Many new couples want to do everything together. When they have separate experiences that are exciting or challenging, they want their spouse to be the first to know about it. Emotional fidelity, the longing to share our highest highs and lowest lows with our spouse first, is such an important part of married life. Husbands and wives share both laughter and tears. When we sail through the stormy seas of life together, we'll reach the shore of eternal joy.

Will remaining faithful guarantee success in marriage? Sadly, it won't. Fidelity alone cannot ensure that you and your partner will remain intimate. A couple can keep their vows, maintain fidelity, do all the right things, and still get into trouble. It's important to keep in mind that conjugal love needs lots of investment and care over a lifetime. From God's perspective, marital fidelity is the most important building block of successful families and a harmonious world. God gave each spouse one key to be shared exclusively with their precious lifelong partner.

Points for Consideration/Activities

- Why would a married couple share their highest highs and their lowest lows with their spouse first?

- What can a couple do to practice fidelity in their marriage and protect themselves from infidelity?

- Did you ever think receiving the Marriage Blessing was a magic pill for a perfect marriage? Why do you think God allows couples to have challenges?

True Love Is Blind

In the movie *Fantastic Four*, Alicia is a blind artist who meets Ben shortly after an accident turns his body to rock, and his fiancé abandons him. Alicia falls in love with Ben, who is now called "The Thing." She helps him accept himself and embrace his new role as a superhero. Ben says, "You don't know what it's like out there. Walking around like some kind of circus freak. People staring, whispering." Alicia responds, "You know, being different isn't always a bad thing." The phrase "blinded by love" is often seen in a negative way when someone fails to see their partner for who they really are. But this expression can also have a positive meaning when it is applied to the husband and wife who choose to see the best in each other.

True Father's Words

142. "One's first love is truly valuable. In the eyes of first love, one's object or subject is mystifyingly beautiful. A woman may think she has an ugly nose—in her mind, a nose so ugly that she would keep it always undercover if she could. But in first love, her beloved says, 'No, put your hands down. I want to see that nose. It is the most beautiful nose I have ever seen.' And he means it! To her husband, that nose is the best possible nose for her. Other people may not be so crazy about it, but that is how first love perceives it. A small woman who always longed to be tall may try to look taller when she gets married. But a husband of true love would say, 'I wish she were even smaller so I could put her in my pocket!'" (1987.8.30)

143. "The innocent, pure baby loves his mother regardless of how she looks. Even if his mother is a hunchback with only one eye, the baby wants to be with his mommy. In the same way, men and women should love each other unconditionally; don't try to evaluate each other. The same way you loved your parents as a child—purely and uncritically—you should love your spouse. Are you confident you can do it?" (1982.6.20)

144. "Do you think Adam in the Garden of Eden was thinking, 'Maybe another woman has a better attitude'? Do you think Eve thought, 'Some other man might be better than this one'? Suppose God happened to make Eve with only one eye? When Adam's first love was ignited, Eve would seem even prettier for having only one eye. First love creates miracles." (1982.6.20)

145. "True love is almighty. There is nothing it cannot do. If someone imagines the ideal, the ideal object that they imagine appears. Even if a husband is not handsome, when his wife comes to love him, he appears handsome to her. Love transforms unattractiveness. We don't know our own faces well. Even though we see them in the mirror every day, we don't know them. When we see ourselves in a photo, we say, 'Oh, so I look like this?' but when we look in the mirror, we don't think that way. According to our mood, we sometimes look like the most repulsive person, sometimes like the most attractive. Sometimes our faces look round, sometimes long. If we look with the eyes of love, no one is better looking than we are. When your eye is very close to something, can you see it well? You need a certain distance in order to focus. If you are too close, you cannot perceive it." (1979.12.16)

146. "A loving husband and wife should not unilaterally stipulate and fix in their minds what their spouse's face should be like. If you imagine the face of your partner as having only one appearance, nothing could be more boring. When you look at your partner's

face with joy, it will appear to be joyful; and if you look upon it with a loving heart, it will look beautiful. You should always see your partner's face as new, like that of water swirling when it flows with new shapes appearing at every turn." (1997)

147. "You should have a creed that you will get married for the sake of your partner and not for your own sake. It is wrong to think that you will get a successful or beautiful person for marriage. If you have understood the principle that a human being should live for the sake of others, then you should consider that marriage also is for the sake of your partner. According to the original view of marriage, you should determine that no matter how ugly your wife may be you will love her more than a beautiful woman." (1997)

148. "No matter how ugly a man's wife is, if he really loves her, he naturally will follow her when she calls. With unity centering on true love, the husband will respond to his wife's beckoning, the elder will follow the younger's call, and the younger will follow the elder's call. None of them will ever want to separate from the other." (1996.9.15)

149. "Twenty-four-karat gold, or pure gold, is worth the same regardless of its origin, be it the land of Korea, a place of scenic beauty, underwater, or some remote spot in a ravine somewhere untouched by human hands. Do you think that, with regard to the spouse you are about to make love to, the sexual organs will protest, 'Oh, I don't like you because your face is ugly'? Once you are in a love relationship, even a pockmarked face will look beautiful." (1996.2.4)

Sharing Thoughts on True Father's Words

The Marriage Blessing begins a lifelong journey in which a husband and wife learn to see beyond the imperfections of the other. Blessed couples should love each other unconditionally without being critical or making comparisons.

Instead of judging our spouse, we see them as God's precious daughter or son. The more we look at our spouse's face with love and joy, the more beautiful they will appear. Unconditional love changes all. It can transform an unattractive spouse into a charming partner. With unity centering on true love, we see the divine nature of our spouse.

This is true not only in the way we look at our spouse but in the way that we see ourselves as well. Young people in particular are most critical of their own appearance. If we don't like one of our features, we can practice looking in the mirror with eyes of love instead of self-criticism. This will allow us to be confident in who we are as God's son or daughter. Instead of focusing on weaknesses, we see strengths. Instead of seeing blemishes, we see inner beauty. True love really is blind!

The Frog Prince

Here's a story about learning to love by the Brothers Grimm:

A Princess was walking in the garden one day when she stumbled and fell against a bush by the pond. Her most cherished piece of jewelry, a sparkling diamond necklace, broke and fell into the murky water. This had been a gift from her parents, the King and Queen, and she was so upset she started to cry. All of a sudden, a talking Frog appeared and told her he could help. She was, of course, surprised that the Frog could speak. But she was so desperate to retrieve the necklace that she ignored her shock and begged the Frog to go fetch it. The Frog responded to her pleas, "I heard you say that you'd give anything to get your treasure back. I'll make a deal with you. I don't want money, or any of your riches as a reward. I just want your friendship. I'll get the necklace if you promise to take me with you to live in the palace for three days and be my friend."

She agreed to this strange request, so the Frog hopped into the water and brought back her necklace. She thanked him and started walking back to the palace. The Frog cried out, "Hey, you promised to take me with you!" Immediately she regretted her promise and tried to ignore him. But the irksome, talking Frog was so persistent she had to let him into the palace. The King and Queen peppered her with questions when they saw the Frog hopping around in the dining room. The Princess explained what had happened. Her parents advised her to keep her promise and be a good friend to the slimy, ugly creature.

Easier said than done, thought the Princess. She didn't like this companion, but she had made a promise, and her parents told her she must be faithful to her words. Meanwhile, the creature had its own struggles. Unknown to the Princess, the Frog was a handsome and benevolent prince who had been put under a curse. Obviously, he was very self-conscious about his appearance as a Frog. The Princess was so beautiful, and he was just a wet amphibian that could talk to humans. He needed her to be his friend in order to undo the curse. But that seemed unlikely, so he was nervous.

For three whole days, the Princess included the Frog in her activities, reading, playing the piano, walking in the garden, eating, and conversing. At first, she was curt and disinterested in this smelly, slimy animal. But as they interacted, she realized that the Frog was very special, and she grew fond of his company. The Princess was human and the Frog amphibian, but this created an interesting bond despite their differences. As they played and talked, she learned all about what it was like to live as a Frog, and it became quite fascinating! The Frog, in turn, no longer self-conscious around the Princess, was able to relax and enjoy her company.

At the end of three days, the Princess realized that time was up, and the Frog would be going back to the pond in the garden. She started to cry and told him how much his friendship meant to her. The Princess begged the Frog to stay and be her friend forever. She covered her face with her hands and sobbed. All of a sudden, something magical happened. As the Princess lifted her head, she saw before her a handsome Prince! The Frog had disappeared and was replaced by this friendly and attractive young man. The Prince thanked her and explained that he had been put under a spell and cursed to live as a Frog until he was accepted as a friend by a human. Eventually, these two fortunate young people enjoyed a royal wedding, and they lived happily ever after!

Making It Real

In this story, the Frog has to overcome his fear of rejection, and the Princess has to look beyond his slimy, ugly appearance so that she can see the Frog for the handsome prince that he really is. As they get to know one another, they become close friends. Both the Frog and the Princess begin their relationship with certain obstacles that they eventually overcome by spending time together and becoming curious about one another.

A marriage can start out this way, but it's more common for a newlywed couple to be so in love that everything about their spouse seems wonderful. Even seemingly annoying habits are cute in the beginning. As time goes on, spouses tend to remove those rose-colored glasses and see each other's faults with remarkable clarity. Dirty socks left on the floor, an unclosed toilet seat, and other habits or mannerisms are less tolerable. What once seemed cute can, over time, become painfully annoying.

As couples age, the wrinkles, grey hair, and other physical changes can understandably make a person critical or self-conscious. But when spouses live by the motto, "true love is blind," husbands and wives become even more attractive to one another and more in love.

God intended for us never to remove those rose-colored glasses. Love is meant to grow, get better over time, and never diminish. A couple's relationship can get stronger as they meet each new challenge, with true love as their constant companion. There are hills and valleys in every marriage, however, when a couple sees each other through the eyes of love, they can endure anything. In the words of the apostle Paul:

"Love is patient, love is kind. It does not envy, it does not boast, it is not proud. It is not rude, it is not self-seeking, it is not easily angered, it keeps no record of wrongs. Love does not delight in evil but rejoices with the truth. It always protects, always trusts, always hopes, always perseveres." (1 Corinthians 13:4-7 New International Version)

Points for Consideration/Activities

- What aspects of your physical appearance do you like the most?

- What do you think God sees when He looks at you?

- Have you ever felt like either the Princess or the Frog from the story, *The Frog Prince*?

Make Love a Verb, Not a Noun

In the Korean language, the word "love" is a very significant word to express your feelings towards another person. In English, we use it to describe an array of experiences. We talk about how we love ice cream and good food, going to movies, and walking on the beach. We use the same word to describe what we feel for friends and family. Then there's a special kind of love reserved just for husbands and wives, but even in marriage, the word love can have several meanings. When we say "I love you" to our spouse, it can mean so much more when it is expressed through thoughtful action and service.

True Father's Words

150. "We can learn conjugal lovemaking not only from nature but also from the experiences of other persons or other places. The important point is that we must use what we have learned for the sake of our spouse. Through these efforts of two persons to become one, a husband and wife can acquire the highest state of love, impregnate the most excellent life, protect the true lineage, and maintain the right conscience. The first purpose of 'transforming your conjugal life into a work of art' is to protect the lineage. Through the Marriage Blessing, your lineage was restored from Satan's lineage to God's lineage. The important thing for the next step is how to keep and protect the restored lineage." (2009.1.1)

151. "If a woman loved by God lives in the heart of a man, and a man who is loved by God lives in the heart of a woman, and they cher-

ish each other, God will rejoice over it, and also all things will be happy together. Their joyful embrace will be of great importance in bringing joy to heaven and earth. The embrace of a man and a woman in mutual adoration is a point where the universe becomes one. This is what the original image is like that is realized under God's ideal." (1985)

152. "The melody God likes most is the laughter of a husband and wife who are happy in their love for each other. When such a couple lives a life with the heart to embrace the world and accommodate the entire universe, that laughter will spring forth naturally. In God's eyes, the beautiful sight of such a couple would be like a flower. This is not just an ideal or abstraction. I am talking about the original world." (1995)

153. "A conversation between a loving husband and wife is more beautiful than any poem or painting in the world. Furthermore, how beautiful and splendid are the words that people who are in love exchange—'just the two of us'!" (1995)

154. "In the eyes of the wife, her husband has to look the best and be number one. Also, in the eyes of the husband, his wife has to look this way as well... The wife should follow and serve her husband well. Such things should not appear just in literature or just as a movie scene. Rather, you should live like that throughout your whole life. Since the best history and best culture have been turned upside down, I have been creating a new history in order to establish such a world and to live in such a way." (1969.5.11)

155. "Love begins with investment. True love begins with the act of giving. This is a universal principle. Because the universe moves according to this law and its rules have this content, if you act only to receive, that is a betrayal of the universe." (1991.8.29)

156. "The male and female organs are the poles, plus and minus, that

can possess God's love. They are the charging plates of a battery. Without them, we could not be charged up with God's love. Since human beings refill their love through that organ, they can do so daily." (1985.7.20)

Sharing Thoughts on True Father's Words

True Father encourages us to learn all we can about the art of lovemaking and the differences between men and women. Our teachers can be nature, people, books, and other resources. There are so many resources, healthy and unhealthy, so it's important to follow the guidance from credible sources that teach an informed approach to blissful lovemaking. The key thing is that we use what we learn for the sake of pleasing our spouse. The Energize Retreat[13] is a High Noon initiative that provides husbands and wives enriching education on topics such as sexual intimacy and conflict resolution.

Love begins with giving. This will allow us to create a heavenly marriage and family and protect our lineage. When men and women who are loved by God cherish each other, this brings joy to heaven and earth. Spouses always want their husband or wife to look their best in front of others and to be number one. When such a couple has the heart to embrace the world, their romantic whispers and laughter become a joyful sound to God.

Making It Real

There are many resources about the differences between men and women that help couples identify the special and endless ways to love one another. Since every woman and man is a unique expression of God, it is important for us all to be a lifelong student of our spouse. How can we become masters of loving our spouse?

When couples consistently perform caring and thoughtful actions for one another, they feel affirmed and loved. Taking time to be helpful and

---

13. More information can be found at our website, highnoon.org.

present, and showing admiration and interest in each other, fosters feelings of affection and safety, especially when life is challenging. Both husband and wife can be impacted by stress and anxiety due to biological and environmental causes; a partner may need extra care, patience and support when this happens. If the couple has developed a deep heartistic bond, they are aware of one another's mood swings and can offer what their spouse needs. As we invest time and effort in understanding and appreciating our spouse, we begin to grasp their hopes, dreams, fears, likes, dislikes, and passions. All these things help us route a "love map" to our spouse's heart. We can make a habit of expressing our affection in the ways that our spouse appreciates, earning a PhD in loving him or her as a unique child of God.

Coming Together

Recognizing differences and learning how to meet the other's needs is a huge part of a successful marriage. It's not merely about making a compromise, although it might feel like it at first. It's God's design for masculinity and femininity to come together in ecstasy and create something greater than just the sum of the two parts.

There are times in every marriage when one partner wants to make love, and the other doesn't. How does a couple with different sex drives express love towards each other? On July 13, 2004, Dae Mo nim[14] spoke about sexual life to women who had received the Marriage Blessing at the 40-day workshop held at the Cheongpyeong Heaven and Earth Training Center in South Korea:

"God explains about the act of love, saying, 'Play as much as you want,' and 'The more you make love, the greater amount of joy and beauty generated.' When a man and woman give and receive beautiful love with each other, an inseparable bond of heart is created between the two. The act of lovemaking creates an emotional bond. It is not because the emotional bond is already formed that you make love. You should not think in reverse. You

---

14. Dae Mo nim is the title given to True Mother's mother, Soon-Ae Hong (1913-1989).

must not say, 'I do not feel love, so how can I make love to my husband?' You are to nurture a loving heart while making love. Then a man and woman can become one in heart and body while nurturing their hearts. Then the family becomes happy. When you act in that way, the wife will not feel discontented, nor will the husband."[15]

Dae Mo nim says the more we make love with our spouse, the more joy and beauty is generated. This is why she encourages us to tease and be playful as often as we can. We shouldn't wait until we feel love to make love with our husband or wife. We can nurture a loving heart while making love to create an inseparable bond of heart.

When we are sensitive to our spouse's natural rhythm and cycles, we can pick up on cues that they are stressed, tired, or feeling unhappy. Especially at these times, we can focus on their needs and keep investing with compassion. We can help with the chores, offer a massage, or just give them space. When a couple has sex on the foundation of real love and care, the act of lovemaking creates the deepest emotional bond between husband and wife. This is how we make love a verb.

True Parents often talk about the benefits of living for the sake of others. This is especially true in marriage. Husbands and wives need to learn to live for each other's happiness in every way.

Heaven, Hell, and Chopsticks

In ancient China, adults would tell this Zen parable to children as a means of teaching them to always serve others first at the dinner table. The parable encouraged children to take food from the communal dishes and place it on the plates of their elders as a sign of respect.

Once upon a time, in a temple nestled on a remote mountainside, there lived a pair of monks, one old and one young. "What are the differences between Heaven and Hell?" the young monk asked the learned master one day.

"There are no material differences," replied the old monk peacefully.

---

15. Yoshihiko Masuda, *True Love, Sex, and Health: As Guided by the Words of True Parents*, (Gapyeong: CheongShim GTS University Press, 2009), 117.

"None at all?" Asked the confused young monk.

"Yes. Both Heaven and Hell look the same. They all have a dining hall with a big hot pot in the center in which some delicious noodles are boiled, giving off an appetizing scent," said the old monk. "The size of the pan and the number of people sitting around the pot are the same in both places. But oddly enough, each diner is given a pair of meter-long chopsticks and must use them to eat the noodles. And to eat the noodles, one must hold the chopsticks properly at their ends; no cheating is allowed."

"In the case of Hell, people are always starved because no matter how hard they try, they fail to get the noodles into their mouths," said the old monk.

"But doesn't the same happen to the people in Heaven?" The younger questioned.

"No. They can eat because they each feed the person sitting opposite them at the table.

You see, that is the difference between Heaven and Hell," explained the old monk.

Chinese people don't think twice about serving others during social eating occasions, sometimes to the bemusement of non–Chinese guests. It has become second nature for them. This was God's plan for marriage. In radiant marriages, husbands and wives joyfully and spontaneously serve each other. When a couple lives for the sake of each other out of love, serving is not a forced act but becomes a joyful and spontaneous expression of their love.

Points for Consideration/Activities

- Why do you think True Father emphasizes the importance of sex in marriage?

- Why do you think God made men and women so differently?

- Can you think of a time when you served someone even when you didn't feel like it, then afterwards felt grateful that you did?

- What are some acts of kindness husbands and wives could do for each other?

Spirit World and Conjugal Love

Have you ever wondered what life will be like in the spiritual world after you ascend?[16] Will you recognize your loved ones? Will you be able to be together with your spouse? What will you do together? What about making love? Certainly, sex in the spiritual realm has got to be out of this world. These were all questions True Father had as a young man. He searched for answers through deep prayer and explored the spiritual world to uncover hidden truths.

True Father's Words

157. "When you go to the heavenly kingdom, you must go through a wedding ceremony. Dressed in ceremonial garments, you enter, stand before God, and greet Him with love. Husband and wife have a love relationship in front of God. When they make love, God Himself rejoices. At the same time, He envelops them from the vertical position. Not only the feelings of the horizontal couple but those of the entire universe flow and intoxicate them. They thus enter an unimaginable world that is like a kaleidoscope. When they love, something amazing happens: two invisible streams of energy come together and unite completely as one and are assimilated into the world of light. This way of life is brought about with true love." (1998.9.23)

---

16. In our faith community we use the word ascension rather than death in celebration of the passing from this earthly life to our eternal life in the spiritual realm.

158. "Couples who were blessed [in marriage] on earth will be together even when they go to the spirit world, which is an eternal world. No matter how many couples and children there are in this fallen world, they are scattered and separated in the spirit world. They are separated, and they do not know where the others have gone. Without a reciprocal connection, they cannot even meet one another. They are all separated in the spirit world according to the state of their spirituality. But as I have told you, if they are united with love at the center through the Blessing, the whole family will dwell together in the spirit world." (1993.10.15)

159. "We were born through love, live our lives in love, and pass away into the afterlife, a world of love. Death is not something to fear. Death is like a marriage; it is a change of locale. It is to leave the realm of limited human love, a realm that until that moment we could not escape, and expand into the unlimited world that transcends time and space. It is to leap into a realm of limitless love." (1988.6.5)

160. "If someone asks a loving husband and wife how long they will be in love, and one of them says, 'Just while we are young,' would the other feel good or bad? For how long do you want to be in love? Eternally, but first of all, until you die, and then you will want to love eternally. Eternity is something that represents the whole in the future. To say that one will love until death is to say that he will love by giving everything he has. Isn't this right? 'Eternally' means the whole, and 'until death' means an intention to love the whole thing. Only then will your spouse be happy." (1970.12.22)

161. "What is the most stimulating and sensitive part of a man? Is it his tongue? Though the organ for tasting may be very sensitive, it could not be as sensitive as the sexual organ. To satisfy the tongue, once you have tasted something, you will desire to have it again the next day, but in the case of the genitals, if you have a spouse

who satisfies your sexual organ, merely thinking about that person would give you satisfaction; that is what the world will be like to you. You can taste something only when you have eaten it, but you will be able to feel your love partner by just thinking about him or her. What can give you pleasure transcending great distances and infinite space and make you desire to love even after death and into the next life? It is the love of your beloved husband or wife, and no other." (1997.8.13)

162. "Do you think God does not see you making love? It is all out in the open. It is open for the universe to see. It is very wrong to be unaware of this fact. Your ancestors are watching from the spirit world; they can see it as if it is taking place right before their eyes, like on the palm of their hands. Therefore, it is very wrong to think making love is embarrassing." (1993.10.15)

163. "What is most precious to us? The sexual organs are more precious than our nations or our ideal families. Without them, our families, races, and nations cannot be established. Eternal life could never come about if they were not united. That is to say, the realm of life through which we can transcend the dominion of the physical world into the spirit world, the limitless world, could never come into being without the male and female sexual organs. God's Kingdom on earth and in heaven would not exist." (1999.1.1)

164. "When a husband or wife is about to go to the spirit world, it is good for them to have a completely private time and place. Looking back at their love relationship, the wife/husband may well clean the dying spouse's sexual organ, which is the palace of love, life, and lineage, with a wet towel. And the wife/husband should gently kiss good-bye to the sexual organ of the dying spouse. Then the wife/husband can let the dying spouse touch her/his sexual organ in order to confirm each other's absolute, unique, unchanging, and eternal love relationship as a husband and wife. This is not what

you must do absolutely, but it is desirable to send the dying spouse to the spirit world in this way if possible." (2000.12.7)

Sharing Thoughts on True Father's Words

Marriage vows in traditional Christian weddings often state that the husband and wife will love each other "until death do us part." True Father explains that God intended blessed couples to be together forever. True Father speaks of death as an ascension into the third and final and eternal phase of our lives: the spiritual realm. When blessed couples are united with love at the center, the whole family will dwell together in the spirit world. That is why death is nothing to fear. In fact, the couple can look forward to a love that will continue to grow forever.

Spirit world is the world where love between a husband and wife is unlimited and eternal. There is no need to hide ourselves even when we make love. When people see or hear a couple making love in the spirit world, they are in awe at the beauty and wholesomeness of the scene. It carries no shame or embarrassment but instead brings the greatest joy to God and to all who behold it. People naturally believe that love is meant to be forever, and it is!

Making It Real

God has been working relentlessly to reveal the truth about the sexual organs and conjugal love. Two thousand years ago, Jesus spoke about the relationship between the physical world and the spiritual world. He summed it up well when he said, "Whatever you bind on earth will be bound in heaven, and whatever you loose on earth will be loosed in heaven." A little over two hundred years before True Father arrived on this earth, Emanuel Swedenborg (1688-1772), a scientist, famous mystic, and Christian theologian, best known for his book *Heaven and Hell* (1758), described his visits to the spiritual realm, where he discovered a correlation between one's experience of conjugal love on earth and in the world after death.

Finally, in this day and age, True Father and his disciple, Dr. Sang Hun Lee (1913-1997), author of *Life in the Spirit World and on Earth*,[17] confirmed that couples who receive the Marriage Blessing on earth stay together in the spiritual realm to continue to grow their love eternally.

It is difficult to believe in life after death because we cannot see it, so we rely on the experiences of those like Dr. Lee and Swedenborg, who have been given the opportunity to visit the spiritual world. We all want to leap into a realm of unlimited love and for that love to have no end. We can have confidence in this because our loving Heavenly Parent would never give us a desire that we could not fulfill!

Do Blessed Couples Enjoy Sex in the Spirit World?

After his ascension, Dr. Sang Hun Lee channeled Mrs. Y. S. Kim, who helped him write his experiences in the afterlife. True Father said Dr. Lee's expression of the spirit world was "mostly correct," and with True Father's approval, we study Dr. Lee's book for Hoon Dok Hwe. Here is what Dr. Lee had to say about conjugal love in the spirit world:

"Conjugal love is the love where men and women are connected physically. On earth, we can feel emotions when our bodies can meet and love. But in Heaven, a man and a woman without physical bodies can love. The conjugal love between those high spirits (those who are close to God) is like a beautiful picture. Since the bodies of the two become one totally when they love, they can feel strong emotion through their bodies and minds which goes beyond the feeling of love they felt on Earth. It is like creating a higher existence from the state of complete absence of ego. It is like feeling you are in a magical world.

"Also, you can actually view the scene of making love with your own eyes. Couples on Earth make love in their bedrooms most of the time. Here, in Heaven, that is absolutely not the case. It is not the hidden love, which only you can do in your bedroom. In Heaven, you might love among wildflowers

---

17. Dr. Sang Hun Lee, *Life in the Spirit World and on Earth: Messages from the Spirit World* (New York: Family Federation for World Peace and Unification, 1998).

in a field, on beautiful land or on an ocean wave. You can even love in the mountains where birds are singing and the scene is so beautiful that those who watch you will become intoxicated. Rather than feeling shame or disgrace as you felt on earth, you can observe the scene with a peaceful mind, admiring the beauty."

When Dr. Lee talks about "bodies" in the spirit world, he refers to our spiritual bodies, which True Father teaches are a mirror image of our physical bodies. The love we give on earth is recorded in our spirit bodies, and that's all we take with us when we go to the third phase of life in the eternal world. That's why True Parents emphasize the importance of living a life of true love on earth. If we are united with love at the center through the Marriage Blessing, our whole family will dwell together in the spirit world.

Points for Consideration/Activities

- What is the best way to prepare for eternal life as a blessed couple in the spirit world while we are alive on earth?

- What do you think about Dr. Lee's description of conjugal love in the spirit world?

- Consider watching the movie "What Dreams May Come," about a husband and wife's experience in the spirit world.

Section IV:
Absolute Sex

What Is Absolute Sex?

There is a great deal of confusion in the world today regarding sex. It seems there is no clear standard. People seek happiness by following their natural desires but often end up disappointed and hurt. It's difficult to figure out what's right and even tougher to stand up for something we don't fully understand. True Father coined the unique expression "absolute sex" to give us clarity about God's absolute ideal for the sexual relationship between husband and wife. This term may seem a little confusing at first. The words absolute and sex are not usually put together, and some may think it refers to wild sexual fantasies or throwing off all restraints. This is the opposite of what True Father meant. What comes to mind for you when you hear the word "absolute" used in reference to sex?

True Father's Words

165. "The ultimate goal of God's Kingdom is the perfection of true families. Within true families, there must be the ideal of a true nation and world. The term absolute sex emerges here as the tradition of true love that can influence a true world and nation. Absolute sex refers to absolute, unique, unchanging, and eternal sex. You can become one in love with your reciprocal partner, to whom you are linked centering on love, an attribute of God, only through sexual relations." (1997.3.9)

166. "Absolute sex is important. What does that mean? People could have the feeling coming from the marrow of their bones that God

for them is a Father of fathers; however, they lived not knowing that He was suffering. Throughout historical ages, they couldn't even imagine this. This is a mistake. So, how huge is our responsibility once we get to know this fact. Heaven and earth must unite; God should be able to play His role as Master and Father. Such a standard should be achieved. This standard established by Heaven begins from absolute sex." (2007.3.7)

167. "I wish that you would center on the absolute sexual organ, unique sexual organ, unchanging sexual organ, and eternal sexual organ, and use this as your foundation to pursue God. You could realize that this foundation could become the foundation of love, life, lineage, and conscience. We also have to realize that the Kingdom of God on Earth and in Heaven will begin on this foundation." (1996.11.1)

168. "What is a key feature of the realm of the Cosmic Sabbath[18] of the Parents of Heaven and Earth? [Absolute Sex.] 'Absolute Sex' is our own patented, professional term from now on. People who are acknowledged officially by heaven and earth and living in heaven and on earth all belong to the realm of... the Cosmic Sabbath of the Parents of Heaven and Earth. The first and absolute prerequisite to entering this realm is absolute sexual ethics, and no one is outside of this realm... Human beings, as lords of all creation, however, have regarded this most precious of all gifts from Heaven as one that should just be used for themselves. They have interpreted it as they pleased, taken advantage of it, and abused it. This has resulted in the creation of all sorts of falsehoods. Since we know this fact, it is urgent that history fully move in the direction of getting the fundamentals in order." (2009.1.2)

---

18. The Cosmic Sabbath is God's ideal of creation established at the cosmic level, representing heaven and earth.

169. "… We need true lineage following Absolute Sex, true love, and true life. True lineage is centered on Absolute Sex, in which true love and true life become one. This is the only way to make a true lineage. If a true lineage is not created, there will be a tattered sphere of sexuality, that is, a tattered lineage." (2009.1.2)

170. "The sexual organs must be liberated. Thus, absolute sex is the opposite of the free sex of today. It is absolute, unique, unchanging, and eternal sex. How lofty and precious are these four concepts! If the two organs remain separate as they are, no development can take place. They must be rooted in true love. True love begins from there." (1996.9.8)

171. "If Adam and Eve had not fallen upon reaching adolescence— around age sixteen or seventeen—but instead had become one with God's love, then their minds and bodies absolutely could not have been divided. With perfect life and perfect love, Adam and Eve would have become a true man and true woman living in a true environment. After the Fall, Adam and Eve always remembered the feeling of anticipation, hoping to stand in that position. Throughout their lives, they longed to find that original position and to think, to live and to love as they were intended to. They surely desired their children to live in that world." (1997)

172. "Try to imagine the intense beauty of the five senses moving in intoxication with true love and the harmony of the five senses moving toward God. Alone, God cannot experience the joy of such beauty. He can experience such beauty only when He has a partner, and this is the reason God created human beings. How would God feel as He observed a beautiful man and woman absorbed into one another through true love-intoxicated eyes, or kissing with true love-intoxicated lips, and playing the melody of a heart of true love? If there is an Eve of true love, God would want to completely traverse her world of heart. God would have

an impulsive desire to explore the breadth and depth of this beautiful Eve's world of heart." (1997)

173. "Even though we all know that we have to preserve Absolute Sex, if we do not rectify the misuse of sexual relations, things will inevitably end in failure. Thus, if we want to seek out and live in the ideal world, we have to abide by this ironclad rule." (2009.1.2)

Sharing Thoughts on True Father's Words

True Father coined the phrase, absolute sex, to describe God's ideal for sexual relationship in marriage. Husbands and wives who embody absolute sex are passionately attracted to one another. Each joyfully lives for the sake of their partner. True Father pairs this term with eternal, unique, and unchanging sex. When we view sex in this way, it heightens the quality of love that we share with our life partner. The only way a husband and wife can become fully one in heart is by engaging all five senses in intoxicating lovemaking. Living within the realm of absolute sex invites God into our marriage and lays the foundation to carry on His true lineage.

Reverend Joong Hyun Pak, Former North American Continental Director of FFWPU, gave a sermon at Belvedere Estates in Tarrytown, New York, based on True Father's teaching about absolute sex on February 1, 1997:

"We now realize that absolute sex is pro-sex, proud sex, positive sex, pure sex, monogamous sex, and joyful, happy sex. We must appreciate True Parents. Without True Parents' revealing of this most deep secret, we could not find it; we were blind. Now we see our purpose for being created. So liberating."

When couples are experiencing absolute sex, they joyfully and passionately satisfy each other's needs and desires. Absolute couples have relationships that glow and radiate with love. Heaven is created wherever they go. Adam and Eve could have enjoyed this quality of conjugal love had they overcome the temptation of self-centered love and invited God into their relationship. Since the world has never seen an example of ideal marriage, it's been difficult for us to understand what absolute sex means or feels like. True Parents are the first to model what an absolute couple looks like and teach how to achieve this quality of love in our own marriages.

Avatar

Avatar, an Oscar-winning movie released in 2009, had phenomenal success. The Na'vi tribe who live on Pandora, a distant moon that resembles planet Earth, are blue-skinned, highly evolved humanoids who live in perfect harmony with their natural environment. The film portrays interesting landforms like the floating Hallelujah mountains and an array of beautiful plants that help balance the ecosystem. Some examples are the Puffball trees that collect and store toxic gases to protect the atmosphere and a bioluminescent rainforest, which is a necessary part of the robust natural environment. Who wouldn't want to live in such a place?

Pandora was achingly attractive, but as viewers left the movie theater, they realized it was an unattainable, utopian dream. Discussion threads about the film were populated with posts from people experiencing depression due to the disappointment that life on Earth had no resemblance to the extraordinary world of Pandora. The desire to live in this healthy, beautiful place was so strong that they couldn't stop thinking about the movie and dreaming of such a life.

Making It Real

Pandora is a place of beauty and wonders that we can compare to the ideal of absolute sex. When we think about a world of absolute sex, we may feel the same pangs of longing *Avatar* fans experienced. Perfection in intimacy can seem beyond our reach, even with our best efforts. The desire for a euphoric relationship of love and connection was placed in us by God. God wants husbands and wives to experience a life filled with intimacy.

Every couple's situation has its own unique set of challenges, so we should never compare our marriage with anyone else's. There are many reasons why couples no longer feel the closeness they once had; some have even given up trying. It's possible they never felt any chemistry in their relationship. Even though both partners may long for intoxicating sexual intimacy, they don't know where to begin to bridge the distance between them. What steps can they take?

We can start by honestly acknowledging where we stand in relation to the ideal and make a plan to move forward. An ancient Chinese proverb reminds us that a journey of a thousand miles begins with a single step. Many couples have found that having open-ended conversations is a great place to start to discover new qualities in each other. Showing affection through non-sexual touch can slowly open the heart for deeper affection. As we take steps to cultivate trust and intimacy in our marriage, True Parents' vision of absolute sex will begin to feel more attainable.

Couples who do the hard work of investing in their relationship begin a lifelong adventure. We may not reach the realm of absolute sex right away, but the journey will be very pleasurable and exciting. God intended for us to enjoy absolute sex through joyful, healthy intimacy with our spouse that will grow forever in the spiritual realm.

Points for Consideration/Activities

- Do you believe absolute sex is possible for you to experience? How does that make you feel?

- Share some steps you can take to experience absolute sex in your relationship with your spouse or prepare for such a relationship.

- Take time to watch *Avatar* with your family or friends.

Absolute Sexual Purity

Have you ever wondered what it must have been like for Adam and Eve before the Fall? The Bible says they had no shame even though they were completely naked. Hard to imagine, isn't it? The world we live in today makes it difficult to keep our hearts free of lust or shame when it comes to sex. Provocative images on billboards, the internet, and TV are everywhere. True Father wants to bring the world back to God's original standard. But how do we bridge this gap? The only way we can restrain our runaway thoughts is to place restrictions in our lives to safeguard ourselves and our loved ones. These boundaries, used effectively, can keep us safe and on track with our goals.

True Father's Words

174. "I have been teaching that belief in absolute sex is the best method of keeping one's purity. This means that once you have formed a bond of love with your spouse, it is eternal, and it is an absolute love relationship that can never change no matter the circumstances. This is because a husband and wife come together centering on God's love, which is eternal and absolute. This is not something that is emphasized only to men, and neither is it applicable only to women. It is the heavenly way that is the same for both men and women; both need to uphold it absolutely." (1997.11.30)

175. "Chastity and purity are the greatest virtues. They are like a blos-

som before it is opened. The sweetness is kept within. So, before you enjoy the divine blessings of marriage, you must be like a blossom shut tight, bearing the fragrance deep within you." (1975)

176. "Ladies and gentlemen, the absoluteness of conjugal love is the greatest blessing that Heaven has bestowed on humankind. Without adhering to the principle of absolute sexual purity, the path to the perfection of one's character and spiritual maturity is closed." (2006.11.21

177. "What was the single word, the one and only commandment God gave to Adam and Eve, the first ancestors, upon their creation? It was the commandment and blessing to maintain an absolute standard of sexual purity until God's approval of their marriage. We find the basis for this in the Bible passage that indicates that Adam and Eve would surely die on the day they ate of the fruit of the knowledge of good and evil. If they had refrained from eating and observed Heaven's commandment, they would have perfected their character and, as co-creators, stood with God, the Creator, as His equals. Furthermore, they would have taken dominion over the creation and become the lords of the universe, enjoying eternal and ideal happiness. It was God's blessing that He told them to preserve their purity so that they could wed as His true children through His Marriage Blessing, become true husband and wife, become true parents, and give birth to true children. This knowledge deepens our understanding of this commandment. It is connected with the principle of absoluteness in conjugal love, which is a principle of God's creation. The profound truth within God's commandment has lain hidden throughout history: human beings must inherit and live by a model of absolute sexual purity that is intrinsic to God's ideal for creation. This is so that they might perfect their individuality as God's children and establish themselves as lords of creation… Therefore, if, upholding absolute sexual morality, Adam and Eve had achieved individual perfec-

tion—the perfection of their character in accordance with God's will, and entered into conjugal relations through His Blessing, they would have attained complete oneness with Him. God would have dwelt within their union. Also, their children would have been linked to this holy order of love, enjoying a direct relationship with God as their Parent. In other words, the marriage of the perfected Adam and Eve, based on their absolute sexual morality, would have been God's own marriage. While God is forever God, also Adam and Eve would have become the embodiment of God. They would have become God's body. God would have settled inside their minds and hearts to become the True Parent of humankind in both the spiritual and physical world, on the foundation of absolute sexual morality." (2006.11.21)

178. "The first stage is maintaining absolute sexual purity prior to getting married. After we are born, we go through a process of growth. We pass through infancy and childhood in a very safe and secure environment embraced in our parents' love and protection. We then enter the time of adolescence, which signals the start of a new and dynamic life as we forge relationships on a totally new level with those around us, as well as with all things of creation. This is the moment when we begin to travel the path to becoming an absolute human being—internally, through the perfection of our character, and externally, by reaching adulthood. Yet, at this time, there is an absolute requirement that people must fulfill, no matter who they are. This is the requirement of maintaining their purity, which is the model of absolute sexual morality for human beings. God gave it to His children as their destined responsibility and duty, to be carried out in order to fulfill the ideal of creation. This heavenly path is thus the way toward perfecting the model of absoluteness in conjugal love." (2006.11.21)

179. "The second stage is the perfection of love between husband and wife. More precious than life is the heavenly law of absolute fidel-

ity. Husband and wife are eternal partners, given to each other by Heaven. Through having children, they become co-creators of true love, true life and true lineage, and the origin of that which is absolute, unique, unchanging, and eternal. It is a heavenly principle that one person alone can never give birth to a child, even in a thousand years. If two people had preserved their purity before marriage and were bound together in marriage by God, how could they ever go astray and deviate from the way of Heaven? People are different from animals; if they understand God's purpose in creating them as His children, they will realize that deviating from heavenly law constitutes an unimaginable betrayal and defiance of the Creator. It is a path of self-destruction on which they dig their own graves." (2006.11.21)

180. "Adam and Eve, up until their teenage years before the Fall, had been growing up in absolute purity... Today, no matter how pure some men and women may be, there is no comparison to the purity of Adam and Eve before the Fall of man. Even though we may live a pure life, we have already received the Satanic lineage and have it within ourselves without even knowing it. It was not our responsibility, but nevertheless, we inherited that Satanic lineage. Adam and Eve, however, did not have that Satanic lineage from the very beginning, so no purity can be compared to Adam and Eve before their Fall. God was so severe, His standard so pure and high, that when Adam and Eve, who were the purest people, committed sin just once, He kicked them out of the garden." (1991.2.21)

Sharing Thoughts on True Father's Words

True Father extols chastity and purity as the greatest virtues that are essential before receiving the Marriage Blessing. The first man and woman were to inherit and model these virtues, intrinsic to God's ideal of creation. God intended for Adam and Eve to perfect their character by honoring the commandment to save their sexual organs for marriage. This was the way to achieve the position of co-creators with God and become lords of creation. Through Adam and Eve, God would have a substantial presence on earth, enabling Him to directly interact with His children and all of creation.

What was the standard of purity in the Garden of Eden? Adam and Eve were growing up naked with no impure sexual thoughts or feelings toward each other. They were untouched by self-centered influence and absolutely pure. After they broke God's commandment by misusing their sexual organs, they covered their nakedness with shame and hid from God.

The time of adolescence is the critical time to preserve sexual purity and create a vibrant and dynamic relationship with God. True Father provided youth with practical advice on how to create that relationship, nurture it and reach maturity. He says it is necessary to prepare oneself during the adolescent years: "The door of love opens only when it is time, and we must wait until it opens before entering. We can open it proudly after becoming an owner of love." The need to follow this principle continues after the Marriage Blessing as well. The heavenly law of absolute fidelity is more important than life itself. Absoluteness in conjugal love is the greatest blessing that Heaven has bestowed on humankind.

The Grand Canyon and Niagara Falls

What do the Grand Canyon and Niagara Falls have in common, besides their unique and awesome natural beauty? Both have extensive guardrails and plenty of danger signs to prevent tourists from falling over the edge and plunging to their deaths. Parks construct guardrail systems made of the best materials to protect us. Unfortunately, they sometimes fail to prevent tragic accidents.

At the Grand Canyon, the visible ground of the rim may look stable, but it's paper-thin underneath due to erosion. What appears to be safe isn't. Risky behavior like walking behind the railings or hanging one's feet over the edge can have fatal consequences. Someone drops the cap off their camera, scrambles to retrieve it, falls off the edge, and dies. Another's hat blows off, lands near the edge, he recklessly goes too close to the rim, and his life is over. People taking photographs in an unsafe way adds to the death toll every year.

Niagara Falls is enticingly beautiful and equally dangerous. Imagine six million cubic feet of water rushing over the falls every minute from speeds of 25 mph in the rapids and up to 68 mph over the brink! Tourists still venture into unsafe places, even though there are many surveillance cameras and warning signs. In 2011, a Japanese student climbed onto a railing to get a cool picture of the impressive Canadian side of the falls. As she straddled the railing, both hands occupied holding the camera and her umbrella, she slipped and fell into the river and then over the edge of the falls. This was just one of many needless, avoidable deaths.

Niagara Falls and the Grand Canyon may tempt us to climb over guardrails so we can taste the unknown and spectacular without restrictions. It is the same with sexual temptation, which can override common sense if we're not careful. We need to construct our own personal guardrails. Ultimately, keeping ourselves safe is a very serious responsibility, and our success depends on the choices we make.

Making It Real

What is needed to guide us on the path of absolute sexual purity so that we can realize God's ideal? Because sex is so enticing, God gave Adam and Eve the commandment. It was to act as a guardrail to prevent them from misusing their sexual organs, protect their lineage, and guard their young hearts from pain. Even though Adam and Eve were purer than any man or woman who has ever lived, they still needed the warning of the commandment in order to keep safe.

We can think we are immune to temptation, but we're not. Guardrails serve a very important purpose. They align us with a standard of behavior that tips off our conscience when we bump into them. We stop and get back on the road before we go over the cliff. Many people refuse to place restrictions in their lives because they feel it's childish or unnecessary. However, by tolerating small inconveniences, we may never have to experience the huge consequences of a terrible accident.

Billy Graham was the predominant evangelical leader of the 20th century, advisor to several U.S. presidents, and revered by millions of people worldwide. Out of concern about the growing number of evangelists who were making the news because of sexual misconduct, Graham led his staff by what is known as the "Billy Graham Rule," which encourages men to not go out alone with a woman unless she's his wife.

The media recently revisited Graham's rule in 2020 when Mike Pence, former Vice-President of the United States (2016-2021), told "The Hill," a political website, that he has always used this rule to build a "safe zone" around his marriage. This self-regulation seems extreme to many people, and it attracted ridicule. But if using such safeguards protects what is most important in life, isn't it worth it? Regardless of whether or not a person believes in the religious or political views of these two examples, the guardrails they've used have protected their marriages. Remember, no one regrets having healthy boundaries in their lives. People do regret ruining their reputation, acquiring an addiction, cheating on their spouse, and hurting their children.

Our sex drive is powerful and beautiful, but it can lead to destructive behaviors. We may have a routine of scrolling through our phones in bed. If this habit leads to watching porn, we may need to leave the phone outside the bedroom at night. Some boundaries we create may be appropriate for our entire life. Others may be necessary for only a short period of time until we can develop the self-discipline to enable us to live without it. What guardrails could you set up to ensure your success?

True Father emphasizes that we should live a life of absolute purity so that we can enjoy a beautiful sexual relationship with our spouse. When we have a clear purpose for our lives, we won't want to risk going over the guardrails for a quick thrill. We can feel secure and grateful for the restrictions that prevent us from trading our future happiness for anything less. When we develop a strong vision for our sexuality and make a great deal of effort, we will eventually live in a new Eden, a world of absolute love that reflects God's original plan.

Points for Consideration/Activities

- Share an experience of when a guardrail saved you or someone you loved. Was there a time when you ignored a guardrail and later regretted it?

- What habits can you instill in your life to protect your purity or to place a safe zone around your marriage?

- Share about your vision for your present or future Marriage Blessing.

Absolute Sexual Ethics in the Family

The presence of God is all around us as we walk in a field of blue lupins and bright yellow sunflowers, float down a cool river on a sunny day or gaze into a baby's adorable face. Nothing expresses the love of God as much as a family that is united and overflows with true love. The innocence and purity of children and the beauty of nature remind us of God's intention for a perfect world. However, we all know this world is far from perfect. How, then, can we create a family rooted in absolute sexual ethics that is free from the influence of this fallen world?

True Father's Words

181. "Where is the palace of God's absolute ideal erected? In the relationship of the absolute ideal husband and wife in a family completely united on the basis of absolute sexual ethics." (2007.12.28)

182. "Without securing the foundation of absolute sexual morality within a true family of perfected individuals, it is impossible for God to manifest with dignity as the incarnate God of character. In order for God, the absolute being, to have direct dominion over our lives and to live and share joy with us, we, who were created as His object partners and children, must assume the form of perfected families based on the standard of absolute sexual ethics, as God intended. Only within the boundaries of a family upholding sexual morality is it possible to create relationships based on an

ideal model of sexual ethics for life as it should originally have existed. This life includes the three-generational realm of grandparents, parents, children, and grandchildren. Please understand that God's eternal life and a person's eternal life are possible only on this foundation." (2006.11.21)

183. "You can simply say, 'God's model for absoluteness, peace and the ideal is the family upholding absolute sexual morality.' In the beginning, there was only one God's family, not two. Family is centered on absolute sexual morality; if we don't go through absolute sexual morality, the family will not come about. The word 'absolute' implies that we unite everything, make overall settlement of accounts, and reach the highest peak. Even with this topic alone, we can unify the world and solve its problems. Absolute sexual morality advocated by God is only one and not two. Two persons should become absolutely one through pure love. No one can fulfill this by himself. Man and woman are two beings, so how can they become one absolute being? The basis for the absolute family, which is a model of absoluteness, peace, and ideal is none else than the sexual organs of man and woman. We cannot make a final solution to the fundamental issues of the universe without referring to sexual organs. That's how precious they are. You all—men and women—have them." (2007.3.7)

184. "Men and women must both preserve their purity. They must not stain themselves before marriage. After chastity, next comes the purity of lineage, of the bloodline. Every person who seeks love has to maintain sexual purity and know about the renewed lineage, the lineage of purity. This is why we speak of chastity, pure love, and pure lineage. When a man and a woman preserve these three, become one through marriage, continuously live for others, do not keep a record of their good deeds, are not swayed left and right, and persevere in sacrificing while forgetting those sacrifices, they will liberate the world for tens of thousands of years, even if the

four corners of the earth relocate, even if up and down reverse, and even if front and back exchange positions. They will bring everything into harmony and realize a world of peace." (2004.2.24)

185. "Now, please go back to your homes and affirm with your spouses that your sexual organs are absolute, unique, unchanging, and eternal. Proclaim that yours is truly your spouse's, and what your spouse has protected so well until now is truly yours. And please pledge that you will live your life with gratitude and in eternal service to your spouse. In such families, God will dwell eternally and, centering upon them, the world-level family will begin to multiply." (1996.8.1)

186. "The thing that is absolutely necessary for a man is not convex. For him, convex repels. There is no happiness there. That which is absolutely convex needs what is absolutely concave. When absolute convex meets absolute concave, God is there, and when it is not like that, God leaves. The fact that it is not like that means that Satan's lineage still remains. Even though 98 percent may be done, if so much as a shadow of Satan's lineage remains, God cannot come down. God can find your family and become its Lord only when vertical and horizontal meet at a ninety-degree angle based on absolute sex, absolute partnership, and absolute love." (2000.8.29)

Sharing Thoughts on True Father's Words

True Father has shown us that God, as a being of absolute truth and love, desires to see His perfect reflection in His children through families who live in the realm of absolute sexual ethics. Embracing absolute sexual purity before the Marriage Blessing and practicing absolute sex afterward is the means through which our sexual organs become the gateway for God's dream to be realized. Wouldn't every generation of these families enjoy harmonious relationships of love? They model the ideal and are the foundation for a peaceful world.

True Father guides husbands and wives to affirm that their sexual organs belong to their spouse. When each couple lives according to the principle of absolute sex with gratitude and service to their spouse, they create harmony in their family and a lineage of purity. As more and more families live like this, they can work together to resolve the world's problems.

The Waltons

In the world of television and movies, it's challenging to find a production that provides a model of a three-generation, God-centered family. Sitcoms that show single-parent families with non-traditional values have been popular since the 1960s, so it was a big surprise when *The Waltons* became a huge success in the 70s. This was a television series about a family in rural Virginia during the Great Depression and World War II. When American families started watching *The Waltons* in 1972, it was like a breath of fresh air. At first, it wasn't expected to succeed because those who embraced traditional family values seemed to be in the minority. After a slow start, the show quickly gained popularity, earning 13 Emmy awards and attracting millions of loyal viewers.

What did Americans like about *The Waltons*? During a time when the divorce rate started skyrocketing, the fictional Walton family stuck together through thick and thin. This was part of the show's popularity. With seven kids, money was tight, but there was always enough love and laughter. Both parents and grandparents showed affection in their marriage and were passionately in love. Even though Grandma was old fashioned and reserved, that didn't discourage Grandpa's playful teasing when he'd plant a kiss on her cheek. The younger generation could tell the fire was still burning in their marriage. Many viewers shared that each episode of the Walton family made them feel uplifted and loved. Ralph Waite, the actor who played the character of the dad, is amazed that he still gets letters of gratitude from fans who appreciated him as a surrogate father, the one they wish they had. *The Waltons* creator, Earl Hamner, reflected on why his show was so successful: "I think the audience needed this affirmation of values, and we supplied that. It lifted their spirits. And the country needed lifting."

In *The Waltons*, God was part of every story, and each character had some formal or informal spiritual beliefs. This was also true for Hamner's family. His grandmother, mother, and some siblings were members of the Baptist church and attended church regularly. His dad didn't like organized religion but had a strong personal life of faith. The entire family was united around the values of loyalty, honesty, and integrity, which they practiced in their relationships with one another and the community. Many of the scenarios and conversations in Earl Hamner's scripts were based on his memories of life in rural Virginia with his own family.

This fictional family inspired many to believe in and embrace a model of a God-centered family. True Father's teaching takes us to a new level where family values are based on absolute sexual ethics.

Making It Real

It may seem like absolute sexual ethics is an unachievable ideal, given the culture we live in today. However, True Father's words invite us to believe that we can do it, with God's help. How do we establish the ideal for ourselves? We can pursue a deeper understanding of the ideal for families living with absolute sexual ethics. What does True Father really mean by this phrase? Parents are committed to fidelity and enjoy a sexual relationship only with each other. They communicate lovingly, openly and regularly with their growing children constantly nurturing their reasons to value absolute sex. Therefore, children learn from an early age to value their sexual organs as sacred and are committed to living with absolute sexual purity until they receive the Marriage Blessing.

Married couples who practice heavenly sex can more easily recharge themselves, heal differences, and relieve stress. Lovemaking affirms their special connection, even though challenges don't disappear. Life is less overwhelming when the husband and wife are united by love. As a married couple develops their conjugal relationship through lovemaking, their faith in and gratitude in God's ideal for the Marriage Blessing grows. When husband and wife are fully committed to each other, experiencing the joy of sex, they prosper in all areas of life. Their emotional security, health, and well-being improve. This lifestyle enables a couple to be role models of sexual morality that impacts their family and community.

In these families, children feel more stable and secure because they have moms and dads who openly express their love for each other. They grow up with a healthy model for conjugal love, a stark contrast to Hollywood romance. Their parents don't depend on schools for sex education. Instead, they take responsibility and have ongoing, honest discussions about sexuality. These conversations become precious, unforgettable memories and help children establish a clear vision for their marriage.

Closeness and filial piety grow as children overcome their fears, speak to their parents about their mistakes, and receive understanding and grace from their parents. Kids are more likely to confide in and learn from parents who share honestly about their own mistakes and how they overcame them. Children who are exposed to porn or discover masturbation, either by accident or from curiosity, can talk with their parents because of the foundation of trust in the family. With unconditional love and guidance, parents can help their children avoid dangerous habits that could harm their future Marriage Blessing and help them stay accountable to their conscience. Parents can listen to their confessions without judgment or disappointment, and consequently, children will feel empowered to reinvest their efforts to protect their sexual organs and recommit to absolute sexual purity.

Parents and grandparents also have a vested interest in helping their children and grandchildren develop sexual integrity and prepare for the Marriage Blessing. With love and life guidance from both parents and grandparents, these young men and women feel fully supported and know their own value and the preciousness of their sexual organs. They honor sexual purity in themselves and others.

Every child longs to grow up in a family with a mom and dad who are committed to staying together forever, who love each other and embrace their children as the fruit of their love. Children would not have been born with this desire if it were an unreachable dream. We can't alter our past, but we can change the future by creating families rooted in absolute sexual ethics.

Points for Consideration/Activities

- What conversations would you have liked to have had with your parents?

- Share a time when you broke something or made a mistake and your parents showed you more grace than you expected.

- Watch an episode of *The Waltons* with your family.

Absolute Sexual Ethics in the World

The first time True Father used the words "absolute sex" was in 1996 in a speech inaugurating Family Federation for World Peace (FFWP).[19] This speech, "In Search of the Origin of the Universe," was advertised in newspapers in every state across America and presented in 185 nations. It was an appeal to world leaders, persuading them to embrace and proclaim a new movement of absolute sex, or sex centered on God, in their own countries.

True Father's Words

187. "Then, what did God expect from Adam and Eve? God expected absolute sex from them. You eminent leaders gathered here tonight, please learn this truth and take it back to your countries. If you start a campaign to secure absolute sex in your country, your families and your nation will go straight to Heaven. When there is absolute sex, an absolute couple will emerge automatically. Words such as free sex, homosexual, and lesbian will naturally disappear." (1996.8.1)

188. "Wherever you may go, please try to spread Reverend Moon's message through television or other media. You will never perish. What force can turn around this world of Hell? It is impossible to achieve

---

19. Reverend Sun Myung Moon, "In Search of the Origin of the Universe," tparents.org, HSA-UWC, August 1, 1996, http://www.tparents.org/Moon-Talks/SunMyungMoon96/SunMyungMoon-960801.pdf#search=%22in%20search%20of%20the%20origin%20of%20the%20universe%22.

this unless our sexual organ is used in accordance with an absolute, unique, unchanging, and eternal standard centering on God's true love, which is absolute, unique, unchanging, and eternal love. God is the original owner of the sexual organs. Let us go forward all together for this common cause. Let us become the vanguard that will carry out God's true love. This is the very mission of the Family Federation for World Peace." (1996.8.1)

189. "What is the purpose of the Family Federation for World Peace and Unification? If humanity were to completely transcend the traditional fields of morality and religion and yet be absolutely in harmony with the sexual organs, earning the welcoming applause of God, what kind of world would it be?" (1996.8.1)

190. "God's attributes are unique, unchanging and eternal; we should regard our sexual organs in the same way, because through these sexual organs we create love. If your spouse truly offers his or her sexual organ to you, then you have to become humble and receive it with a humble attitude. Love cannot be achieved without a partner." (1996.8.1)

191. "Reverend Moon has lived an entire life overcoming a suffering path in order to initiate this kind of movement worldwide. Now the time has come for Reverend Moon to trumpet the fanfare of victory and move the entire world. Therefore, I am grateful to God. The family sets the cornerstone on the road to world peace. The family also can destroy that road. It was Adam's family in which the destruction of the foundation of human hope and happiness took place. Therefore, when we establish the Family Federation for World Peace, the road going 180 degrees opposite the direction of the satanic world will be open, and for this, we cannot help but give thanks to God. Without following this road, there is no freedom, happiness, or ideal! I wish that you would center on the absolute sexual organ, unique sexual organ, unchanging sexual

organ, and eternal sexual organ, and use this as your foundation to pursue God. You should realize that this foundation should become the foundation of love, life, lineage, and conscience. We also have to realize that the Kingdom of God on Earth and in Heaven will begin on this foundation." (1996.8.1)

192. "Well, you can live absolutely for the sake of your spouse and create absolute love. If you truly believe in this teaching, go back to your country and utilize all the means you can find to spread this message throughout your country. As long as you do that in a true spirit, you will always prosper. We can see this world of hell change into a world centering on God's absolute love. You need to love with an unchanging love and use your sexual organ as an instrument of unchanging love. Satan has been using the sexual organs, but God is the original owner of sexual organs, isn't He? Can you deny that? Now that you clearly understand let's all take action together. How can we create unique, unchanging, eternal, absolute love? How can we protect this organ? This is the task of the Family Federation for World Peace. Without this concept, we cannot liberate the world. Those who agree with my teaching tonight and are determined to live according to this spirit, could you show your hands to me as your promise? Keep your sexual organ absolute, unique and unchanging. Go home tonight and recognize your spouse's sexual organ as yours and offer your sexual organ to your spouse. Through this recognition and exchange, you can build your true family and expand your true family to a true society, true nation, and true world. This is the very spirit of the Family Federation for World Peace." (1996.8.1)

Sharing Thoughts on True Father's Words

True Father was very concerned about sexual immorality as a leading cause of family breakdown. In the pivotal speech, "In Search of the Origin of the

Universe," he addressed world leaders to promote the education and practice of absolute sexual ethics in their countries. When a nation fails to curb immorality and makes no effort to enforce and promote proper standards for sexual behavior, this causes ruin and breakdown of the family and eventually the whole country.

True Father warns world leaders that the only way they can turn their nations away from destruction is to guide their citizens to use their sexual organs in accordance with God's eternal standard of true love. God-centered families who honor the sexual organs and live according to an unchanging standard of healthy sexuality contribute to prosperous nations and a world of peace.

A Remarkable Declaration

"The Family Federation was formally launched on August 1, 1996. True Father called together a very illustrious group of people to Washington, D.C. There were many influential and highly qualified people, including three former presidents of the United States. Everyone was intrigued to learn what the Family Federation could bring to bear on the problems of humanity.

When True Father got up to give his closing speech, I think many people believed that he would speak about how the family was the first institution, or that the family was the school of love. Or perhaps he would speak about how people of different faiths could work together to make one human family. I was there, and that's what I expected. But True Father cast convention aside, and to everybody's surprise, he chose to speak about the sexual organs.

He asked, 'What will the world be like in the future if it is a world that values the sexual organs? Will that world prosper or perish?'

There was nervous laughter in the audience. And Father said, 'This is not a joke! When God was investing in human beings, which part did he invest the most? What is the purpose of the Family Federation? If humanity were absolutely in harmony with the sexual organs, what kind of world would it be? When we come to clearly understand the ownership of our sexual organ lies with the opposite sex, the world will not remain in its present condition.'

That was a remarkable declaration. There are many scholars and PhDs, but none of them have ever thought about this. That was the founding purpose of the Family Federation." —Michael Balcomb, FFWPU Europe and Middle East Region President

Making It Real

In Dr. Martin Luther King's famous speech, "I Have a Dream" he imagined a world at peace, without racism and division. Similarly, we are encouraged to imagine a world in which absolute sexual ethics are practiced. True Father, in the opening banquet to inaugurate the Family Federation, spoke boldly to heads of state about the important role of sex in their nations. He implored these leaders to return to their people and educate them about the sacred value of the sexual organs. True Father challenges leaders to imagine a better future when he asks, "What will the world look like in the future if it values the sexual organs?" We invite you to open your hearts and imagine it with us.

The media, government, and schools are actively promoting a culture of sexual integrity by emphasizing the sacredness of the sexual organs. All people are respected as children of God, not treated as objects for self-indulgence. Porn is no longer mainstream or cool because it is widely viewed as a destructive habit. Human trafficking is a thing of the past. Parents don't worry about their children's innocence being lost. Their kids can play safely in their neighborhoods and online since the pornography industry and sexual predators are long gone.

There is a significant reduction in juvenile delinquency and problems with drugs, alcohol, and other addictions because intact, God-centered families provide a safe and nurturing environment for children. Family courts where couples argue over the custody of their children are not needed. The number of single-parent families declines, and children feel more secure because they all have stable homes with a mom and dad. Hollywood features stories that are uplifting and family-friendly. Casual sex and sexually explicit content is no longer glorified in movies or shows.

Couples are happily intimate, and they have no desire to look else-where for sexual satisfaction. Sexual integrity and lasting marriages are the greatest source of pride. People are living longer because sex is a health-promoting activity when shared with a lifetime partner in mar-riage. Media often features married couples celebrating their 50th or even 80th anniversary.

We are capable of imagining this world because we know in our hearts that it was always meant to exist. How can we create such a world? When we master our impulses and act according to our original mind, this integrity manifests in all our relationships, creating harmony and prosperity in the family, nation, and world. If we set our mind and heart on this image of the ideal when it comes to sex, we can marry knowing we will share a pure, selfless love with our spouse, and raise a family that understands and lives with sexual integrity. True Father boldly proclaimed his message everywhere in the world.

Likewise, we can be clear and courageous when we talk about God's intention for sex. A world in which all people value the sexual organs will emerge as we authentically grow our sexual integrity and help others do the same.

Points for Consideration/Activities

- What do you think world leaders thought of True Father's momen-tous speech, and how may it have impacted them after they returned to their countries?

- How can your family and community work together to contribute to a world that values the sexual organs?

- How would absolute sexual ethics help the world achieve interde-pendence, mutual prosperity, and universal values?

Section V
The Fall

The Root

Imagine you were adopted and didn't know your biological parents. Even if your adopted parents were loving and awesome, most likely, you'd still wonder where you came from and whether you had any brothers or sisters. You'd want to know who your parents are, and why they left you. Then, one day, you find out where they live, so you go to their house and knock on the door. Perhaps you recognize that they were the ones who were always sitting in the back at every recital, all of your baseball games and graduation. As you begin to introduce yourself, they tell you that they know who you are. They've been keeping track of you since you were a baby, and then they pull out a scrapbook full of pictures. How would you feel when your birth parents put their arms around you and tell you they have always loved you?

True Father's Words

193. "Imagine a huge tree which is really beautiful to behold. Although you can't see its roots, they will be deeply laid. The tip of its root is small and lies hundreds of feet below the surface. Can you see that the tiniest leaf on the top is connected to that root? It is so high in one direction and so deep in the other that the connection is hard to see. Yet, without a relationship with the root, the leaf will eventually die. By the same token, if we human beings say, 'I don't care about my roots; they are separate from me,' then we, too, will start to die. The underground roots must grow and expand in order for the rest, the visible part, to grow and be strong. Fertilizer is put on the ground to feed the part of the tree which we can't see. The

fertilizer for human beings is thought and prayer. These give nourishment to our roots. We have to constantly give more and more
nourishment to the underground root." (1988.4.3)

194. "In my strenuous efforts to find the answer to the fundamental
problems of humankind, and the root of the universe, I realized it
was the sexual organs. Once I realized it was them and thought the
whole matter through, I found that the harmony of heaven and
earth was swirling around the sexual organs. It is an amazing fact."
(1990.1.7)

195. "God is the motivation within our hearts. He is our original source
and the root of our ideals. Without a cause, there can be no result.
Therefore, the universe cannot exist apart from God. Dwelling on
this earth, we are like orphans who have lost our parents. Imagine
the joyful shout of someone who finds his or her lost parents. That
joy would be incomparably greater than the joy of a general who
conquers the world and gains a material fortune." (1969.10.2)

196. "The wrongful use of love is the cause of the Fall. Through an
illicit sexual relationship, Adam united with Eve, who had already
united with the archangel, and thus they became husband and wife
and formed a family, centering not on God but on Satan. Therefore, all humankind as their descendants came to inherit Satan's
lineage. Accordingly, although Adam and Eve's sons were originally
to become God's first and second sons, because Eve established
a relationship of illicit affection with the archangel, her first and
second sons fell into Satan's possession." (1997)

197. "Adam and Eve should have united centered on God, however,
they united with the archangel, a servant of God; that is what the
Fall refers to. Human beings, who should have inherited the lineage of God, inherited the lineage of the servant instead. That is
why fallen people may call God "Father," but they do not actually
feel that He is their Father. This is because they have inherited the

primary characteristics of fallen nature, which makes them think of everything in a self-centered manner, with no regard for God or anything else. Thus, people became contradictory beings, forming tribes and nations. Therefore, these tribes and nations come to be divided very quickly. This is how the sphere of satanic culture developed." (1977.2.23)

198. "Could the original sin appear through eating the fruit of the tree of the knowledge of good and evil? Even if a father ate the fruit and thus committed a sin, what kind of fruit was it that made thousands of generations of his descendants into sinners? It was a relationship that involved lineage. Once planted in the lineage, the root of sin continues eternally by the law of inheritance. This can only be possible through a relationship of love. Improper love is the cause of the Fall." (1969.5.18

199. "Where did the Fall start from? What is the fall that occurred in the family? Is it eating the fruit of the Tree of the Knowledge of Good and Evil? The fall that can occur in the family can be nothing other than that which involves the act of love. Do you think they fell by eating a fruit? Does original sin result from eating a fruit? It is said that the parents' eating of the fruit was the sin, but what is that fruit through which the descendants of thousands of generations have become sinners? This has to do with the blood relationship. If the root of sin is planted through lineage, it lasts forever by virtue of the law of heredity. The only thing that can make this happen is the wrongful use of love." (1969.5.18)

200. "If you carefully study the contents of the Bible, you cannot deny the fact that due to the illicit love, the human ancestors connected themselves to the devil, Satan, with a relationship of father and children. Human beings are precious beings who were supposed to inherit God's lineage and be born as His own sons and daughters within His absolute love. However, they were born into the lineage

of the devil, Satan, as his sons and daughters. In the eighth chapter of Romans, it is recorded, '...but we ourselves, who have the first fruits of the spirit, groan inwardly, as we wait for adoption as sons, the redemption of our bodies.' An adopted child has a lineage different from that of his adoptive parents. This is the reality of human beings." (1972.3.1)

201. "What is the fruit of the tree of the knowledge of good and evil? If you misuse love, you inherit the eternal fruit of evil. If you love righteously, you inherit the eternal fruit of goodness. Is this fruit of good and evil an actual fruit? ... This fruit refers to the male and female sexual organs." (1992.2.2)

202. "You are now living in an era of grace in which, after receiving the Marriage Blessing from True Parents, completing the conversion of lineage, and leading a life that is vertically aligned with Heaven, such that no shadow is cast, you can automatically enter the kingdom of heaven. That is to say, if you establish a true family on earth and lead a heavenly life, once you die, your life will be connected to the kingdom of God in heaven, and you will enjoy eternal life." (2006.10.14)

203. "In Eden, God was unable to conduct the wedding ceremony of Adam and Eve. They married of their own accord and thus connected to Satan's lineage instead of God's lineage. The Blessing Ceremony uproots this and reconnects Adam and Eve to God's lineage. That is why through the Blessing Ceremony, we receive the citizenship that enables us to live in our original homeland, the liberated kingdom of heaven in heaven where there is no Fall, and to attend God as our Father." (2006.3.30)

Sharing Thoughts on True Father's Words

True Father uses the word "root" often as a metaphor, especially in reference to lineage. What does it mean when he says the sexual organs are the root of the universe? Adam and Eve were originally created as God's children. According to God's design, they were supposed to inherit God's lineage and give birth to His sons and daughters by using their sexual organs. Because the sexual organs create a blood relationship, they are the root of lineage and the means by which His love could expand forever.

When Adam and Eve misused their sexual organs, the original root was defiled. Consequently, thousands of generations created to be God's children were born into Satan's lineage instead. Out of unconditional love and commitment, God determined to reverse the tragic course of history and provide a way to retrieve His lost lineage.

We are now living in the era of grace when we can receive the Marriage Blessing from True Parents and change our lineage from Satan's back to God's. True Father tells us that in order to return to God, we must cut everything off from the satanic world and graft ourselves to the true root. The way that men and women use their sexual organs determines whose lineage they will perpetuate. If we misuse our sexual organ, we inherit the fruit of evil. If we love righteously, we inherit the fruit of goodness. Blessed husbands and wives make a commitment to preserve their sexual organs for one another exclusively and create radiant families who understand and practice Heavenly intimacy. From these families, God's good lineage begins and expands.

Making It Real

Roots are the anchor of a tree, like the foundation of a house, supporting everything above ground. They provide a system through which nutrients can be collected from the soil and transported to its branches and leaves. Tree roots amaze and impress engineers who wish they could build such complex and efficient systems. Tree roots know where to find the richest organic matter and water within the top 18 inches of soil. But a tree's root system can extend much further than that. A tree can have hundreds of miles of roots, some as thin as a human hair. The quality of life a tree enjoys depends on its roots.

A Healthy Ancient Cherry Tree in Japan

Jindai Zakura (神代桜), in Yamanashi's city, Hokuto, is about 2,000 years old. This cherry tree is the oldest sakura (cherry tree) in Japan and possibly in the world, but it still blossoms every spring. In 2011, this tree survived a terrible earthquake. Centuries before that, it endured countless challenges like wars and famines. What is the secret to its success? The root system! A cherry tree has an intricate system of substantial permanent roots with a network of smaller feeder roots. This complex system under the ground ensures a long life for the cherry tree. When it's taken care of properly, a tree can survive to fulfill its purpose, producing beautiful blossoms every spring.

The story of the cherry tree is one of a successful life that brings joy to all who behold it. When we commit to take care of our roots, which connect us with all of our ancestors, descendants, and even with God, we are investing not only in our Marriage Blessing but in God's beautiful ideal for the whole universe. Nothing else can do what the sexual organs do, so their function is irreplaceable and unique. This is why True Father calls the sexual organs the root of the universe. He said it is the palace of love, life, and lineage. By connecting their sexual organs, husband and wife nourish their love for each other. God designed sex as an important part of the Marriage Blessing as it is essential for our lifelong journey towards perfection.

Points for Consideration/Activities

- Have you ever searched for information about your ancestors? If so, what did you find?

- What kind of legacy would you like to leave behind?

- How can blessed couples take care of their roots?

Crossroads to Heaven or Hell

Have you ever wondered what your life would be like now had you made a different decision about an important course of action? When we look back at some of these crossroads, we realize that at the time, we never could have imagined where our choice would lead us. Sometimes, we carefully considered what lay ahead, but at other times, we made the decision that seemed easiest. True Father understands the significance of our choices, especially involving sex. His words can be shockingly strong at first, but when we understand the heart behind them, we feel grateful.

True Father's Words

204. "If you use your sexual organ as if you are wandering aimlessly and without direction, it will undoubtedly lead you, as its owner, to hell. By the same token, if you use your sexual organ according to the standard of God's absolute love, you will be led high up into heaven. That is a clear conclusion. Today, we face a serious youth problem because Adam and Eve, during their youth, planted the seed of free sex in the shade through their Fall in the Garden of Eden. In the Last Days, which is the time of harvest, we see the worldwide phenomenon of rampant free sex among youth." (1996.9.15)

205. "You need to know that the sexual organs were the dividing point between heaven and hell. If you use them wrongfully, you are bound for hell, and if you use them rightfully, you will automatically reach heaven. There is only one starting point, not two. This shows the

importance of lovemaking. When all women and men return home and say, 'Now I know the truth. Let's put it into practice henceforth. It is the basis of hope for our family,' then universal liberation will take place. The conclusion is that, in conjunction with the universal proclamation, we should understand its contents and preserve the sanctity of the sexual organs." (1996.5.24, 2)

206. "Where did heaven and hell begin? In midair? Where? At the sexual organs. This must be serious. They have turned heaven and earth upside down. Can anyone deny that? There is no way to deny the logic of The Fall in Reverend Moon's *Divine Principle*. Ask God. Examine everything. Not having received any answers from that, you would not be able to oppose what I have arranged in systematic order, including theories and contents that you could never imagine even in your dreams." (1996.8.1)

207. "In today's satanic world, the sexual organs have ruined everything. Free sex, homosexuality, and drugs are reigning supreme. Drugs make you lose your senses. They make you like animals, not human beings. They make you think nothing but animalistic thoughts. The Kingdom of Heaven, on the other hand, is diametrically opposite to this. It follows the concept, not of free sex, but of absolute, eternal, unchanging, and unique love. They connect to the Kingdom of Heaven instantaneously. When such a foundation is laid on earth, it will become God's Kingdom on earth. This is the undeniable logical conclusion. You should exercise great care toward the foundation of love." (1996.5.26)

208. "What is the Fall? What is the fundamental problem...? It is that Adam and Eve considered their sexual organs to belong to themselves and acted freely. Had they reached full maturity centering on God, Adam's was to belong to Eve and Eve's to Adam, and through them, they were to lay the foundation of absolute love with the eternal God. However, they were unfaithful and instead

made the organs their own. Hence, that foundation was completely destroyed. Those who live for themselves are bound for hell, and those who live for their spouses are bound for heaven. This is where the crossroads are. The sexual organs are the boundary between hell and heaven. You must know this." (1996.11.1)

209. "Throughout history, the sexual organs came to be regarded as most evil. Think about it—the starting points of heaven and hell lead in diametrically opposite directions. Until now, humankind was ignorant of how the true sexual organ is the starting point to heaven, and the false sexual organ leads to hell. That is the sexual organ. Misusing the genitals leads to hell, and the rightful use of love leads to heaven. It is simple." (1996.5.26)

210. "What is the fruit of good and evil? It becomes good if you enter into a relationship with a good man: if you marry a king, you'll give birth to a prince, but if you marry a gangster boss, you'll give birth to a future gangster boss. That is what the fruit of good and evil is: the thing that is able to bear the fruit of good or evil is the female sexual organ. It must not be violated." (1997.4.16)

211. "Everything flows vertically, coming to fruition in the sexual organs. That is where everything is bound to come together, whether bad or good. Hence, those who use them well become people of goodness, and those who use them wrongly become the worst people." (1996.11.11)

212. "God never sends people to hell. When people go to the spirit world, they go to hell on their own account. When people who live an evil life go to places of goodness, they cannot breathe... Who sends people to hell? It is not God. You go to hell on your own." (1990.2.25)

213. "Therefore, heaven is not a world found in outer space on the other side of the galaxy, nor is it the product of imagination exist-

ing only in the human brain. It refers to a substantial kingdom, heaven on earth, which can be created only when you lead a life of true love. When you leave the physical world on that foundation, you automatically enter the kingdom of heaven in the spirit world. This means that only when you have led a heavenly life on earth can you lead such a life in heaven." (2006.4.10)

214. "You, the young ones, are standing at the crossroads of good and evil. If you take one wrong step, you might fall into a steep and deep pit of death. Although it is difficult, take the step that will make you stand tall. Then you can be victorious princes and princesses who look out at the hope for a shining tomorrow that lies on the broad plane. Therefore, you need to watch every step. Be careful as you walk on the snow-covered road." (1972.7.16)

215. "Dear guests, do you know the dividing line between heaven and hell? Is it in the air? Is it in a church sanctuary? Is it in a national government? No, the dividing line between heaven and hell is found in your reproductive organs. This is where the greatest tragedy in human history occurred, which turned heaven and earth upside-down. If you use your reproductive organ recklessly and blindly, you will surely go to hell. On the other hand, if you use it in accordance with the standard of God's absolute love, you will go to Heaven. Who can deny this? If you doubt it, I ask you to carefully read the *Divine Principle*, which contains the laws of Heaven that were revealed to me. If that does not satisfy your doubts, please pray about it sincerely. I am sure that God will answer your prayer." (2004.10.26)

Sharing Thoughts on True Father's Words

True Father discovered the powerful role of the sexual organs in realizing God's dream. Adam and Eve had the choice to obey God's commandment to use their sexual organs in the way God intended. Their decision to disobey took them and the rest of humanity down a long and painful road. The road not taken would have been a beautiful, thriving journey towards the realization of God's ideal. At the crossroads, they defied their Heavenly Parent, ruining everything. They chose not to take the step that would allow them to stand tall. The mistake of a single moment began a history of human suffering that continues to this day.

True Father's insights about how the first man and woman fell away from God can help us to make better choices with our purity. The inclinations for making wrong decisions are always with us, but now we are more informed about the serious consequences of our choices. True Father encourages us to pause at our crossroads and look far into the distance to the place God is guiding us, difficult though that may be to do.

Like our original ancestors, we often find ourselves standing at a fork in the road regarding choices about sexual integrity. True Father likens these times to a crossroads to heaven or hell because he knows if we go one way we can create a beautiful and happy life for ourselves and our families. If we go the other way our life will become difficult and will cause much suffering. What we do in our second phase of life factors in the choice we make for ourselves in our final phase of life: to choose to live in heaven or hell. That's on us alone. Have you reflected seriously on how you will live out the second phase of your life?

True Father wants us to avoid the natural consequences of our mistakes, so he gives us this harsh warning. Despite these strong words, he clearly teaches that hell is not a permanent circumstance; it's a choice we make. God will never give up on His children; likewise, can we believe in ourselves to stand tall in the face of difficult choices? As a loving, forgiving Heavenly Parent, He will always provide a path for each person to reach heaven. Can we also be the people who can provide a path for ourselves and each person we love to reach heaven?

Making It Real

Have you struggled at a crossroads, indecisive about the choice of going down one road or the other? Depending on which path we take, we can either get to a better place or end up worse off. When we repeatedly make healthy choices, we establish good habits that lead to a happy and fulfilled life. Unfortunately, the opposite is also true. Unhealthy and self-centered decisions put us on a conflicted and troubled path, full of regret.

One of the most challenging crossroads we face in life is how we choose to use our sexual organs. The promise of instant gratification can be easy and enticing, but the pleasure we experience as a result is always short-lived. It doesn't take much effort to watch porn in the middle of the night when we're alone, but that will never leave us fulfilled. Misusing our sexual energy will slowly erode our self-discipline, a quality that is necessary to be a loving spouse and parent. When a serious addiction develops, this can lead to heartache and tragedy for the individual and everyone they love. Our ability to experience true intimacy in conjugal love will be more difficult as long as these habits perpetuate.

When we make the choice to defer immediate gratification, we are investing in our present and long-term happiness. When we reserve our sexual energy exclusively for our spouse, it becomes a powerful bonding agent between husband and wife. In a marriage where both partners live for the sake of each other, there is comfort, connection, and empowerment. This couple fulfills their highest aspirations for love. They lead a joyful, productive life that is an inspiration to others.

The road that leads to the lifestyle God intended for us is indeed a challenging one. We may face many crossroads in our lifetime. Heavenly Parent has a big heart and will always provide a way back to the life we are meant to live. Getting back on track after a mistake begins with honesty and reaching out for help. Through grace and a lot of effort, what was broken can be mended.

Splitting the Atom

God created atoms as the essential basic building block for everything in the universe. A pin head is made up of millions and millions of atoms, and within each one are even smaller particles. In the 1940s, scientists discovered a process to release the powerful energy that holds these subatomic particles together by splitting the nucleus of the atom. What was considered a miraculous discovery was put to use with catastrophic consequences.

The atomic bomb that hit Hiroshima on the morning of August 6, 1945, weighed more than 9,000 pounds and was dropped by parachute from an American airplane. When the bomb exploded 2,000 feet above the ground, it created sudden and swift devastation through heat, light, shock waves, and nuclear radiation.

Almost all structures within a one-mile radius were leveled, but the human cost was the most tragic consequence. It was estimated that this bomb immediately killed 80,000 people in Hiroshima alone. The explosive blasts from the bombs and firestorms and the acute radiation poisoning eventually killed 200,000 people in Hiroshima and Nagasaki. Large numbers of civilians continued to die for years afterward from the effects of burns, radiation sickness, and other injuries.

Nuclear energy has caused extreme devastation, but it does have the potential to produce amazing benefits. The Hiroshima bomb was 15 Kilotons and could have powered Los Angeles for about a week![20] When compared with other energy sources, nuclear energy is better for the environment, and its efficiency is unbeatable. It can release one million times more energy from one atom than fossil fuels. A nuclear-powered submarine can travel underwater for a whole year without refueling! Imagine that!

The Path We Choose

Nuclear energy and the sexual organs have something in common. They

---

20. Nikolas Martelaro, "Turning Nuclear Weapons into Nuclear Power," (course work, Stanford University, March 23, 2017), http://large.stanford.edu/courses/2017/ph241/martelaro2/.

both have the potential for contributing to a thriving world or for bringing devastation. It depends entirely on how we choose to use them. The effect of the misuse of sex is more subtle than the firestorms of nuclear blasts but still an ever-present part of society.

The world is riddled with examples of the destructive force of sex when it is misused. Not a week goes by without the news broadcasting a scandal of a politician, religious leader, or celebrity whose indiscretions have destroyed their relationships, reputations, and careers. When sex is devoid of respect and commitment, it leads to a loss of intimacy. Without understanding God's vision for sex, we cannot effectively make a stand against larger societal issues, such as human trafficking, pornography, and many more. These complicated problems inevitably trickle down to the family and influence the way we view sex.

The crossroads in our lives are always times of great challenge, but also enormous opportunities. The decisions we make about sex have an especially profound impact on our lives. We yearn for the joy of a sexually fulfilling relationship with true love that lasts forever. When we find ourselves at a turning point, we can move toward the outstanding life we envisioned. Like nuclear energy, sex is an incredibly powerful force that must be used in accordance with its true purpose if we are to experience the bountiful fruits it was meant to deliver. The right choice at the crossroads may be unpopular or less traveled by, but it will make all the difference. As Robert Frost says,

"Two roads diverged in a wood, and I—
I took the one less traveled by,
And that has made all the difference."

Points for Consideration/Activities

- Share a time in your life when you were standing at an important crossroads, where your decision would lead to very different outcomes.

- What helped you to make your decision? Did you ask anyone for advice? If so, what was the advice?

- What do you think about True Father's analogy that the main crossroad of our life is how we use our sexual organs?

The Odyssey

The Odyssey by Homer is a Greek classic partially inspired by the timeless theme of temptation. It is as relevant for us today as it was to the ancient Greeks. Another well-known Greek writer, Aesop, wrote fables, like this one about temptation.

> *One day a bee farmer left a pot of honey on the picnic table outside his house. The sweet-smelling honey attracted a family of flies. The bees that made the honey noticed the flies and warned them. "Watch out; it's not safe. Don't go there; you'll get stuck!" The bees swarmed around the pot, forming a wall to prevent the flies from getting stuck in the honey. The flies broke through and ate voraciously, unaware that their wings and legs were getting heavy and sticky with honey. Unable to fly or walk out of the pot, the whole family of flies drowned in the tasty but dangerous honey.*

God gives us warnings to help us avoid sticky situations where we could get trapped, unaware of impending danger. True Father's teachings about sexual temptation reveal just how important it is to be educated about its challenging and dangerous presence in our society.

True Father's Words

216. "When a man enters into a spiritual state of deep prayer, a woman always appears to tempt him. Something like this inevitably occurs, blocking the religious path. Why does this happen? It is because

history was formed through illicit love. The fact that the teaching that asserts that human beings fell by eating of the fruit of the tree of the knowledge of good and evil remained intact for two thousand years is surprising." (1971.2.17)

217. "The free sex rampant in this world is a trap Satan made to cause people to fall and to prevent them from coming closer to God. Once caught in this trap, they will die and be controlled by Satan or become his prey. In today's western societies, the USA in particular, due to the prevalence of free sex, it is becoming more and more difficult to form ideal families, and the number of people failing to form families is increasing daily. Thus, in the not-too-distant future, the majority of people will not have families at all." (1993)

218. "The private parts of a man or a woman are like a poisonous snake. They are the trap of a poisonous snake. What does it mean to say that a serpent tempted Eve? It is a reference to the reproductive organ. Are there not many women out there whose female organ is more deadly than a viper? Men, too, do they not use their serpent-like organ to tempt and seduce women? If you mistakenly take that bait, you will get into serious trouble. Because of it, a nation can perish; even a world can perish. In fact, it can block your way to heaven and eternal life." (1992.2.16)

219. "Through the Fall, Satan diabolically injected self-centeredness into the mind-body relationship. He planted this poison mushroom in the human heart. Although the embrace of self-centeredness may lead to a beautiful appearance, worldly fame, and earthly comfort, it is a trap. To enter it is reckless, for it becomes an addiction and leads to hidden suffering that is difficult to escape." (2004.10.26)

220. "Do you suppose I am a different kind of man because of who I am? I am not immune to temptation. I'm even more receptive to

all kinds of sensations. If I didn't know how to control myself, I would react even more strongly than you to such stimulation. So do you think my struggles are easier than yours or more difficult? I had to fight a hundred times harder in order to control these sensations and gain the victory for God and humankind." (1983.6.12)

221. "The devil destroys completely women's sexual organs, and then he uses them to destroy men… Once men are set on fire by lust, they can do outrageous things throwing their dignity and honor away." (2007.12.28)

222. "By misusing your sexual organ, you might destroy your family or nation. The most fearful enemy of the world is lineage—the sexual organ if you misuse it. The Kingdom of God might be torn apart. Our five senses should not be misused—manipulated by sexual desire. There must be absolute unity between mind and body." (2001.2.18)

223. "Satan, in disguise, will tempt you, saying he is going to make you whatever you want to be. To the male members, a most beautiful girl may appear and try to entice you. On the worldly level, you cannot help but be tempted by such beauty. What will you do? Answer me. You will be seduced if you are absent-minded, and you cannot pledge to safely guard yourself. If so, you will collapse in the hands of Satan. What will you do? If and when you are faced with anything, think of things in light of the *Divine Principle*." (1974.2.13)

224. "If that kind of temptation comes, however beautiful such a girl may be, you must kneel before God and ask Him what to do, and He will guide you. Do you understand? This means you have to pray. Whenever any temptation comes, you must pray—pray for a decision. For instance, you female members, some of you may think, 'Well, I'm over thirty; when can I be married?' … And there comes, without doubt, a handsome man tempting you. He looks

like a king and looks as though he's qualified for anything and everything. What will you do? This is nothing to laugh at. You are apt to be tempted. At that moment, you must kneel down before God in prayer—question in your prayer. What God is going to make out of you, and what I am going to make out of you, is that you become the person who can win over Satan, win over the worldly way. Do you realize that?" (1974.2.13)

Sharing Thoughts on True Father's Words

True Father's explanation of the Human Fall offers valuable insight into the danger of sexual temptation in our own lives. He describes the thoughts and actions of the first man and woman that led to the misuse of their sexual organs. Even though they were innocent and completely pure, Adam and Eve became susceptible to deception and outright lies, leaving them vulnerable to sexual temptation. We learn how Lucifer, a cunning angel motivated by self-centered thoughts, convinced Eve to ignore God's word and focus on her own desires. True Father's message is an appeal to be proactive, patient and prepared so that we are not subject to the self-centered thoughts sexual temptation creates.

When we embark on a religious path, temptation will always appear. Self-centered love is a trap that we can fall into if we are not careful. It always leads us to suffering and is difficult to escape. True Father uses a poisonous snake as a metaphor in describing the sexual organs and warns us that Satan may disguise himself in the form of a beautiful woman or handsome man who makes false promises. He describes his own experience, how he encountered all kinds of temptations and eventually gained victory for God and humanity. When we pray and ask God for help with an open mind and humble heart, we will be guided. We can ask God, "What kind of person do You want me to become?"

Making It Real

Literature, poetry, and music have provided countless variations on the topic of sexual temptation and its tragic consequences. Why is this theme so popular? Audiences and readers are moved by stories that are real to them. Most of us know of people who have been sexually exploited. Victims of sexual exploitation experience paralyzing fear and shame that can overshadow them for the rest of their lives.

Sexual temptations that influence us to make poor choices are all too common. A naïve high school girl becomes obsessed with someone older who seems wiser and more attractive than the boys her own age. She begins to spend time alone with him, which can easily result in unforeseen and negative consequences. Like Adam and Eve, we tend to justify our actions and hide them from those who love us. Sexual desire is a powerful and relentless force that can have damaging effects when misused.

The 21st century has brought a new form of sexual temptation on an unprecedented scale. Internet pornography is influencing people's attitudes towards sex in a way and on a scale like never before. What makes internet porn such a phenomenon? Today's porn is accessible, aggressive, affordable, anonymous, and addictive. These five A's of internet porn are fueling the greatest threat to sexual integrity the world has ever seen. In previous generations, softcore pornography was available primarily through books, magazines, and films. If a person wanted to view pornography, they had to go out and look for it. For most would-be consumers, it simply wasn't accessible or worth the risk. Enter the age of the world wide web, and we find ourselves in a time when everything from immodest swimwear to the most vile and graphic pornographic videos are easily within reach, not just in the home but in our pocket. Billions of pornographic images are available on the web at no cost. Accessing pornography on the internet requires no face-to-face contact with the vendor and provides a low risk of detection. The anonymous nature of internet pornography creates the perception of being immune to consequences.

True Father emphasizes how serious we need to be about sexual temptation. God's heart is one of compassion and grace, but the path back from these kinds of mistakes can be difficult. We can easily become discouraged and left with feelings of shame following the short-term reward of a sexual high from watching pornography. It takes tremendous courage and self-discipline to acknowledge our problems and change our behavior. The wise thing to do is to avoid the pitfall altogether.

The Odyssey

Seduction is always deceitful, but it's not always subtle. In Homer's ancient tale, *The Odyssey*, Odysseus is faced with a very obvious and blatant form of temptation.

The protagonist, Odysseus, is trying to get back home to his family. There are many obstacles set up by jealous gods who want to prevent his return. One of the most fascinating trials Odysseus faces is when his ship passes a dangerously rocky island where the infamous and bewitching Sirens live. These are creatures bent on destruction, with feathery bird bodies and large women's heads. The seductive lure of the Sirens' songs is deathly, as sailors, bewitched by their music, steer their ships into the rocks and crash. The island is littered with their dead bodies.

> *"'Come closer, famous Odysseus—Achaea's pride and glory—moor your ship on our coast so you can hear our song! Never has any sailor passed our shores in his black craft until he has heard the honeyed voices pouring from our lips, and once he hears to his heart's content sails on, a wiser man.'"*[21]

When their ship approaches the island, Odysseus cleverly has his shipmates plug their ears with wax so they can't hear. He then tells the sailors to tie him to the mast with no wax to block the singing and orders them to keep him tied up while they sail past the island. He knows if they untie him,

---

21. Homer, *The Odyssey*, trans. Robert Fagles (New York: Penguin Group, 1996), 277.

he would throw himself into the sea and drown. Their ship successfully sails past the rocky island, and the hero goes on to face more exciting adventures.

It is important to understand that seduction can take many forms. Our temptations will likely be more subtle than that which Odysseus faced. However, the loss of control we experience can feel the same. We may not be on a ship that is destined to capsize on the rocks, but we can be confronted with a very real danger that could wreck our lives and the lives of the people we love. This is why we need others to help us, just as Odysseus had his fellow sailors support him. God wants us to be vigilant so that we can see the danger that lies ahead. If we are resolved to set sail for the distant shore of an exciting, happy Marriage Blessing, we will need to navigate around the dangerous rocks we encounter along the way.

Points for Consideration/Activities

- Share a time you gave in to temptation and what it felt like afterwards.

- What can you do to protect yourself from sexual temptations?

- Share a time when you were tempted by something and overcame the temptation.

Immorality and Youth

Within the past century, people's attitudes about sex have dramatically changed. Many sexual activities that are accepted nowadays were criminal a century ago. Back then, it was scandalous for a woman to show her ankles in public, and people could be arrested for having sex without being married. The largest evidence of this change in attitude is the widely accepted, multibillion-dollar porn industry. Today, the average teenager can see far more images of nudity in one afternoon than their grandparents could have seen during their entire lifetimes. How can we protect our young people from this pornified culture?

True Father's Words

225. "Today, we face a serious youth problem because in the Garden of Eden, Adam and Eve planted the seed of free sex in the shade through their fall during their youth. In the Last Days, harvest time, there must be the worldwide phenomenon of rampant free sex among the youth. Satan knew that the Lord of the Second Advent would come in the Last Days with the strategy to save human beings, who are in the realm of the fall, by lifting them up to the realm of absolute love, centered on God's true love. Satan cannot find any other standard of love other than free sex, as the archangel introduced in the Garden of Eden. Therefore, we see that the entire world is stripped naked and being pushed in the direction of death by free sex." (1996.8.1)

226. "The morality of young people has declined. While Adam and Eve were growing up as teenagers, they misused their sexual organs. Following the law of cause and effect, in the last days, we see the problem of immorality among the youth; they engage in free sex, and these problems multiply throughout the world." (1996.9.15)

227. "During the time when children are growing, they do not know love. These days, children see through TV, and through parents, the love affair before they really mature and sense by themselves. In Adam and Eve's case, they had nothing to see. They did not know about sexual love... Through natural growth and development, they would have matured and learned to know of love. Then God could have blessed them in marriage. They were just to grow naturally, and when they reached the point when they came to know one another, then God wanted to bless them. It is different from the state of children today. They know things before they actually mature." (1965)

228. "True Parents finished all preparations for removing Satan's lineage. The Fall occurred because there was no protection. We have now completed pure love education in some middle schools and high schools. Nonetheless, the purity of students is being destroyed. The Internet's influence is terrible. How can we remedy this situation? Mothers and fathers everywhere have to protect their children because parents represent the position of God... During their adolescence, Adam and Eve were supposed to prepare themselves to meet their partner. In spite of their pledge, they fell during their teenage years when they had reached the top of the growth stage. God could not intervene directly under the Principle, so to eliminate the risk that they might fall under Satan's sovereignty, He gave them the warning, 'Do not eat.'" (1999.4.25)

229. "Also, in every nation, there has been a breakdown in sexual morality among young people through the misuse of their special,

precious sexual organs. Since we clearly recognize that those young people are to marry and the resulting new man–woman relationships are meant to be the absolute prerequisites for laying the ideal foundation of a nation's future and the life or death of its history, we know very well that the issue of young people's sexual ethics is the most important one for us to deal with. People who have not thought about this issue or heard of it until now might ask why we need the concept absolute sex. We absolutely need it. Do you understand? ... We now realize that absolute sexual ethics are absolutely needed. When they are subverted, destruction comes to a nation." (2009.1.2)

230. "Human history began from Adam and Eve's mistake of leaving the heavenly way of God and loving each other as they wished when they were still a boy and girl of sixteen years of age. We can say that the corruption of today's young people results from this cause. This is the same as harvesting when autumn comes. The young generation's acting as they wish and falling is the harvest of the wrong seeds which their ancestors sowed. The Unification Church has appeared in order to completely cleanse and demolish these problems." (1998)

231. "I would like to pass on to you a truly precious teaching today. People, particularly young people, must understand correctly about the value of the love organs and treat these preciously. The love organs in their original state are the center and origin of love, life, and lineage. The completed fruit of love, as well as the conception of new life, is possible only by means of the love organs. Without utilizing the love organs, the parents' lineage cannot be passed down to the next generation. For this reason, the love organs are the most important parts of the human body. Unfortunately, in fallen modern society, the love organs are misused in too many instances. The global trend is that social and cultural environments, manifesting particularly through movies, music, journalism,

and the Internet, are misleading people into the misuse of their love organs. Young people are easily swept away by the waves of free sex that are ruining countries, and families are breaking apart. This is a tragic reality. It is time that religious leaders and other leaders of conscience raised their voices loudly in support of what is right." (2003.7.10)

Sharing Thoughts on True Father's Words

The Lord of the Second Advent comes in the last days to save humanity. Satan's primary weapon to control God's children is to employ the same strategy he used against Adam and Eve, enticing them to engage in unprincipled or "free" sex. Today, internet pornography and social media tempt young people to misuse their sexual organs, fueling a global pandemic of immorality among the youth. Because of this unregulated environment, children learn about sexual love before they are ready. True Father urges parents everywhere to stand in the position of God to protect their children and help them keep their purity in preparation for the Marriage Blessing. An ideal foundation for the future will arise when our youth begin to live by absolute sexual ethics.

Making It Real

God created the family to be a school of love where family members learn about healthy love relationships from one another. However, the current reality is that most children learn about sex from other sources. The breakdown of traditional family values and sexual norms that the world witnessed during the latter part of the 20th century has accelerated. Families are drifting apart, and young people are becoming more and more isolated.

Technology has created an imitation world through internet porn that sucks viewers into a fake reality. Pixels on a screen can appear much more stimulating than real relationships. Young people are presented with a distorted view of sex and acquire unrealistic expectations that can never be met in real life. This can drive them deeper into their fantasy world as they seek to satisfy their real need for connection and intimacy. Children who acquire a porn habit during their formative years can warp their sexual template. They condition themselves to look at people as objects of pleasure rather than precious individuals who have an incredible, unique value and whose purity should be honored and respected. Even more concerning is that young people can learn to associate violence and abuse with the sacred act of love. In today's hookup culture, young people go from one unsatisfactory partner to the next as easily as if they were clicking on porn sites. This diminishes their capacity to develop authentic relationships and causes them to lose hope for a happy and fulfilling marriage.

True Parents teach that the root of immorality has a spiritual cause that began when our first ancestors misused their sexual organs in the Garden of Eden. Since then, history has been littered with stories of leaders and empires falling from greatness because of this problem. In spite of these moral failures, societies have always sought to protect their children. However, today's culture has reached a new low in which children as young as seven years old can easily find the vilest pornographic images and videos online.

True Parents have come to reverse Adam and Eve's mistake by modeling and teaching absolute sexual ethics. They have taken the road less traveled and initiated a pure love movement in order to address the destructive trend of immorality among the youth and promote God's standard of love in the Marriage Blessing. When we begin to create healthy families and communities, young people can regain hope for their own future.

It Takes a Village

Most of us have heard the phrase, "It takes a village to raise a child." Rene Messora, a filmmaker and mother of a newborn, spent some time with the Kraho people in Brazil. One day, she was with a Kraho mother, when suddenly the mom picked up Rene's baby and started breastfeeding! This tribe believes that every member of the community should help raise children. It's even common to see a three-year-old taking care of a one-year-old. Children are taught to be aware of their natural and social surroundings, so they enjoy a close relationship with both nature and people. Women help deliver each other's babies and share in the responsibility of disciplining all the children. When elders point out a needed change in a child's behavior, it's done in a stern voice without yelling. Messora noted in her article that the Kraho children are the happiest she's ever encountered.[22]

Other cultures express similar messages that guide their communal lifestyles and child-rearing approaches. A Swahili proverb, "One hand does not nurse a child," and a Sudanese saying, "A child is a child of everyone," encourage community members to be actively engaged in a collective approach to raising children. In other words, it is through interdependence and mutual support that we survive and prosper.

The youth of today need a village like that of the Kraho people in Brazil. If we all watch out for each other's children, we can overcome the dangerous environment that preys on our youth in our neighborhoods, schools, and communities. A study from the Barna Group that was published in *The Porn Phenomenon* states that 72 percent of 13- to 24-year-olds look up porn at least once or twice a month, and most of them reported that their first exposure was unintentional. Since internet pornography is everywhere, it's not a matter of if your child will ever see porn, but when. Parents need to prepare for when their children see pornography and learn how to respond to their children without shaming them.

How can parents support their children's natural interest in sex as they grow up in this overly sexualized world? Here's an example from a mom whose son stumbled upon some suggestive content on the television.

"I remember the look in his eyes like it was yesterday. My sweet tween boy was channel surfing and paused when he saw a barely dressed rockstar. She moved close to the screen with what I call the porn-look in her eyes. Gone were the preschool days of innocence; my son had awakened to the

---

22. Rene Messora, "A child raised by many mothers: What we can learn about parenthood from an indigenous group in Brazil," *The Washington Post*, September 6, 2019, https://www.washingtonpost.com/lifestyle/2019/09/06/child-raised-by-many-mothers-what-we-can-learn-how-other-cultures-raise-their-children/.

allure of the female body. The day my son found that video on television, I counted to 10 before I responded. I sensed it was better to acknowledge the sexual awakening that was happening than encourage a lifetime of shame by ignoring his interest. 'Hey, buddy,' I said softly. 'What do you think of her?' He thought carefully and then said the most profound thing: 'I think she wants to be beautiful, but she's very confused.' I turned off the television. Then, I asked what other great thoughts he was thinking. Thus, began an ongoing conversation that has lasted into his young adult years."[23]

The task of reversing the immoral direction of today's world may seem impossible, but when enough of us get involved, we can reach a tipping point and turn the tide. We can solve the problem of immorality among our youth by modeling a lifestyle of honesty and sexual integrity and initiating healthy conversations about sex. When we work with others in our village, we can begin to counteract the misinformation from schools, the government, and the media. True Parents are calling on us to get involved in the movement to create a new culture in which young people embrace a lifestyle of purity in preparation for the Marriage Blessing.

Points for Consideration/Activities

- How can we work together as a community to protect children and help them have a healthy understanding of sex?

- Share some examples of immoral messages in our culture that young people are exposed to on a daily basis.

- What would you say to your child if they told you they've been watching pornography?

---

23. Dannah Gresh, "Healthy Sexuality: Sending the Right Message to Your Kids," *Focus on the Family*, June 27, 2017, https://www.focusonthefamily.com/parenting/healthy-sexuality-sending-the-right-message-to-your-kids/.

Immorality in the Family and World

The sexual revolution took America by storm in the 1960s. Americans, followed by people of other western nations and, eventually, most of the world, gave themselves permission to be "liberated" from all sexual constraints. This was the beginning of the sexualized culture that exists today. Things that were prohibited and avoided became accepted and sought after on a global scale. It promised freedom but instead enslaved men and women in destructive behaviors. In this way, the free sex lifestyle robbed people of what God intended, a deeply satisfying sexual intimacy that one can only experience in an exclusive, husband-and-wife relationship.

True Parents' Words

232. "Immorality among youth and family breakdown are among the
     bad fruits reaped from the seeds sown by the first human ancestors.
     When Adam and Eve fell, they turned the family upside down.
     The fruits of the Fall have become manifest throughout the world,
     with the result that we are now in a time of great suffering. The
     fallen family is the root and is at the heart of all the problems of
     societies, nations, and the world. People do not know which way
     to turn. It is a time when grandfathers cannot fulfill the role of
     grandfathers, parents cannot fulfill the role of parents, husbands
     and wives cannot fulfill the roles of husbands and wives, and chil-
     dren cannot fulfill the role of children. As selfish individualism

takes root, God is not present, both the world and its nations are lost, and a good society cannot emerge." —True Father (1997.4.8)

233. "People say that today is an age of globalization. What is the center of this age, as they describe it? They usually speak of it in terms of economics, academics, sports, and so on, and they do not realize that globalization should focus on the family. The problems of the world are not primarily rooted in economics or politics but in the family. Families are breaking down, especially in developed nations. Many families have been destroyed by free sex. People have to understand that the authentic movement for globalization must be based on the family. In other words, people have to know True Parents' teachings about the ideal family." —True Father (1996.5.5)

234. "The reason people strive for everlasting, unchanging love between a husband and wife, yet can't seem to achieve it, is Adam's and Eve's original separation from God, the Fall, which was caused by false love and adultery. The reason the original sin is inherited throughout the generations, and the reason we, in what the Bible calls the last days, are witnessing wide-scale immorality and family breakdown, is due to this. What God dislikes the most is when a person goes against the law of love and becomes immoral... These phenomena are more fearful than starvation, war, or any disease. Why is that? These problems are not just our problems today they are the problems that will destroy humanity's hope in future generations. Today's immorality has direct consequences for our descendants... Immorality, sexual promiscuity, and divorce are grave mistakes that violate heavenly law." —True Mother (1995.8.23)

235. "Among all violations, the one that pains God most is free sex. A world of free sex is absolutely contrary to the Will of God. Love needs to come from the stimulation of unblemished emotion. However, free sex is totally devoid of purity or true emotion.

How many of us have been touched by the cruelty of infidelity and divorce? Where is God in a one-night stand? What about the nightmares where children are sexually abused by a parent or relative? Is free sex worth the price of a broken child?" —True Mother (1993.7.28)

236. "Literature, films, and the media have been highlighting and fanning the flames of free sex. Now, leaders of all spheres of life, including politicians, business people, writers, journalists, and religious leaders, must stand as one to rid the culture of its obsession with free sex. This disease cripples individuals, families and nations." —True Father (2004.10.26)

237. "Look at the world in which we are currently living. The people of the world are caught in the trap of extreme selfishness, clamoring for material gain. They have lost all sense of value, and the desire for self-gratification drags them into the depths of degradation. The world is filled with alcoholics. As if drug addiction and free sex were not enough, there are even those who commit incest, an act not even seen in the animal world, and still strut around with their heads held high. This world has become one wherein beasts with human faces roam freely, even after violating women, grandmothers, mothers, wives, and daughters. The swapping of spouses among couples is rampant. Such circumstances represent without a doubt the pinnacle of the destruction of morality and the last of fallen acts. This world has become hell on earth, in which we cannot even dream of the perfected world embodying the ideal that God envisioned at the creation." —True Father (2006.4.10)

238. "Our lives testify to the truth of the proverb, 'You shall reap what you sow.' What seed did Adam and Eve sow in the garden of Eden? They planted the seed of free sex through an illicit sexual relationship. That is why it is written that after they fell, they hid their lower parts. It was certain that in the Last Days, the time of

harvest, rampant free sex among young people would manifest throughout the world. Through promiscuity, Satan is carrying out his last campaign to deter anyone from returning to God. Satan's goal is to destroy human beings and perpetuate hell on earth." — True Father (2004.10.26)

Sharing Thoughts on True Parents' Words

We have all, without a doubt, struggled with the question of why the world has become hell on earth, filled with all sorts of terrible problems related to the misuse of sex. True Father has unique insight into the cause of this problem. He explains that it began when Adam and Eve shared an illicit sexual relationship and planted the seed of free sex. True Father contrasts free sex with absolute sex. Free sex is devoid of intimacy and causes people to fall into the trap of extreme self-centeredness. Families break down and are destroyed.

Many of us may feel troubled by the growing trend of literature, films, and the media glorify this view of sex. Among all violations, True Parents have explained the one that pains God most is the misuse of sex. Absolute sex is God's way of building healthy, loving, radiant Blessed families, which are the cornerstone for a peaceful world. We can support this worldview in our lives by standing tall in the face of our own difficulties. We can inspire others as we engage ourselves to live this way. Some people may even want to engage politicians, business people, writers, journalists, and religious leaders to work together to rid our culture of its unhealthy obsession with free sex and be part of creating the world God envisioned. Political and economic reform alone will never solve the problem of immorality. The world is in need of true family values, and true family values, start with me.

Making It Real

The revival of true family values is the main goal of True Parents' ministry. God's original design was to multiply goodness and true love through the institution of the family. True Parents called the family "a school of love" because it is meant to be the most natural and healthy place for raising a child to become a person capable of giving and receiving true love. While technological and medical advances improve our efficiency and life span, comparable developments have not been achieved in the areas of human well-being and happiness. In reality, we have an expanding moral crisis with more single parents and fewer marriages.

Attempts to stem the tide of family breakdown haven't been enough to change the culture fundamentally. Public attitudes toward the value of marriage and traditional family values remain ambivalent. Cohabitation, single-parent families, and divorce are widely accepted and have become the norm, despite growing evidence of their negative impact on children. Religious institutions, which are expected to provide guidance on these matters, are divided over how to revive the faltering American family and question whether it's in need of revival. It is undeniable that it is; family matters. Through all the ups and downs of life, families provide a permanent set of relationships to care for us and help us to grow.

Central to True Parents' teaching about the family is that it is essentially a school of love. It is the primary school of moral and ethical development and the source of our most deeply held values. What is the teaching about God's design for the family? We learn that the ideal family is where God dwells as a partner. Blessed families participate in God's work of establishing the Kingdom of God, even as we overcome our own inadequacies to become families of true love. When a family gives itself to God and lives for the sake of others, God gives His love to the family, easing their burdens and transforming their relationships.

Clean Up

When we contemplate life today with all of its struggles, especially those that exist within families, we can't help but think that God must want to do something to help us clean up our act and solve our problems. While these challenges may seem insurmountable, we can gain hope from the remarkable efforts of scientists around the world to find solutions where others thought there were none.

It is common knowledge that the ocean is filled with garbage, from soda bottles to microplastics. Many of the animals and plants that live in the sea are dying because of this. According to the United Nations Environment Program (UNEP), 13 million tons of plastic waste find their way into the ocean every year. Not only that, but beaches are being destroyed by trash. Is there any hope of ever cleaning this up?

Five-foot-high piles of garbage on a beach in Mumbai did not prevent Afroz Shah, a lawyer and environmentalist, from accepting the challenge to solve this problem. This became known as "The world's largest beach clean-up project," according to the United Nations. In 2015, with the help of a neighbor, he began clearing the beach of trash. Before long, he was joined by 1,000 volunteers from all walks of life, rich and poor, all concerned about saving the beach. Once the beach was cleared of garbage, they planted 50 coconut trees and installed toilets. Mr. Shah's goal is to plant 5,000 coconut trees and restore the pristine coconut lagoon to its original condition.

This is an example of what one person can do to transform a dump into a paradise. We are reminded of a story about a little girl on the beach collecting stranded starfish and throwing them back into the water. Her grandfather, who'd been silently watching her, finally commented, "Young lady don't you realize there are miles of beach ahead with so many starfish? It's useless and won't make much of a difference." She wisely replied after gently placing one back in the sea, "It made a difference for that one!"

The environmental challenges we face today seem insurmountable, but because of a few people like Afroz Shah, there is hope. Likewise, when we look at the problems of sexual immorality, it seems impossible to ever reverse this historical trend and create a moral society. The vision seems to be buried underneath the pain, suffering, and mistakes; it's all too deep and wide. We'd like to make a difference, but then we think that one person can't really change things. True Father acknowledged this challenge, and his solution was to create a pure love movement based on absolute sexual ethics.

True Father blew people away when he gave his pivotal speech in 1996. He instructed heads of state to go back to their countries and teach about absolute sex in an all-out effort to defeat the global pandemic of immorality. Because of his clear understanding and courage, there is hope. We might not be able to change the entire world by ourselves, but at least we can change a small part of it. Like the little girl who believed that her efforts were making a difference, we can have faith that our actions will contribute to cleaning up the mess. As each of us models a pure love lifestyle, we will create a ripple effect that will spread to our community and beyond, building the world God originally intended.

Points for Consideration/Activities:

- Do you have ideas on how your family or future family can intentionally practice being a school of love?

- Share about an inspiring person or group who is creating a positive change.

- Next time you go to the beach or a park, bring trash bags for everyone in your group and pick up some garbage.

Section VI
Restoration

Learning about Sex
from Our Parents

While you were growing up do you remember what, if anything, your parents taught you about sex? Sexuality has been wrapped in shame throughout human history with the consequence that the great majority of parents have avoided talking with their children about sex. Parents and children typically feel embarrassed and shy away from the subject. But if we consider how precious sex is, then this would be the most important education that parents impart to their children.

True Parents established a sacred tradition when they educated blessed couples in preparation for their lives as husbands and wives. Reverend Joong Hyun Pak shares about the intimate education True Father provided to the early blessed couples in the Unification Church. "I participated in the 430 Couples Marriage Blessing Ceremony.[24] At that time, I was a church leader in the countryside in South Korea. True Father came with True Mother to my region. True Father called all the blessed couples of the 430 Blessing Ceremony to gather. We were in the middle of our 40-day separation period.[25] True Father sat down with us and taught us about husband-wife sexual relations. Honestly, at that time, I so appreciated True Father. I thought he is truly *my* father. So close a feeling he stirred within me. The most deepest secret of human life he gave to me. That meant he was truly my parent. Even

---

24. The Marriage Blessing Ceremony is typically held once a year and is officiated by True Parents and attended by thousands of couples taking their vows in marriage.

25. This sacred period of separation is considered an offering of gratitude and appreciation to God. During this time, couples prepare to consummate their marriage.

my physical parents didn't teach me like this. But True Father did. I remember deeply, tearfully appreciating True Father."[26]

True Father's Words

239. "I'm the one who teaches that men should become the owners who closely safeguard their sexual organs and that women too should safeguard their sexual organs carefully forever. The people who bear the responsibility of making men and women safeguard themselves are the parents having the name of True Parents. Being True Parents is very simple. They are the ones who have the power to assemble licentious men and women and make them men and women who will never again be unfaithful but remain absolutely chaste." (1995.8.28)

240. "In the inner conjugal relationship, a man and woman are different in the required time. The woman is two to five times slower than the man. Some women are more than five times slower than men. Therefore, even though they have a conjugal sexual relationship, some women finish their lives without knowing the real taste of conjugal lovemaking. That is a man's fault. If conjugal lovemaking is not satisfactory, its negative vibrations will continue for the whole day or the whole month. Sexual satisfaction is absolutely necessary for a woman's health… We need to educate everyone about this. A father has to educate his son, and a mother has to educate her daughter. It will cause trouble if daughters marry without knowing it. Do you understand? Therefore, I am educating everyone well here. You should consult and ask women around you, 'How do you do it?' and if you want your husband to extend

---

26. Joong Hyun Pak, "Absolute Sex—Exploring Its Meaning" (sermon, Belvedere Estate, Tarrytown, NY, February 1, 1997), tparents.org, http://www.tparents.org/UNews/Unws9702/jpak9702.htm.

the time of lovemaking because you cannot feel a sexual climax yet, you should ask him to do foreplay much longer. Do you understand? This is an important talk." (1993.12.21)

241. "Some may still think that as the founder of the Unification Church, I should not refer to the sexual organs in public. Ordinarily, Christian ministers don't refer to sexual organs in a sermon. God created the human sexual organs to be a sacred place, not what they have become since Adam's fall. Do you understand? It is supposed to be a holy palace. In God's original plan, the sexual organ is a love palace. This is the truth." (1997.6.5)

242. "We are abused and called the scoundrels of the Unification Church because its founder teaches such things, aren't we? I don't care if we are called scoundrels. Isn't it better to win a real gold medal rather than a false one? The male and female sexual organs are gifts inherited from the Creator and the ancestors, unchanged and connected as they are. They are precious gifts that not even God Himself will interfere with and which our ancestors cannot violate. Those who violate them would become the flesh and blood of the devil, destroying the original palace of love, the center of the great laws of heaven. The sexual organs are the original palace of life, giving birth on the foundation centered on eternal true love as the pure essence. They are also the source of a new lineage. Why were the sexual organs created? Certainly not just for one individual person or another. They were given to you for the great Way of heaven and earth and the great providential governance of heaven and earth. How will the ideal world come upon the earth in the future? If the way of the rightful use of the sexual organs is not revealed, the world will come to ruin. We would never be able to find the world of peace." (1989.10.3)

Sharing Thoughts on True Father's Words

Some people feel it is inappropriate for a religious leader to talk about sex in public, but True Father reminds us that our sexual organs are a precious gift from God. They are the original palace of love, life, and lineage, created not just for individual pleasure but also for bringing husband and wife together in deepest intimacy. Since God created the male and female sexual organs as sacred, couples should remain forever faithful.

The family is the place where God intended for children to learn the divine value of their sexual organs. Prior to consummating their marriage, they can receive education from their parents about how to please their spouse. If married couples are not having satisfying sexual relations, the marriage will suffer. Learning to be a skilled communicator about what they like and dislike in the bedroom will help to deepen the satisfaction and connection. Only when all people understand and practice heavenly sexuality will the peaceful world of God's ideal come about.

Making It Real

School of Love

True Father calls the family the school of love because it is where members of the family learn all kinds of love. When children are young, they receive love from their parents and practice loving their brothers and sisters.

Most parents avoid talking with their children about sex, but it is important for parents to understand that they need to educate their children about the precious value of their sexual organs. By giving age-appropriate guidance, parents can instill a healthy perspective of sexuality in their children and protect them from making serious mistakes and acquiring destructive habits that can harm their future.

School of Love was initiated by High Noon in response to the need for family education about sex. Its goal is to empower parents to engage their children in open conversations about heavenly sexuality from a young age. An online curriculum is available to help parents teach that the sexual organ is a holy place where their children will experience love exclusively with their future husband or wife and create their own future family. Parents are encouraged to study and discuss the lessons together with their children. They lovingly instruct about the dangers of pornography and premarital sexual relationships. Parents who don't know how to talk about sexuality can find support to make these conversations easier.

Children discover that their sexual desires are natural and God-given. They learn how to manage their impulses in today's sexualized world and create positive habits that will help them maintain a standard of purity. As they develop a mature understanding of heavenly sexuality, they look forward to one day experiencing this beautiful gift that awaits them in their future marriage.

Sex is a beautiful, exciting, and stimulating part of marriage. Creating a thriving sex life is not only important for our marriages but also an inspiring example for our children. When children see their parents happy and in love, they will naturally want to seek that same kind of blessing for their own lives. As we align ourselves with True Parent's vision for the family as a school of love, we will create radiant families with true parent-child relationships, which actively contribute to God's plan for an ideal world.

The Scream

This cute story was shared by Yeunhee Chang, PhD candidate at SunHak Graduate School in South Korea. She is originally from Canada. Her husband is from Korea.

I am a second generation blessed child[27] and received the Marriage Blessing in 2009. My husband and I have five children ages four to eleven. As my children get older, I talk to them about the opposite sex and ask questions like, who do you like, or who do you think is a nice person? I always try to keep this kind of subject light and joyful, hoping that later on, this will help

---

27. Blessed child is a term used to refer to children born of couples who have received the Marriage Blessing.

when they get older. I don't want them to feel guilty for liking someone we may disapprove of, and I want them to trust us enough to share their deep feelings without worrying we will freak out.

I observed that my daughter was interested in love, as she drew pictures of the Walt Disney couples kissing. She is different from my boys and was always curious about men and women expressing love and being intimate. She also asked me questions about how babies were born and how they came out of my body. Up until our "sex talk," I told her, and our boys, that whenever daddy and mommy kissed for more than ten seconds, a baby would start to grow in mommy's belly. Then later I told my daughter that there was a seed in daddy's body that touched mommy's belly button and a baby would start to grow. She thought that was funny and accepted the answer, but I could tell she wasn't satisfied.

When she was in the third grade I found a comic book from the school library in her school bag. The book had drawings showing a man hovering over a young girl as his hand was running up her thigh. The drawing showed the young girl with her skirt up and her panties exposed. I was very upset at the school and demanded to know why this kind of comic book was even in their library. Their answers were not enough to calm me down. At this point, I felt that I, as the parent, had to be the one to teach my daughter about love and sex. I felt like I needed to do it quickly before some warped idea of love was imprinted in her mind. I didn't want this image of a sexual interaction between a man and a girl to be left in my child's very young mind. I never thought I would talk to my child so early about sex, but I felt that I had no choice. I needed to explain to her that love between a man and woman was supposed to become physically expressive only between a married couple, like mommy and daddy, and only when their parents permitted them to be together through the Marriage Blessing.

So I called my daughter to my room. I had the anatomy book next to me. I let her know that the book she brought from school was not something I wanted her to read because it didn't teach about the love mommy and daddy wanted her to learn. As we were sharing, her younger brothers were running in and out of my bathroom, naked, because they were taking turns showering. My daughter had seen her brothers' sexual organs, so I suppose she was somewhat desensitized. She always laughed when she saw her little brothers with an occasional erection. She would say, "Mommy why is his 'go-chu' (means penis in Korean) sticking up like that!"

I told my daughter that I was going to explain how babies were made, for real this time. She was all ears. I said, 'the reason why a man's penis gets big and sticks upward is because…' I turned to the page of the drawing showing a man's penis when it was and was not erect. Then I showed her the drawing of a woman's internal sexual organ. I continued saying, 'look here. There is a hole in the woman's body because a man's penis, when it becomes big, goes inside the woman's body and the baby seeds come out of the man 's "go-chu" leaving them in the woman's body.' I turned to the page showing a drawing of a woman who was eight months pregnant. My daughter's eyes opened wide. Both her hands shot up to the sides of her temples, like in the Edvard Munch painting, *The Scream,* as her naked brothers ran out of my room. She yelled, 'Ahhh mommy!' She was quite upset about what I had told her and for a few minutes she looked at her naked brothers and screamed. She said it was so disgusting and she was never going to get married, ever.

At this point, she is more interested in her girl friends, making things with her hands, learning and reading, and keeping her distance from boys. Hopefully, as she watches my husband and I interact with one another in a loving and respectful way, it will be enough for her to want to create a loving relationship with her future husband when she is ready. For now, I am very happy that our sex talk resulted in her wanting to keep the boys at bay. Maybe this story can give other parents confidence to have this kind of conversation with their children.

Points for Consideration/Activities

- What do you think is the best way for children to learn about sex?

- What are some healthy ways you can imagine educating your kids in the future, or right now? If your kids are grown up already, how can you support them to have a sexually thriving Marriage Blessing. How can you be a treasure of wisdom supporting them in their own parenting journey with their children?

- How can we take the "awkward" out of sex conversations? And should we try to?

Why Does the Messiah Come?

We watch blockbuster movies about heroes with supernatural powers whose mission is to save the world. When the world is saved from destruction by the end of the films, we feel a sense of hope for the future. Historically, people have believed the Messiah is a superhuman who comes to save the world. At the time of Jesus, the Jewish people thought the Messiah would defeat their enemies and lead them into military conquest. Christians believe Jesus will return to save all believers. Despite the many claims of what a Messiah will do, nobody has ever proclaimed the Messiah comes to restore the sexual organs. What does that even mean? Why are they in need of restoring, and how will that save the world?

True Father's Words

243. "Until now, because of Satan, we were ignorant regarding the owners of the sexual organs and how they came to be created. In order to disclose this truth, and to clean away the evil and foul tumult and turmoil of Satan, both on earth and in heaven, I came forth and hoisted my banner." (1989.10.3)

244. "Through free sex, Satan wants to stop every last person from returning to God. In other words, Satan wants to destroy all humanity and create Hell on Earth. Is not the world in which we live today Hell on Earth? Therefore, we will find the road to Heaven by going 180 degrees opposite the direction of this Hell on Earth. When the Lord of the Second Advent comes, he will show

us the 180 degrees opposite path as a means to save the world and lead us to Heaven. Then what is the road that is 180 degrees opposite the way of free sex? The path of free sex was laid because of the false parents. Therefore, True Parents have to come to straighten the wrong path. God cannot intervene. No authority nor any military, economic, or political power can do it. It was caused by false parents. Therefore, it takes True Parents to cut it open with a scalpel." (1996.8.1)

245. "When the Parents of Heaven and Earth unite in conjugal love, they will make a home where God can dwell peacefully. In their home untouched by the Fall, they will realize absolute sex. Now that I have reached the level of the True Parents of Heaven, Earth, and Humankind, I am speaking more freely about absolute sex. When I speak about absolute sex, I am not referring to self-centered, individualistic sex." (2009.4.10)

246. "Because the first marriage was a false marriage, True Parents come to straighten out marriages and give them the right direction. That is the mission of True Parents. Through True Parents, God will introduce absolute sex in place of free sex. So from now on, if you go back to your country and your home and practice my teaching, eventually your home and your country will be restored back to God." (1996.8.1)

247. "Through this messiah, all humankind will be replanted and connected back to God. If this world is supposed to end and a new heavenly world is to begin, we have to turn 180 degrees around. Then we will end up with the Kingdom Of God on Earth. Since Satan spread the concept of free sex and turned the world around, now God comes with the concept of absolute sex. With this concept, we will build the Kingdom of God on Earth. Have you heard of the concept of absolute sex? This term, just coined, means only God can take control." (1996.8.1)

248. "We now think that only True Parents can solve the problem on earth. I am the one who has taught people over several generations that the experiences and details related to sexual immorality create a certain bad influence, and I know very well that absolute sexual ethics are absolutely needed. Do you understand?" (2009.1.2)

249. "So, the Lord at his Second Advent had to become an absolute and unchanging king. I got first place in terms of following the absolute sexual ethics. Now this royal position cannot be invaded." (2007.12.28)

250. "The sexual organs were misused. A revolution is needed here. For that, you need the Mother and the Father. Women are to be mobilized with Mother as the leader. Mobilizing the Women's Federation settles Mother's position. Is that not where the returning Lord appears? What would the Messiah bring with him? Absolute sex. He is coming for the perfection of absolute, unique, unchanging and eternal sex." (1996.9.22)

251. "In finding those events and the persons who played roles in the fulfillment of God's dispensations and failed, and in finding the history of the providence of God's restoration, I shed so many tears. I not only understood the Principle[28] but lived it. When I came to the fall of Adam and Eve, I felt as if it were my own concern. I felt the sorrow of God to see Adam's fall. I felt Adam's sorrow in himself. It was not Adam's story, but mine." (2000)

252. "I declare again and proclaim in the name of True Parents that within the realm of the Cosmic Sabbath of the Parents of Heaven, Earth, and Humankind, that on the basis of the unity of these three—Absolute Sex, the seed of True Father's love, and the ovum

---

28. It is common for those familiar with *The Divine Principle* text to abbreviate it in this manner.

in True Mother's womb—we will recreate a victorious universe embodying the right of the true lineage." (2009.1.15)

253. "You have to realize that Reverend Moon overcame death hundreds of times in order to find this path. Reverend Moon is the person who brought God to tears hundreds of times. No one in history has loved God more than Reverend Moon has. That is why even if the world tries to destroy me, Reverend Moon will never perish. It is because God protects me. If you step into the realm of the truth Reverend Moon teaches, you also will gain God's protection." (1996.8.1)

Sharing Thoughts on True Father's Words

With tearful prayers, True Father discovered the sacred value of the sexual organs and how God grieved when His first son and daughter misused them. Since then, God had been searching for someone who could reverse this terrible mistake and redirect the tragic course of human history. God needed to send the Messiah to restore what was lost in the Garden of Eden. "What would the Messiah bring with him? Absolute sex." With blood, sweat, and tears, True Parents resolved to restore the absolute, unique, and eternal sexual organs of men and women. Their path of suffering laid the foundation to begin speaking about absolute sex. This was necessary in order to build the Kingdom of Heaven on earth where God can finally dwell with His children.

Superman

True Father's mission can be compared to that of the well-known hero, Superman, who tells us who he is and what he stands for in these familiar words: "I am Superman. I stand for truth, for justice, and for the future." The big "S" on his shirt is the Kryptonian symbol for hope. With his superpowers, Superman becomes a savior in a world riddled with crime and injustice. He is aware of his mission from an early age, when his birth father, Jor-El, tells him, "Even though you've been raised as a human, you're not one of them.

They can be great people, Kal-El. They wish to be. They only lack the light to show the way. For this reason above all—their capacity for good—I have sent them you, my only son."

In the 2006 movie *Superman Returns*, the hero comes back after a five-year hiatus, still intent on saving the people on Earth whom he loves. With his god-like listening powers, he hears people crying out for help and performs amazing rescues daily. Of course, there's a villain, Lex Luthor, who plots to destroy civilization and kill billions of people. Superman uses his powers to save humanity and thwarts Luthor's plot. He succeeds in his mission to rid the world of Luthor, at the cost of his own life. As Superman nears death, he remembers the words of his father, Jor-El, who told him that his good actions would inspire others to "moral betterment."

According to the director, Bryan Singer, "Superman is the Jesus Christ of superheroes." Superman's willingness to sacrifice himself for the sake of his mission is clear. When he is beaten and pierced, we are reminded of the fate of the Messiah and True Father's experience of being ruthlessly tortured.

Superman Returns conveys a clear message of humanity's need for salvation, emphasizing that it will take leadership and sacrifice for that to happen. The movie stimulates hope, even though it is a fantasy with a superhero who has special powers. True Father proclaims the same message that humanity can recover what was lost in the Garden of Eden. He makes it clear that the means by which that happens is not supernatural.

> 254. "The Messiah is the true man with the new seed of life. He guides people of the fallen lineage to deny their life and then engrafts his new seed onto them. Even though the Messiah is rooted in God, as the second Adam, he must clean up what Adam did. This is the reason God cannot send the Messiah as a superman having God's almighty power." —True Father (1996.4.16)

The path of the Messiah is one in which blood, sweat, and tears are shed in order for God's ideal world to be established. True Parents have no special powers. Nevertheless, they do have a heart of longing to serve God and save humanity and the willingness to do whatever it takes to make that happen.

Making It Real

Wouldn't it be nice if the Messiah could appear with superpowers and solve all the problems of the world? Historically, that's what most messianic religions have thought. However, the mission of the Messiah is to restore what was lost in the Garden of Eden, which was God's ideal of absolute sex. How would the Messiah achieve that?

God intended for Adam and Eve to experience conjugal love only after they reached maturity. But they fell when they had sex prematurely. Since the sexual organs were lost in a relationship, they could only be restored through a relationship. The Messiah could not restore the sexual organs by himself. That is why God needed to send True Parents. Only when a true man and a true woman become one flesh and incarnate Heavenly Parent could the sexual organs be perfected.

True Father first used the term "absolute sex" at the age of 76. Why did he wait so long before he began teaching about this fundamental pillar of God's kingdom? We know from studying Providential history that for every heavenly victory, there is a price to be paid in order to move forward with God's plan for restoration. Sacrifice is always needed to lay the foundation for the next step. For example, through Jesus' sacrifice on the cross, spiritual salvation was granted to believers. It is the same in the time when Christ returns as the Second advent to fulfill the mission of True Parents.

True Father went through unimaginable suffering in order to proclaim the era of absolute sex. When we look at how he endured endless life and death challenges, we can appreciate how precious the teaching of absolute sex is. True Father was unjustly put into prison six times, where he was mistreated and tortured, almost to the point of death. Like Superman, True Father was willing to sacrifice everything for the success of his mission.

Points for Consideration/Activities

- Why is sex so important to God?

- How do you see Satan working against the restoration of the sexual organs?

- What role can we play in restoring the sexual organs?

Midway Position

All of us, without exception, have found ourselves in the midway position at some time or another where we feel a deep conflict about which path to follow. Our heart pushes us to do the right thing, but at the same time, we desire that which is immediate and satisfying. Even the apostle Paul, who was the greatest champion of Christian faith, lamented in Romans 7:22-24, "For in my inner being I delight in God's law; but I see another law at work in the members of my body, waging war against the laws of my mind and making me a prisoner of the law of sin at work within my members. What a wretched man I am? Who will rescue me from this body of death?"(New International Version). What can we do when we find ourselves in this state of turmoil which causes us to anguish?

True Father's Words

255. "Your original mind does not need a teacher. It is your second god. Do not try to follow a teacher or me; instead, try to serve your mind. What about the mind? You wake up at daybreak, all alone, and it is so quiet that you can hear even the squeak of a mouse or the buzz of a fly, and you think to yourself, 'Well, I should like such and such a thing. I should try to do a good deed.' Your original mind will then tell you, 'Good! Good! Do it now!' On the other hand, if you harbor only evil thoughts in your mind, it will chide you with words like 'No! No! You fool!' Would it not know what you are thinking? Of course, it knows. That is the way it is. It knows only too well." (1986.1.19)

256. "Do you know when your mind and body began fighting? They began fighting right after the Fall; they became infected at that moment. Unless we completely cure this infection, we cannot enter heaven. The person whose mind and body are in conflict cannot enter heaven. I have struggled to fulfill this standard: 'Before seeking to master the universe, attain mastery over yourself.' The further you advance and the deeper your spiritual level, the more fearsome the Satan you will have to face." (2006.5.28)

257. "Your spirit will show plainly whether you have led a wholesome life ripening in goodness or a wormy, rotten life of sinfulness. What this means is that God will not judge you; you will be your own judge. If you are aware of this astonishing rule of Heaven, will you spend your life on earth in selfishness and immorality, succumbing to the temptations of Satan in pursuit of nothing but pleasure? You will not; rather, you will abstain from injuring and scarring your spirit body, even at the risk of your earthly life. Please bear this truth in mind: your thoughts, words, and deeds in each moment determine whether you are bound for heaven or hell." (2006.12.20)

258. "You must decide which path you will go. There is always a tug of war between the visible self and the invisible self, and temptation is always trying to pull you in one direction, while God's truth is trying to pull you in the other. Each person is caught in the middle and usually goes a zigzag course, being pulled from one side to the other. This is a very realistic analysis." (1979.1.1)

259. "You should know that there is a happiness, ideal and love which Satan likes, and another happiness, ideal and love which God likes. God's criteria are based on eternal things, and Satan's criteria are instantaneous or temporary things. Which happiness would you choose? I'm sure you would choose eternal happiness, and you should. You should prepare and try hard to search for eternal love.

If you only seek instantaneous love, you will eventually die. When an instantaneous impulse or desire arises within you, pray for the power to seek eternal love and to avoid the darkness of death." (1998)

260. "If the first human ancestors had not fallen but had reached perfection and become one in heart with God, then they would have lived relating only with God. However, due to their Fall, they joined in a kinship of blood with Satan, which compelled them to deal with him as well. Immediately after the Fall, when Adam and Eve had the original sin but had not yet committed any subsequent good or evil deeds, they found themselves in the midway position—a position between God and Satan where they were relating with both. As a consequence, all their descendants are also in the midway position." (1996)

261. "How does God separate Satan from fallen people who stand in the midway position? Satan relates with them on the basis of his connection with them through lineage. Therefore, until people make a condition through which God can claim them as His own, there is no way God can restore them to the heavenly side. On the other hand, Satan acknowledges that God is the Creator of human beings. Unless Satan finds some condition through which he can attack a fallen person, he also cannot arbitrarily claim him for his side. Therefore, a fallen person will go to God's side if he makes good conditions and to Satan's side if he makes evil conditions." (1996)

262. "How can you end up going to the most terrible part of hell? If you use your sexual organ in a way that violates heavenly law, you are bound for hell, whereas if you go the opposite way, that is, the path of God's absolute love, you will go to a higher place in heaven. This conclusion is only too clear." (1996.8.1)

263. "Your spirit self grows, matures, and is finally perfected only

within your physical body, through an earthly lifetime of having actualized true love, bringing your mind and body into a smooth, unified relationship of give and take. Nevertheless, undeniably, your outer self and inner self are in a constant relationship of conflict and struggle. How much longer will you allow this fighting to continue? Ten years? A hundred years? In contrast, there is undeniably a proper order for all forms of existence in the universe. This indicates that God did not create human beings in this state of conflicted disorder. You need to know that it is your duty and responsibility as a human being to dispel all temptations directed at your outer self (your physical body) and achieve victory in life by following the way of your inner self (your conscience). Heavenly fortune will be with those who lead their lives in such a way. They will attain the perfection of their spirit selves." (2006.4.10)

Sharing Thoughts on True Father's Words

We can all identify with that internal tug of war that True Father spoke about. We feel it on a regular basis. True Father revealed that this inner conflict is a tragic consequence of the fall. Immediately after the fall, Adam and Eve were in the midway position where they could relate to both God and Satan. As a result, all of their descendants are also in the midway position. Until people make an effort and fully invest themselves, there's no way for God to restore them to His side. Likewise, we will be pulled to Satan's side when we make bad conditions.

We move to God's side when we take action that is aligned with His ideals, such as preparing conscientiously for a future marriage by keeping our purity. When we seek immediate gratification, with no concern for anyone's long-term happiness, we move to Satan's side.

Temptation pulls us in one direction, while God's truth is pulling us in the other. This is the human condition; we dwell in both God and Satan's realms, caught in the middle. If we seek only instantaneous love, our relationships will be negatively affected because of self-centeredness. When an immediate impulse or desire arises within, pray for the power to seek eternal love and avoid the suffering that comes with sexual immorality. Our thoughts, words, and deeds in each moment determine whether we are bound for heaven or hell. The person whose mind and body are in conflict cannot enter heaven. The greater your spiritual level, the more fearsome the Satan you will have to face.

Making It Real

Two Wolves

One evening, a Cherokee elder told his grandson about a battle that goes on inside people. He said, "My son, the battle is between two wolves inside us all. One is evil. It is anger, envy, jealousy, sorrow, regret, greed, arrogance, self-pity, guilt, resentment, inferiority, lies, false pride, superiority, and ego. The other is good. It is joy, peace, love, hope, sincerity, humility, kindness, benevolence, empathy, generosity, truth, compassion, and faith." The grandson thought about it for a minute and then asked his grandfather, "Which wolf wins?" The old Cherokee simply replied, "The one that you feed."

The moral of the Cherokee story is *what you feed grows and what you starve dies.* What can we do when we find ourselves in the midway position, being pulled in opposite directions? Self-centered thoughts and emotions are like poison. When we dwell on them, their attraction becomes stronger, and the temptation to go the wrong direction increases. The most challenging of all is sexual temptations and compulsions.

Given that the misuse of the sexual organs is the cause of all evil in the world, it's not surprising how powerful it is. If we have a habit that we want to get rid of, we need to starve that habit; stop having give and take with it. The longer we starve the bad wolf, the weaker it will become. By feeding it, we will only end up torturing ourselves and remain stuck in the midway position.

What kinds of conditions can we make to rise above self-centered thinking and instant gratification? When we make good conditions through daily prayer and studying God's word, we restrict our bodies' influence and fortify our conscience. It's akin to exercising our muscles by doing pushups, running, and other physical activities. As we examine True Parent's lifestyle of living for the sake of others, we see that denying their physical bodies was a condition to advance God's providence. In a North Korean prison, where men often starved to death, True Father divided his portion of rice into two and gave half to other prisoners. After True Father's passing, True Mother traveled extensively even though she suffered from fatigue and health problems. She pushed her body to bring God's blessing to people around the world. These are examples of a lifetime of sacrifice they made to support God's side and defeat the enemy.

When we push ourselves in order to accomplish a greater good, we make a very powerful condition to distance ourselves from temptation and come closer to God. The more we invest, the stronger and more clear our conscience will become. As we do good deeds and live for the sake of others, we feed the good wolf inside ourselves and create a divine spirit.

Points for Consideration/Activities

- Share an example about something you "starved" or "fed" that resulted in your personal growth.

- What kind of conditions can we use to protect ourselves from sexual temptation?

Ending Shame

Have you ever seen a toddler running around naked and laughing after taking a bath? As children, we are not born with shame. God created our sexual organs as the most precious and sacred part of our bodies. He wants us to maintain that innocence as we grow up and eventually marry. The act of lovemaking is meant to be the most beautiful, intimate, and joyful expression of love between husband and wife. However, the messages we receive from our parents, schools, and entertainment often project a distorted version of sex. Our sexual behaviors and beliefs have been influenced by what we've learned as children. The shame we've developed about sex can block us from true sexual intimacy with our spouse. We may become frustrated, not knowing what to do about it. True Father encourages us to get rid of shame and self-consciousness and embrace God's vision for sexual joy.

True Father's Words

264. "Do you think God sees you making love or not? Would God, who transcends time and space, close His eyes at night, when the five billion people of the world make love? How would He feel when He sees them?" (1991.11.3)

265. "In your family life during marriage, in order to feel true joy, you should bring God into the center and make a relationship where you can love each other while watching God rejoicing together with you. A man and a woman getting married and making love is

not something you should be ashamed of. This is something most dignified, holy, and beautiful." (1997)

266. "If we read the Bible, it tells us that Adam and Eve fell by eating of the fruit of the tree of the knowledge of good and evil, but then what does it mean that they covered their sexual parts? ... Why were Adam and Eve ashamed of their sexual parts? Why did they cover them? They should have covered their mouths and hands. There is nothing wrong with sexual organs. However, since people fell through them, these parts of the human body became a palace of shame where heavenly love was violated. A spring of true love should have welled forth from there, but a fountain of false, devilish love gushed out instead. That place, therefore, became the stronghold of the worst kind of love." (1990.5.2)

267. "Into what did Satan drive his roots? Into the body. God created Adam and Eve, but they fell when they were underage. God commanded them not to eat of the fruit of the tree of the knowledge of good and evil, but it was not a commandment concerning a literal fruit. If they had plucked the fruit with their hands and eaten it with their mouths, then they would have hidden their hands and covered their mouths. So why did they cover their sexual parts? This is a deadly trap, the cause of the destruction of human culture. The word 'love' is the most sacred word, but why have words related to love become obscene in spite of this? Why do we consider them foul words? It is because the misuse of love destroyed the great Principle of heaven and earth." (1990.1.25)

268. "Thunder and lightning caused by negative and positive electricity on a cloudy day symbolize the marriage of the universe. A loud noise is audible at such times, right? Are not pigeons noisy when they make love? Do you cry out when making love? I'm sure you have a hard time stifling the cry that threatens to come out of your mouths lest your mother and father hear you. Be spontaneous.

There is no need to hide such things. It is no longer a sin to shout until the window panes shatter all at once. Just as lightning flashes with a peal of thunder, so should you blaze. In marriage, you should attain that state of living in attendance of a holy woman or man, and God." (1990.6.26)

269. "In the fallen world, love has turned into the most dangerous thing. It is because of the Fall that mismanaging love shatters the world and turns it upside down. People have not clearly realized why love has become false and dirty but have still tried to keep and protect it because of their instinctive desire that true love should appear." (1997)

270. "The original palace of love, the historical palace of love, comes to be where the male and female sexual organs unite. It becomes the place of repose. No one can move this place; it is eternal and absolute. In that love nest, the life of man and the life of woman assimilate, boil over, and finally explode, giving rise to a new life. Through the explosive power thus generated, a new life is brought into existence. That is why when making love, even doves make explosive noises of coo-coo. Thus, in lovemaking, man and wife should not be embarrassed at making a noise loud enough for their parents to hear them." (1989.10.3)

271. "Where do man and woman join together at ninety degrees? They connect at the genitals. This is not a laughing matter; it is holy. The genitals are the original palace of love. The principle palace of love is not the eyes or the head. Which parts of man and woman are used for lovemaking? Is it the eyes, the head, or what? It is the sexual organs. So don't think of them as evil. They are considered bad due to the Fall. Satan made them the original palace that ruined this world. Aren't the sexual organs the original palace of love and life? Where does life come from? Isn't it from the genitals?

What enables the connection of lineage? Is it at the head or on the back of the hand?" (1990.2.11)

272. "When a husband and wife dance naked in the room, is this something to be concerned about? Between the husband and wife, who cares what they do, whether they dance naked or do other strange things? What does it matter when a husband and wife do it by themselves?" (1968.11.24)

Sharing Thoughts on True Father's Words

From God's perspective, the center of the kingdom of heaven is where blessed couples make love. Then why is there so much shame around it? True Father explains that the origin of shame was in the Garden of Eden when Adam and Eve misused their sexual organs. At the time of the Fall, the innocence of love and sex was lost. The palace of love became a palace of shame. Even though humanity has not understood why sexual love has become false and dirty, we still long for sexual love because that is how God created us.

True Father openly talks about conjugal love. He describes what God intended for sex and contrasts that with the viewpoint that sex is something dirty. True Father once spoke about making love like the animals, saying:

273. "What is shameful? Is there anything you feel ashamed about? Why do you feel ashamed? I do not feel ashamed at speaking such a story as this. It is natural. If you feel ashamed, it is a habit of the fallen world." (1996.5.1)

He advises couples to be spontaneous and passionate in their lovemaking, without fear of making noise. Even if their parents or children might overhear them making love, a husband and wife should not feel ashamed. True Father encourages us all to remove the shame we feel about sex by understanding that our sexual organs are the very origin of love, life, and lineage.

Making It Real

True Father teaches that sexual relations were meant to be the most beautiful and holiest expression of love between husband and wife, much more than just a physical expression of our sex drive. We were created to make love with every fiber of our being, intentionally meeting all of the spiritual, emotional, and sexual needs and desires of our spouse. Since God created us to fully enjoy conjugal intimacy, why is it so often physically and emotionally challenging?

A common barrier to sexual enjoyment is the presence of shame. True Father emphasizes that God never intended for Adam and Eve's descendants to experience shame. This is something we inherited from Satan, causing us to believe God could not love us if He knew our mistakes. We may have a guilty conscience because of something we've done wrong. When we don't receive forgiveness and come to believe that we are bad, the guilt we feel can turn into shame. Guilt is a message from the conscience, meant to help us resolve a mistake. It has a positive purpose, to get us back in alignment with God's intention for our lives. Shame, on the other hand, fosters self-loathing and causes us to lose hope. Shame tells us, "you're no good," "you'll never kick this bad habit," or "you're worthless and pathetic." Those words don't come from God; they come from Satan. With shame, we forget we are unconditionally loved as children of a Heavenly Parent who wants to forgive us. God is always telling us, "You are my child. I will always love you. You have a bright future. Try one more time."

There's confusion around sex because of conflicting messages. Some people treat sex casually, making those who want to live with integrity and keep their purity feel embarrassed. Others think that sex is vile and dirty. We may have been influenced by preachers and other authority figures who have only spoken about the misuse of sex, labeling it as sinful and shrouding it in shame. Nevertheless, parents have the greatest impact on our ideas about sex. Ironically, it is often because of parents' hesitation to talk freely about sex that children assume there is something inherently shameful about it.

It is also the case that, in some families, children have suffered from sexual abuse and carry the shame of that experience into their adult lives.

These negative memories regarding sex can block us from experiencing the deepest expression of intimacy in marriage. Overcoming the negative messaging in our lives is possible through practicing sexual integrity, which starts with open and honest communication with those we love and trust; our parents, our spouse, or mentors. It can include exercising self-control by avoiding pornography and other self-centered sexual activities. When we learn to talk openly and honestly, we can lift the heavy weight of shame from our lives. Married couples can experience healing and a new level of intimacy when they are able to share their needs and wants with an understanding spouse.

We were created by God to experience the most beautiful love and sexual freedom of expression within a Marriage Blessing. We prepare for this during our adolescent and young adult years. It's important to use that time well to develop our sexual integrity so that when the time comes, we are ready to receive the Marriage Blessing and all it has to offer. When a blessed couple can share their love physically, emotionally, and sexually they can radiate love wherever they go and through whatever they do.

God Loves Us

Everyone has struggled at some point or other with shame. The biggest problem with shame is that it makes us believe we are unlovable. Shame blocks us from feeling God's love and love from others. It also blocks us from loving ourselves. Shame gives us a distorted understanding of ourselves. The children's book *You Are Special*, by Max Lucado, gives a message to young and old about how the heavy weight of shame can be lifted from our lives.

You Are Special is about a town of wooden puppets called "Wemmicks" who govern themselves with artificial concepts about what is right and acceptable. What looks good on the outside, such as talent, beauty, and intellect, is publicly rewarded, while those who are "different" are made to wear dot stickers on their clothes to embarrass them. Those who fit in by meeting the community's standards of excellence get to wear special star stickers. The protagonist, Punchinello, has no outward specialness and doesn't ever get these star stickers. His self-esteem suffers, and, covered with dot stickers, he finally goes to the village woodcarver, Eli, for advice.

Eli tells Punchinello that he is a special, unique, and authentic creation, a precious work of art. "The stickers only stick if they matter to you. The more you trust my love, the less you care about their stickers."[29] Until that moment, Punchinello, influenced by an environment filled with misinformation and distortions, had almost given up all hope. Now he knows the truth; Eli, his creator, designed him to be special and loved. As he celebrates this new realization, the sticker dots fall off his clothes, and, for the first time in his life, he is filled with a deep sense of pride, gratitude, and joy.

Just as the puppet maker created Punchinello to be a precious work of art, God created us as His children and infused His divine nature into every part of our bodies. Because of our True Parents' we know God invested the most in designing our sexual organs. He is reaching out to us with the truth about who we really are as sexual beings. Punchinello needed to be reminded of his true essence, and so do we. As we embrace God's intention for sex and grow our sexual integrity, the heavy weight of shame will be lifted from us.

Points for Consideration/Activities

- Share a time when you felt shame over something, as a youth, or adult. Were you able to work through it, or has it remained with you?

- How would you like to respond the next time someone shares a mistake they made? What response would you like to receive from a loved one when you reveal a mistake you have made?

- Do you have any thoughts about how to resolve any shame you may experience in your life?

---

29. Max Lucado, *You Are Special* (Wheaton: Crossway, 1997), 29.

Life Without Shadows

If you had the power to become invisible, would you act the same as you do now, or would you do things like spy on people or sneak into places? Although the question is somewhat childish, it becomes relevant when we think about how we act when no one is watching. True Father broaches this topic when introducing the concept of high noon. He encourages us to live in "high noon settlement"— to remove and live without shadows in our lives. What would it be like to live with a sense of pride in everything you did with nothing to hide?

True Father's Words

274. "High noon is the time of the brightest sunlight. There is no darkness anywhere, only brightness pervades the atmosphere. It is the condition of fullness, there is nothing lacking." (1983.1.2)

275. "God's throne is currently situated in the middle of hell on earth, and it must rise like the sun. When it does, all creation will enter the era of high noon settlement, where there is no shadow. The phrase 'high noon settlement' means there is no shadow for all eternity. When you go to the spirit world, you will see the sun high up at the center of the sky all the time. You will not see any shadows. If a shadow were to appear, all the good spirits would immediately come and blow it away. It would vanish. In the same way, good spirits will come to the earth and punish this world of shadows." (2005.7.14)

276. "High noon settlement is possible when there is no shadow. When the mind and body become one, the shadow disappears. When a couple becomes one, the shadow disappears... A shadow can be cast in any of the four directions. However, at high noon, when you stand at the very center, there is no shadow. You should have such relationships with your parents, spouse, children and siblings. Only then can God be positioned as the owner of the eight stages of love. If you are unable to establish a high noon position, the amount of devotion you offer does not matter. Without establishing this high noon position free of shadows, you are not able to be with or go to God, who has no sliver of a shadow, because you are not in a perpendicular position. You should establish such a position in which you cast no shadow for all eternity." (2000.9.26)

277. "High noon settlement! For this, there should not be any shadow in the four-position foundation. If we can achieve such a state, God will descend and everyone will rejoice. No matter how vast the area, everyone in it will be happy. Thus, you should each become a mother or father, husband or wife, and son or daughter who can find high noon settlement. If you cast a shadow in any of those positions, you will bring all the misfortunes of heaven and earth to take root in your family. These are terrifying words. This is the one formula and model to which we all have to conform." (2000.9.25)

278. "You are not to live a life with shadows. Therefore, I proclaimed the high noon settlement. It is a marvelous concept. For there to be no shadows, mind and body must be united, and the family must be united as a four-position foundation. If the father did something wrong, he would create a father's shadow. If the mother did something wrong, she would make a mother's shadow. If there were four members in the family and the four could not settle down, then the light would be blocked. No one likes the place of shadows. That is why we must achieve the high noon settlement.

There shouldn't be any shadows, even after we go to the next world. God travels through the vertical line of eight stages from the shadow-free individual to the shadow-free family, tribe, people, nation, world, cosmos, and God. Can there be any shadow cast on God's love? It is purity itself. That is why everyone wants that purity, even in his or her flesh and blood. No one likes shadows. The shadow is Satan. This is why whenever we do wrong, we tend to cover it up. That is the enemy. That is the barrier. You must break down that barrier if you are to have the high noon settlement. I am not saying this just symbolically. It must be done." (2000.9.27)

279. "You must become families who can settle at the position of high noon, where no shadow is cast. The garden of Eden was a place of true love, without any shadows. In love, there are no shadows. That is why everything in the world wants to come and be in that place. In the position of high noon, no one asserts himself or herself. It is the place of absolute faith, absolute love, and absolute obedience. There is no assertion of self. This is what happens to everyone in the presence of true love. Adam's family must be established as a family without shadows. Then from it will emerge Adam's tribe, Adam's people, Adam's nation, and Adam's world." (2000.10.1)

280. "The Unification Church was the first to declare the concept of the settlement of noon. At noon, no shadows are cast. When you are standing still at noon, you can see that the sun shines brightly, so brightly that even the glittering of diamonds and jewels would be nothing compared to that light, and yet there are no shadows, no darkness at all. In that light, all that is dark breaks apart, leaving not a trace. It is the same in God's presence. Even the light of fireflies cannot shine out of the blackest darkness, but in God's presence, the light emitted by God, the bright light that is hundreds of times brighter than the sun, absorbs all other kinds of light. You cannot fight it, because it absorbs every kind of light" (2003.10.25)

281. "I am asking you to analyze and scrutinize the innumerable different situations in daily life each moment and determine whether you are right or wrong. In the same way Korean teachers grade tests, give yourself an O if you are right or an X if you are wrong. When you meet a situation and act in an affirmative and hopeful way, you get an O. By this action you set a vertical axis up to heaven, and you live as at 'high-noon' without casting a shadow. Your life undoubtedly had such depth and breadth that you forgave and embraced an enemy in the spirit of true love. When you act shamefully, however, give yourself an X. Most likely, your heart was filled with negative emotions such as insecurity, irritation, bitterness, or envy. Your mind and thoughts were narrow and intolerant, and you were selfish and individualistic to the point that you did not see what was happening to others around you. I believe that your choice could not be clearer... Please pursue the true O so that you can stand in the brightly burning sunlight and not be ashamed, face the vast and infinite universe with honor, and stand before all of creation having nothing to hide." (2004.10.26)

Sharing Thoughts on True Father's Words

When True Father first spoke about high noon settlement, he said it means there is no shadow for all eternity. Without establishing a high noon lifestyle in our family relationships, we will bring misfortune to our lineage. We should eliminate shadows in all of our relationships; with our siblings, parents, spouse, and children. In fact, God's plan is for humanity to create a world without shadows through eight stages from the individual to the family, tribe, people, nation, world, cosmos, and even God. When we can live a life without shadows, we can rejoice together with God.

The garden of Eden was a luminous place filled with God's absolute, unconditional love for His first son and daughter. When Adam and Eve misused their sexual organs, a shadow was cast upon them. They were overcome by fear and shame and attempted to hide their mistake by covering their lower parts. These shadows blocked them from the love of God, plummeting them into darkness. Since then, we have inherited their fallen nature. When we hide our mistakes from the people we love, our hearts become filled with negative emotions.

True Father says we must analyze ourselves every moment of the day to see if we are being self-centered, individualistic, or intolerant. He wants us to meet each situation in a hopeful and positive way so that our hearts will be filled with gratitude for every circumstance.

Making It Real

In 2015, a concerned blessed couple decided to address the worldwide pornography pandemic. They were inspired by True Father's teaching about high noon settlement and felt this would help those suffering from compulsive sexual behaviors to come out of the shadows and live according to their ideals. Even though sex is meant to be a divine experience, many of us experience shame, confusion, and secrecy in this area of our lives.

How do we live a high noon lifestyle? We can look from God's point of view, not our own. When we are living in the settlement of high noon, we are in alignment with God's ideal in all of our relationships. Parents and children have open, ongoing conversations about everything. Couples feel free to share their most intimate desires with one another. Communities enjoy a culture of trust and acceptance, in which we consciously uplift and honor each other's dignity as children of God. This allows us to ask for support when we need it. The important virtues that create this culture of high noon are honesty, grace, integrity, accountability, and courage.

Honesty

282. *"People who try to hide their mistakes cannot develop. On the other hand, honest people develop because the universe pushes them and supports them wherever they go."* —True Father (1987.10.8)

Honesty is foundational for any genuine relationship. Most of us have learned to hide our mistakes and pretend to be someone we're not because we're afraid of what others may think. We feel it's impossible for someone to fully trust and accept us if they knew our faults. Being honest about ourselves to the people who care about us allows us to experience real, unconditional love.

Grace

283. *"... There will be some tribulation, but when this is overcome, God's grace will pour upon you. No matter how violent the storm, it is followed by sunshine."* —True Father (1980)

Unlike God, we tend to judge a person's shortcomings instead of seeing their original value. Even though we may not approve of the behavior, we can still love the person as a child of God. Grace is a necessary element that nourishes our spirit. Grace is the experience of forgiveness and unconditional love. It is freely given, not something to be earned. Our hearts open to receive grace when we are able to tell the truth about ourselves. Grace is something we must give ourselves as well as others. When we let go of our inner dialogue that says, "I'll never succeed," or "I'm so stupid," we allow ourselves the opportunity to learn and try one more time. Honesty and grace are the foundation for creating a high noon life.

Integrity

284. *"Give the ideal with your words, show the practice by your character and give love with your deep heart."* —True Father (1980)

To live with integrity means we honor and practice our ideals. We constantly check ourselves to see if we are aligning our actions with our words and ultimately with God. We can never be in full integrity unless we live in accordance with God's design for our lives. This applies to everything—our health, relationships, and sexuality. Because sex is the most private part of our lives, it can be the most challenging area in which to maintain integrity. True integrity means living our ideals, especially when no one is watching. Living this way is powerful and rewarding.

Accountability

285. *"We need companions in our life of faith. People without companions are lonely people. Those who have companions can support and protect each other. They can find ways to overcome the challenges that arise in their life. Those with no companions have to resolve by themselves any problems that crop up."* —True Father (1971.3.21)

Accountability in a relationship requires a commitment to practicing integrity and grace. When we are vulnerable and share honestly about things we have or have not done, we can be kept accountable for our actions. We become increasingly responsible as we learn to fulfill the promises we make.

An accountability partner is encouraging and reminds us of our goals, praising even small steps along the way. They listen without judgment. By sharing about how we want to improve and grow, we are empowered to make choices that will bring us closer to living a life without shadows.

Courage

286. *"The bolder, more courageous, and more adventurous you are, the greater will be the blessing which you can receive from God."* —True Father (1980)

Courage is the cornerstone for developing and practicing honesty, grace, integrity, and accountability. It takes courage to be vulnerable, even when it hurts and may be embarrassing. Trusting others allows us to feel understood, forgiven, and receive grace. We need courage to realign ourselves daily with our hopes and ideals. A leap of faith is required to invite accountability into our lives. Living a high noon life can be scary at times, but it is the only way we can experience freedom and unconditional love.

Finding Hope through High Noon

Here is a testimony from a young man who experienced a major change in his faith and relationships when he began to live a high noon life.

"I started to have problems with pornography when I was 15 years old. Porn caused a lot of issues in my life, but the biggest problem for me was the fact I couldn't talk and pray to God honestly. Every time I would pray or read True Parents' words, I felt ashamed. This problem also blocked me from being honest with my parents, siblings, and friends at church. Over time I started to feel that I was alone, that I was different from other second generation, and that I didn't want to be in the church anymore.

However, through High Noon, I learned that purity is not something that you lose but something I could nourish, and I determined to start by confessing to my parents. Through the conversation with my parents, I could feel God's love. I realized that God wanted to help me, but I wasn't opening my heart to Him. After that, the first change that I experienced was that I could pray to God honestly, and my relationship with my parents and siblings became closer."

Points for Consideration/Activities

- Which of the five virtues do you see as most important for you to work on?

- Share a time when you were tempted to do something when no one was watching.

- Share a shadow that you successfully removed and how you felt afterward.

The Pure Love Movement

Every movement has an inspiring leader who is willing to make any sacrifice, even if it means going to jail or giving up their life for what they believe. Martin Luther King Jr. was a prominent leader of the American Civil Rights Movement of the 1960s. When a righteous leader hones in on moral injustice, which threatens our human dignity and passionately inspires others, a movement is created. The power that fuels a cause is generated when a mass of individuals embrace a singular vision. At that point, it begins to develop a life of its own, igniting a ripple effect throughout an entire nation and even the world. True Father had this level of commitment his entire life in the pursuit to defeat the forces of evil and build God's kingdom on the earth. His greatest passion was to rally people around a movement for pure love.

True Father's Words

287. "I directed you to create the pure love movement. None of the teachers in the colleges, high schools, and middle schools can carry out the pure love movement; we are the only ones. Nobody can argue with this. It is only we who can do it. We have been ordained by heaven to take this historical responsibility." (1998.8.17)

288. "We have to accomplish a revolution in education, for all people to value absolute sex, that is, the constitution of Heaven, with God as their vertical, absolute axis. This is the only way to pass on the true, good lineage to all humankind. That is the path to achieving God's ideal of true families. From now on, sexual purity, purity of

lineage, and purity of love will be the essence of the philosophy of education for the true human race." (2006)

289. "Satan's tradition has reached even small towns, so we have to manifest the pure love movement just as widely... The pure love movement should be developed focusing on the family. It is not the nation that will take the initiative. This is why I encouraged you to start holding demonstrations right away. If we are not successful with the true love movement, we will lose everything. It is crucial that we establish in people's minds that the true love movement is our movement. It is like being the ones who first apply for a patent." (1999.6.30)

290. "Hundreds of thousands of young people throughout the world stopped indulging in free sex after accepting the teachings of the Reverend Moon. The message of the pure love movement, which advocates absolute sex, is now spreading like wildfire. While free sex is based upon false love and motivated by selfish desires that come from Satan, absolute sex is the expression of absolute love centered on God." (2004.10.26)

291. "We have to establish the pure love movement and the true family movement on university and college campuses. What can we do to deal with the problems of youth? Where can we establish the true family ideal? We can do so by connecting to the middle schools, high schools, and colleges. Today young people are easily influenced and polluted by corrupt thoughts. Students ages 12 through 24 have this affliction. How can we cure them? Respected civic and social leaders must act as a fortress to protect them. Families need to be protected against being destroyed by homosexuality and free sex. Families should be models of true love. Families have to stand tall, based on traditional Christian values, but in reality, they are becoming weak. We have to rebuild all these things. We have to restore families and young people. This level of restoration will not emerge from the

family alone; support is also needed in the schools. Focusing on elementary schools, middle schools, high schools, and colleges, the nation's leaders should unite and establish the tradition of the family. We have to educate people thoroughly about family ethics and advocate absolute family values." (2000.8.8)

292. "We need to educate young people in order to prevent them from falling. To do that, we made the pure love movement. In promoting the pure love movement, we should publicly recognize young people who exemplify the pure love ideal in their towns or regions. Such students should be treated with respect in their schools. Teachers and principals should honor those students who keep purity." (1995.10.5)

293. "In today's world, things have degenerated to the point where even discussing the value or importance of the term 'pure love' is deemed outmoded. Yet it is the absence of pure love that is the fundamental cause for the breakdown of families that is darkening the future of humanity." (1997.11.30)

294. "The reason people throughout history emphasized pure love and treasured it is because pure love directly connects to the dignity of life. The heart that respects pure love is the heart that values life. It is the heart that esteems one's own tribe and all humanity. Furthermore, the heart that respects pure love is closest to the heart that can meet with God." (1997.11.30)

295. "Although the United States is a powerful nation, in reality, you cannot deny that it is not at all powerful when it comes to this issue of pure love. Moreover, if Washington, D.C. wishes to maintain its reputation as the capital city of the world, above all else, it needs to become the leading city in this matter of pure love. The day Washington, D.C. becomes the holy city of pure and true love will be the day when the entire world will respect and love the United States." (1997.11.30)

296. "Innumerable heroes and sages in human history, including our first ancestors Adam and Eve, were unable to overcome one critical issue, this very issue of pure love. Today's problem is that no one can take responsibility for this matter of pure love—not the family, schools, churches, or even the government." (1997.11.30)

297. "As can be seen, the purpose of the World Culture and Sports Festival is to inculcate maturity on the part of individuals, who can go on to form and strengthen true families that are the basis of true love. The meaning of pure love, then, is all the more special and important to you who have been taking part in this festival. This pure love movement you are carrying forward, once established throughout the world, will be the most important pillar of the true family movement." (1997.11.30)

Sharing Thoughts on True Father's Words

In 1997, even though much of the world considered purity to be old-fashioned, True Father boldly proclaimed that pure love is absolutely needed for the future of the world. Today, young people who believe in abstinence are often challenged by their peers, but True Father said those who commit to sexual purity should be publicly recognized and honored.

The misuse of sex causes us to see ourselves and others as objects instead of God's divine children. This naturally impacts all of our relationships, especially within the family. How can we be a loving and supportive couple when we don't understand each other's value? As parents, how should we raise our children to recognize their own value as sons and daughters of God? True Father called us to guide people to value their sexual organs. He said that we are the only ones who can create a pure love movement that deals with the problems of young people and give them hope for their future. The heart that respects pure love is the heart that values all humanity and can meet with God.

The Civil Rights Movement

We can learn a lot from the Civil Rights Movement. Racial segregation during the Jim Crow era was a system that relegated African-Americans to the position of second-class citizens. Schools for African-American children received second-hand books, and the school day was cut in half because they had too many children and not enough funds. African-Americans were forced to ride in the back of the bus and were forbidden from entering many establishments. The most common types of segregation mandated that public institutions and business owners keep people of color and white people separated. Interracial marriage was strictly forbidden.

The Civil Rights Movement (1954-1968) was a response to this travesty of justice and is perhaps the most iconic movement in recent history. Tens of thousands of men and women dedicated their lives to ending racial discrimination in the United States. Millions more supported by participating in rallies, sit-ins, and boycotts.

Making It Real

Just as Martin Luther King Jr. responded to the hatred and bigotry of segregation, True Father committed himself to end moral decline throughout the world by calling upon us to become leaders of a pure love movement. He had the utmost respect for Martin Luther King Jr., calling him one of the greatest Americans in history. The Civil Rights Movement was needed to address the flagrant injustices African-Americans faced at the time. Likewise, a pure love movement is necessary to address the moral crisis facing the world's youth.

The Pure Love Alliance (PLA) was founded as a global organization in response to True Father's call to create a pure love movement. The PLA encouraged young people to treat their sexuality as God's gift for their future spouse and commit to abstinence until marriage. They wanted to demonstrate that pure love was a worthwhile life choice. Young people held rallies in America, Asia, and Europe to promote sexual purity as an alternative to pop culture's typical portrayal of casual sex. The PLA's approach of hosting large outdoor events with thousands of teenagers proclaiming their commitment to saving sex for marriage was radical in the 90s. It caused a notable stir and was featured on many major news outlets.

A modern pure love movement is needed to counter Satan's strategy to spread false sexuality across the globe. Internet pornography portrays a distorted and often violent view of sex, which is confusing the world's youth. It ensnares millions in compulsive sexual behavior, destroys marriages, and fuels the hook-up culture and human trafficking.

High Noon, a Modern Pure Love Movement

High Noon is responding to the urgent need to address the global pornography pandemic by educating people about its harmful effects and providing recovery support. Armed with True Parent's vision for heavenly sexuality, we are speaking boldly about their profound understanding of the sexual organs as God's original palace of love, life, and lineage. We offer marriage enrichment to help couples grow in their relationship and resources to empower parents to have open, ongoing conversations with their children about sex and purity.

Through these activities, we are witnessing a level of authenticity never before imagined. Singles and couples throughout the world have been inspired as they share God's beautiful ideal for sex and gather others in the cause of pure love. Men and women of all ages find the courage to share honestly about their challenges in the area of sex and seek the support they need to create a fulfilling marriage. However, more than what we've accomplished, we're inspired by the initiative taken by others in response to High Noon's work. We often hear about people whose lives have been changed because somebody who attended one of our events reached out to them to ask how they were doing with their sexual integrity. We receive emails from people we don't know, living in countries we've never been to, who tell us that they have formed their own accountability groups to support each other in quitting porn. Additionally, university students have organized campus events to discuss the topic of sexual integrity. This ripple effect extends far beyond High Noon's immediate impact.

True Father's mantra was, "Before I seek to master the universe, I must first seek to master myself." True Mother eloquently reminds us that, "Peace starts with me." The first step is for each of us to develop our own sexual integrity and become blessed couples who embody heavenly intimacy and radiate God's love. Upon that foundation, we can share God's intention for sex with the people in our lives.

Points for Consideration/Activities

- What do you think would be an effective way to create a modern day pure love movement?

- Who are the people in your life with whom you feel comfortable enough to have a conversation about sex?

- What are some ways you can nurture your sexual integrity and experience heavenly intimacy in your marriage (current or future)?

Conclusion

We hope you have found something within these pages that has touched your heart and mind. Each of us has had a different experience when it comes to learning about sex. True Parents' teaching about the holy sexual organs are both profound and challenging. We strongly believe that it is possible for every person to create a radiant marriage and to experience sexual fulfillment that leaves them with a deep feeling of connection and love. One day we will all live in a world that honors the sexual organs as God intended.

To learn more about High Noon please visit our website, highnoon.org. We have many resources for people battling unhealthy habits involving pornography and masturbation, for couples seeking to experience deeper sexual intimacy, and for parents wanting to learn how to educate and protect their children in this hyper-sexualized world. When you come and explore High Noon, you'll find there is support and community for everyone.

We'd love to hear from you about what you thought about the contents of this book. Please write us at admin@highnoon.org and share your thoughts and feelings with us.

Thank you for taking the time to read this book. We pray it continues to guide you and your family to experience God's beautiful vision expressed to us in the eternal words of our True Parents.

References for True Parents' Words

Section I. Core of the Universe

Core of the Universe

1. *Cheon Seong Gyeong*, Book 11, Chpt. 2, Sec. 1, p. 1708
2. *Cheon Seong Gyeong*, Book 11, Chpt. 2, Sec. 2, p. 1711
3. *Cheon Seong Gyeong*, Book 11, Chpt. 2, Sec. 2, p. 1712
4. *Cheon Seong Gyeong*, Book 11, Chpt. 2, Sec. 2, p. 1713
5. *Cheon Seong Gyeong*, Book 11, Chpt. 2, Sec. 2, p. 1718
6. *Cheon Seong Gyeong*, Book 11, Chpt. 2, Sec. 2, p. 1724
7. *Cheon Seong Gyeong*, Book 11, Chpt. 2, Sec. 2, p. 1717
8. *Cheon Seong Gyeong*, Book 11, Chpt. 2, Sec. 2, p. 1723
9. *Cheon Seong Gyeong*, Book 11, Chpt. 2, Sec. 2, p. 1723

The Original Palace of Love

10. *Cheon Seong Gyeong*, Book 11, Chpt. 2, Sec. 2, p. 1717
11. *Cheon Seong Gyeong*, Book 11, Chpt. 2, Sec. 2, p. 1717
12. *Cheon Seong Gyeong*, Book 11, Chpt. 2, Sec. 2, p. 1715
13. *Cheon Seong Gyeong*, Book 11, Chpt. 2, Sec. 2, p. 1717
14. *Cheon Seong Gyeong*, Book 11, Chpt. 2, Sec. 2, p. 1724-1725
15. *Cheon Seong Gyeong*, Book 11, Chpt. 2, Sec. 2, p. 1712
16. *Cheon Seong Gyeong*, Book 11, Chpt. 2, Sec. 5, p. 1767
17. *Cheon Seong Gyeong*, Book 11, Chpt. 2, Sec. 1, p. 1708
18. *Cheon Seong Gyeong*, Book 11, Chpt. 2, Sec. 1, p. 1706-1707
19. *Cheon Seong Gyeong*, Book 11, Chpt. 2, Sec. 5, p. 1767

The Original Palace of Life

20. *Cheon Seong Gyeong*, Book 11, Chpt. 2, Sec. 2, p. 1712
21. *Cheon Seong Gyeong*, Book 11, Chpt. 2, Sec. 2, p. 1714
22. *Cheon Seong Gyeong*, Book 15, Chpt. 2, Sec. 2, p. 2257
23. Dr. Hak Ja Han Moon, "The Journey of Life," speech given in various locations on the World Tour, 1999
24. *Cheon Seong Gyeong*, 2nd Edition, Book 5, Chpt. 4, Sec. 2, Verse 15, p. 556-557
25. *Cheon Seong Gyeong*, Book 11, Chpt. 2, Sec. 2, p. 1716
26. *Cheon Seong Gyeong*, Book 11, Chpt. 2, Sec. 2, p. 1714

The Original Palace of Lineage

27. Reverend Sun Myung Moon, "Purity, Blood Lineage, Device Which Creates Life (sexual organ)," sermon given at Belvedere Estate, Tarrytown, NY, February 2, 2001
28. *Cheon Seong Gyeong*, 2nd Edition, Book 3, Chpt. 2, Sec. 3, Verse 27, p. 316
29. *Cheon Seong Gyeong*, 2nd Edition, Book 3, Chpt. 2, Sec. 3, Verse 29, p. 316
30. *Cheon Seong Gyeong*, Book 11, Chpt. 2, Sec. 2, p. 1724
31. *Cheon Seong Gyeong*, Book 11, Chpt. 2, Sec. 2, p. 1714
32. *Cheon Seong Gyeong*, Book 11, Chpt. 2, Sec. 2, p. 1712
33. *Cheon Seong Gyeong*, Book 11, Chpt. 2, Sec. 2, p. 1716
34. *Cheon Seong Gyeong*, Book 11, Chpt. 2, Sec. 2, p. 1723
35. *Cheon Seong Gyeong*, Book 11, Chpt. 2, Sec. 3, p. 1733

Section II. God's Design for Sex

God's Purpose for the Sexual Organs

36. *Cheon Seong Gyeong*, Book 11, Chpt. 2, Sec. 2, p. 1719
37. *Cheon Seong Gyeong*, Book 11, Chpt. 2, Sec. 2, p. 1720
38. *Cheon Seong Gyeong*, Book 11, Chpt. 2, Sec. 2, p. 1725

39. *Cheon Seong Gyeong*, 2nd Edition, Book 4, Chpt. 4, Sec. 3, Verse 15, p. 460
40. *Cheon Seong Gyeong*, 2nd Edition, Book 3, Chpt. 2, Sec. 3, Verse 17, p. 313
41. Reverend Sun Myung Moon, "In Search of the Origin of the Universe," speech given in Washington, D.C., August 1, 1996
42. *Cheon Seong Gyeong*, Book 11, Chpt. 2, Sec. 2, p. 1713

The Chemistry of Love

43. *Cheon Seong Gyeong*, Book 3, Chpt. 2, Sec. 5, p. 366
44. *Cheon Seong Gyeong*, Book 3, Chpt. 2, Sec. 5, p. 367
45. *Cheon Seong Gyeong*, 2nd Edition, Book 3, Chpt. 1, Sec. 4, Verse 25, p. 291
46. Reverend Sun Myung Moon, "True Parents' Completion of Responsibility in View of Providence," sermon given at Belvedere Estate, Tarrytown, NY, December 26, 1999
47. Reverend Sun Myung Moon, "The Purpose of Life, Coming and Going," sermon given at Belvedere Estate, Tarrytown, NY, January 8, 1984
48. *Cheon Seong Gyeong*, Book 11, Chpt. 2, Sec. 2, p. 1722
49. *Cheon Seong Gyeong*, 2nd Edition, Book 4, Chpt. 4, Sec. 2, p. 455

The Chemistry of First Love

50. "The Center of Responsibility and Indemnity," Belvedere Estate, Tarrytown, NY, January 30, 1983
51. Reverend Sun Myung Moon, "The Center of Responsibility and Indemnity," sermon given at Belvedere Estate, Tarrytown, NY, January 30, 1983
52. Reverend Sun Myung Moon, "The Present Time," sermon given at Belvedere Estate, Tarrytown, NY, February 4, 1979
53. Reverend Sun Myung Moon, "The Way of Victory of God," speech given at the World Mission Center, New York City, NY,

August 20, 1987
54. *Cheon Seong Gyeong*, Book 6, Chpt. 1, Sec. 4, p. 829

First Night

55. *Cheon Seong Gyeong*, Book 4, Chpt. 7, Sec. 8, p. 489
56. *Cheon Seong Gyeong*, 2nd Edition, Book 3, Chpt. 2, Sec. 3, Verse 21, p. 314
57. *Cheon Seong Gyeong*, Book 11, Chpt. 2, Sec. 3, p. 1744
58. *Cheon Seong Gyeong*, Book 11, Chpt. 2, Sec. 3, p. 1733
59. *Cheon Seong Gyeong*, 2nd Edition, Book 4, Chpt. 4, Sec. 3, Verse 19, p. 462
60. *Cheon Seong Gyeong*, Book 11, Chpt. 2, Sec. 3, p. 1744
61. Reverend Sun Myung Moon, "Heavenly Life," sermon given at Belvedere Estate, Tarrytown, NY, November 20, 1983
62. Reverend Sun Myung Moon, "Parents, Children and The World Centered upon Oneself," sermon given at Belvedere Estate, Tarrytown, NY, June 5, 1983
63. Reverend Sun Myung Moon, "World Era of Blessed Families," sermon given at Belvedere Estate, Tarrytown, NY, May 4, 1997
64. *Cheon Seong Gyeong*, Book 11, Chpt. 2, Sec. 3, p. 1744
65. *Cheon Seong Gyeong*, 2nd Edition, Book 7, Chpt. 3, Sec. 4, Verse 2, p. 758-759

God's Wedding

66. *Cheon Seong Gyeong*, Book 11, Chpt. 2, Sec. 3, p. 1735-1736
67. *Cheon Seong Gyeong*, Book 11, Chpt. 2, Sec. 3, p. 1736
68. *Cheon Seong Gyeong*, Book 11, Chpt. 2, Sec. 3, p. 1734
69. *Cheon Seong Gyeong*, Book 11, Chpt. 2, Sec. 3, p. 1737
70. *Cheon Seong Gyeong*, 2nd Edition, Book 1, Chpt. 2, Sec. 2, Verse 19, p. 66
71. *Cheon Seong Gyeong*, Book 11, Chpt. 2, Sec. 3, p. 1734
72. *Cheon Seong Gyeong*, Book 11, Chpt. 2, Sec. 3, p. 1734

73. *Cheon Seong Gyeong*, Book 11, Chpt. 2, Sec. 3, p. 1734

74. *Cheon Seong Gyeong*, Book 11, Chpt. 2, Sec. 3, p. 1736

75. Yoshihiko Masuda, *True Love, Sex, and Health: As Guided by the Words of True Parents* (Gapyeong: CheongShim GTS University Press, 2009), p. 240

Guardians of the Universe

76. *Cheon Seong Gyeong*, 2nd Edition, Book 3, Chpt. 2, Sec. 3, Verse 28, p. 316

77. *Cheon Seong Gyeong*, Book 9, Chpt. 1, Sec. 3, p. 1289

78. *Cheon Seong Gyeong*, Book 9, Chpt. 1, Sec. 3, p. 1287

79. *Cheon Seong Gyeong*, Book 9, Chpt. 1, Sec. 3, p. 1288

80. *Cheon Seong Gyeong*, Book 9, Chpt. 1, Sec. 3, p. 1288

81. *Cheon Seong Gyeong*, Book 11, Chpt. 2, Sec. 2, p. 1722

82. *Cheon Seong Gyeong*, Book 11, Chpt. 2, Sec. 4, p. 1757

Sexual Purity in Mind and Body

83. *Cheon Seong Gyeong*, 2nd Edition, Book 5, Chpt. 3, Sec. 1, Verse 20, p. 537

84. *Cheon Seong Gyeong*, 2nd Edition, Book 4, Chpt. 4, Sec. 2, Verse 11, p. 454

85. *Cheon Seong Gyeong*, 2nd Edition, Book 5, Chpt. 2, Sec. 1, Verse 3, p. 498-499

86. *Cheon Seong Gyeong*, Book 11, Chpt. 2, Sec. 3, p. 1736

87. *Cheon Seong Gyeong*, Book 4, Chpt. 1, Sec. 5, p. 427

88. Reverend Sun Myung Moon, "The Master Speaks on Satan, The Fall, and Evil (Question and Answer Sessions)," talks given at various locations throughout the United States, March-April 1965

89. Reverend Sun Myung Moon, Blessed Family and the Ideal Kingdom Vol I, (HSA-UWC, 1997), p. 443

90. *Cheon Seong Gyeong*, 2nd Edition, Book 8, Chpt. 2, Sec. 4, Verse 1, p. 847

91. *Cheon Seong Gyeong*, 2nd Edition, Book 4, Chpt. 1, Sec. 2, Verse 34, p. 377

92. *Blessed Family and the Ideal Kingdom Vol I*, HSA-UWC, p. 444, 1997

93. *Blessed Family and the Ideal Kingdom Vol I*, HSA-UWC, p. 53, 1997

Why Do We Marry?

94. *Cheon Seong Gyeong*, Book 11, Chpt. 2, Sec. 3, p. 1739

95. Reverend Sun Myung Moon, *As a Peace-Loving Global Citizen*, (Washington D.C.: The Washington Times Foundation, 2010), p. 207

96. *Cheon Seong Gyeong*, Book 3, Chpt. 3, Sec. 1, p. 385

97. *Cheon Seong Gyeong*, Book 11, Chpt. 2, Sec. 3, p. 1743

98. *Cheon Seong Gyeong*, 2nd Edition, Book 5, Chpt. 2, Sec. 2, Verse 5, p. 504

99. *Cheon Seong Gyeong*, Book 11, Chpt. 2, Sec. 3, p. 1746

100. *Cheon Seong Gyeong*, 2nd Edition, Book 5, Chpt. 2, Sec. 2, Verse 13, p. 506

101. *Cheon Seong Gyeong*, Book 11, Chpt. 2, Sec. 3, 1743-1744

102. Reverend Sun Myung Moon, "In Search of the Origin of the Universe," speech given in Washington, D.C., August 1, 1996

103. *Cheon Seong Gyeong*, 2nd Edition, Book 5, Chpt. 2, Sec. 2, Verse 16, p. 506-507

104. *Cheon Seong Gyeong*, Book 11, Chpt. 2, Sec. 3, p. 1744-1745

105. *Cheon Seong Gyeong*, Book 11, Chpt. 2, Sec. 3, p. 1744

Section III. Conjugal Love

The Sacred Value of Sex

106. *Cheon Seong Gyeong*, Book 11, Chpt. 2, Sec. 1, p. 1705-1706

107. *Cheon Seong Gyeong*, 2nd Edition, Book 3, Chpt. 2, Sec. 3, Verse 29, p. 316

108. *Cheon Seong Gyeong*, 2nd Edition, Book 3, Chpt. 2, Sec. 3, Verse 30, p. 316-317

109. *Cheon Seong Gyeong*, Book 8, Chpt. 2, Sec. 4, p. 1146

110. *Cheon Seong Gyeong*, Book 11, Chpt. 2, Sec. 2, p. 1713

111. *Cheon Seong Gyeong*, Book 3, Chpt. 3, Sec.1, p. 387

112. Reverend Sun Myung Moon, "The True Owners in Establishing the Kingdom of Peace and Unity," speech given at the Cheon Jeong Peace Museum, Cheongpyeong, South Korea, April 10, 2006

Heaven's Gift Exchange

113. *Cheon Seong Gyeong*, Book 4, Chpt. 12, Sec. 1, p. 531

114. Reverend Sun Myung Moon, "In Search of the Origin of the Universe," speech given in Washington, D.C., August 1, 1996

115. *Cheon Seong Gyeong*, Book 11, Chpt. 2, Sec. 4, p. 1750

116. *Cheon Seong Gyeong*, Book 11, Chpt. 2, Sec. 4, p. 1751

117. *Cheon Seong Gyeong*, Book 11, Chpt. 2, Sec. 4, p. 1752

118. *Cheon Seong Gyeong*, Book 11, Chpt. 2, Sec. 4, p. 1753

119. *Cheon Seong Gyeong*, Book 11, Chpt. 2, Sec. 4, p. 1754-1755

120. *Cheon Seong Gyeong*, Book 4, Chpt. 12, Sec. 3, p. 532-533

121. *Cheon Seong Gyeong*, Book 4, Chpt. 12, Sec. 3, p. 533

122. *Cheon Seong Gyeong*, Book 4, Chpt. 12, Sec. 3, p. 533

Two Become One

123. *Cheon Seong Gyeong*, Book 11, Chpt. 2, Sec. 3, p. 1743

124. *Cheon Seong Gyeong*, 2nd Edition, Book 3, Chpt. 2, Sec. 3, Verse 26, p. 315-316

125. *Cheon Seong Gyeong*, 2nd Edition, Book 5, Chpt. 2, Sec. 2, Verse 10, p. 505

126. *Cheon Seong Gyeong*, Book 3, Chpt. 3, Sec. 1, p. 387

127. Yoshihiko Masuda, *True Love, Sex, and Health: As Guided by the Words of True Parents* (Gapyeong: CheongShim GTS University Press, 2009), p. 127

128. Dr. Hak Ja Han Moon, "Women Will Play a Leading Role in the Ideal World I," speech given in Incheon, South Korea, May 11, 1992

129. *Cheon Seong Gyeong*, Book 3, Chpt. 2, Sec. 4, p. 356

130. *Cheon Seong Gyeong*, Book 11, Chpt. 2, Sec. 3, p. 1744-1745

131. *Cheon Seong Gyeong*, Book 11, Chpt. 1, Sec. 3, p. 1661

132. Reverend Sun Myung Moon, "Nothing Was Created for Its Own Sake," sermon given in Seoul, South Korea, August 10, 1997

133. *Cheon Seong Gyeong*, 2nd Edition, Book 5, Chpt. 2, Sec. 2, Verse 3, p. 503

Fidelity in Marriage

134. *Cheon Seong Gyeong*, Book 11, Chpt. 2, Sec. 4, p. 1752

135. *Cheon Seong Gyeong*, 2nd Edition, Book 13, Chpt. 1, Sec. 3, Verse 7, p. 1384

136. Dr. Hak Ja Han Moon, "Let Us Become the Living Embodiment of the True Family Ideal," speech given in Washington, D.C., November 17, 1997.

137. *Cheon Seong Gyeong*, 2nd Edition, Book 5, Chpt. 2, Sec. 1, Verse 15, p. 502

138. *Cheon Seong Gyeong*, Book 3 Chpt. 2, Sec. 5, p. 363-364

139. *Cheon Seong Gyeong*, Book 9, Chpt. 1, Sec. 3, p. 1292

140. *Cheon Seong Gyeong*, Book 3, Chpt. 3, Sec. 2, p. 390

141. Cham Bumo Gyeong, Book 4, Chpt. 3, Sec. 1, Verse 10, p. 376

True Love Is Blind

142. Reverend Sun Myung Moon, "The Way to Grow," sermon given at Belvedere Estate, Tarrytown, NY, August 30, 1987

143. Reverend Sun Myung Moon, "Blessed Family," sermon given at Belvedere Estate, Tarrytown, NY, June 20, 1982

144. Reverend Sun Myung Moon, "Blessed Family," sermon given at Belvedere Estate, Tarrytown, NY, June 20, 1982

145. *Cheon Seong Gyeong*, 2nd Edition, Book 3, Chpt. 1, Sec. 4, Verse 28, p. 292

146. *Cheon Seong Gyeong*, Book 3, Chpt. 2, Sec. 4, p. 358-359

147. *Cheon Seong Gyeong*, Book 3, Chpt. 3, Sec. 1, p. 386

148. Reverend Sun Myung Moon, "In Search of the Origin of the Universe," speech given in Seoul, South Korea, September 15, 1996

149. *Cheon Seong Gyeong*, Book 11, Chpt. 2, Sec. 1, p. 1707

Make Love a Verb, Not a Noun

150. Yoshihiko Masuda, *True Love, Sex, and Health: As Guided by the Words of True Parents* (Gapyeong: CheongShim GTS University Press, 2009), p. 42

151. *Cheon Seong Gyeong*, Book 3, Chpt. 3, Sec. 2, p. 391

152. *Cheon Seong Gyeong*, Book 3, Chpt. 2, Sec. 4, p. 355-356

153. *Cheon Seong Gyeong*, Book 3, Chpt. 2, Sec. 4, p. 356

154. *Cheon Seong Gyeong*, Book 4, Chpt. 7, Sec. 8, p. 489

155. *Cheon Seong Gyeong*, 2nd Edition, Book 3, Chpt. 2, Sec. 3, Verse 31, p. 317

156. *Cheon Seong Gyeong*, Book 11, Chpt. 2, Sec. 4, p. 1753

Spirit World and Conjugal Love

157. *Cheon Seong Gyeong*, 2nd Edition, Book 7, Chpt. 2, Sec. 2, Verse 21, p. 718-719

158. *Cheon Seong Gyeong*, 2nd Edition, Book 7, Chpt. 3, Sec. 4, Verse 10, p. 761

159. *Cheon Seong Gyeong*, 2nd Edition, Book 4, Chpt. 4, Sec. 4, Verse 17, p. 471-472

160. *Cheon Seong Gyeong*, Book 4, Chpt. 7, Sec. 8, p. 488
161. *Cheon Seong Gyeong*, Book 11, Chpt. 2 Sec. 2, p. 1718-1719
162. *Cheon Seong Gyeong*, Book 11, Chpt. 2, Sec. 3, p. 1747
163. *Cheon Seong Gyeong*, Book 11, Chpt. 2, Sec. 2, p. 1725
164. Yoshihiko Masuda, *True Love, Sex, and Health: As Guided by the Words of True Parents* (Gapyeong: CheongShim GTS University Press, 2009), p. 158

Section IV. Absolute Sex

What is Absolute Sex?

165. *Cheon Seong Gyeong*, Book 15, Chpt. 2, Sec. 4, p. 2268
166. Reverend Sun Myung Moon, "Absolute sex is important," sermon given at Cheon Jeong Peace Museum, Cheongpyeong, South Korea, March 7, 2007
167. Reverend Sun Myung Moon, "In Search of the Origin of the Universe," speech given at Washington, D.C., August 1, 1996
168. Reverend Sun Myung Moon, "Twenty-sixth Day of Victory of Love: In the Realm of the Cosmic Sabbath There is Absolute Sex," sermon given at Cheon Jeong Peace Museum, Cheongpyeong, South Korea, January 2, 2009
169. Reverend Sun Myung Moon, "Twenty-sixth Day of Victory of Love: In the Realm of the Cosmic Sabbath There is Absolute Sex," sermon given at Cheon Jeong Peace Museum, Cheongpyeong, South Korea, January 2, 2009
170. *Cheon Seong Gyeong*, Book 11, Chpt. 2, Sec. 4, p. 1764
171. Reverend Sun Myung Moon, Blessed Family and the Ideal Kingdom Vol I, (HSA-UWC, 1997), p. 17-18
172. *Cheon Seong Gyeong*, Book 4, Chpt. 5, Sec. 6, p. 465
173. Reverend Sun Myung Moon, "Twenty-sixth Day of Victory of Love: In the Realm of the Cosmic Sabbath There is Absolute Sex," sermon given at Cheon Jeong Peace Museum, Cheongpyeong, South Korea, January 2, 2009

Absolute Sexual Purity

174. Reverend Sun Myung Moon, "The Youth Culture Must Become a Pure Love Movement," speech given in Washington, D.C., November 30, 1997

175. Reverend Sun Myung Moon, *A Prophet Speaks Today, the words of Sun Myung Moon*, ed. W. Farley Jones, (New York: HSA-UWC, 1975) p. 33

176. Reverend Sun Myung Moon, "Peace Message 10: The Family Rooted in Absolute Sexual Ethics, Which is the Model for God's Absoluteness, Peace and Ideal, and the Global Kingdom," speech given in Ilsan, South Korea, November 21, 2006

177. Reverend Sun Myung Moon, "Peace Message 10: The Family Rooted in Absolute Sexual Ethics, Which is the Model for God's Absoluteness, Peace and Ideal, and the Global Kingdom," speech given in Ilsan, South Korea, November 21, 2006

178. Reverend Sun Myung Moon, "Peace Message 10: The Family Rooted in Absolute Sexual Ethics, Which is the Model for God's Absoluteness, Peace and Ideal, and the Global Kingdom," speech given in Ilsan, South Korea, November 21, 2006

179. Reverend Sun Myung Moon, "Peace Message 10: The Family Rooted in Absolute Sexual Ethics, Which is the Model for God's Absoluteness, Peace and Ideal, and the Global Kingdom," speech given in Ilsan, South Korea, November 21, 2006

180. Reverend Sun Myung Moon, talk untitled, talk given at the Blessed Couples' Conference, New York City, NY, February 21, 1991

Absolute Sexual Ethics in the Family

181. Reverend Sun Myung Moon, "Establishment of the Royal Palace," sermon given in Cheongpyeong, South Korea, December 28, 2007

182. Reverend Sun Myung Moon, "Peace Message 10: The Family Rooted in Absolute Sexual Ethics, Which is the Model for God's Absoluteness, Peace and Ideal, and the Global Kingdom," speech given in Ilsan, South Korea, November 21, 2006

183. Reverend Sun Myung Moon, "Absolute Sex is Important," sermon given at Cheon Jeong Peace Museum, Cheongpyeong, South Korea, March 7, 2007

184. *Cheon Seong Gyeong*, 2nd Edition, Book 8, Chpt. 2, Sec. 5, Verse 3, p. 857

185. Reverend Sun Myung Moon, "In Search of the Origin of the Universe," speech given in Washington, D.C., August 1, 1996

186. *Cheon Seong Gyeong*, 2nd Edition, Book 3, Chpt. 2, Sec. 3, Verse 37, p. 318-319

Absolute Sexual Ethics in the World

187. Reverend Sun Myung Moon, "In Search of the Origin of the Universe," speech given in Washington, D.C., August 1, 1996

188. Reverend Sun Myung Moon, "In Search of the Origin of the Universe," speech given in Washington, D.C., August 1, 1996

189. Reverend Sun Myung Moon, "In Search of the Origin of the Universe," speech given in Washington, D.C., August 1, 1996

190. Reverend Sun Myung Moon, "In Search of the Origin of the Universe," speech given in Washington, D.C., August 1, 1996

191. Reverend Sun Myung Moon, "In Search of the Origin of the Universe," speech given in Washington, D.C., August 1, 1996

192. Reverend Sun Myung Moon, "In Search of the Origin of the Universe," speech given in Washington, D.C., August 1, 1996

Section V. The Fall

The Root

193. Reverend Sun Myung Moon, "Early Spring of Life," sermon given at Belvedere Estate, Tarrytown, NY, April 3, 1988

194. *Cheon Seong Gyeong*, Book 11, Chpt. 2, Sec. 1, p. 1708

195. *Cheon Seong Gyeong*, 2nd Edition, Book 1, Chpt. 1, Sec. 2, Verse 6, p. 35

196. *Cheon Seong Gyeong*, Book 4, Chpt. 10, Sec. 2, p. 511-512

197. *Cheon Seong Gyeong*, Book 8, Chpt. 2, Sec. 2, p. 1140

198. *Cheon Seong Gyeong*, Book 8, Chpt. 2, Sec. 4, p. 1146

199. *Cheon Seong Gyeong*, Book 4, Chpt. 10, Sec. 2, p. 511

200. *Cheon Seong Gyeong*, Book 8, Chpt. 2, Sec. 1, p. 1130-1131

201. *Cheon Seong Gyeong*, Book 8, Chpt. 2, Sec. 4, p. 1148

202. Reverend Sun Myung Moon, "The True Owners in Establishing the Kingdom of Cosmic Peace and Unity in Heaven and on Earth," sermon given at Cheon Jeong Peace Museum, Cheongpyeong, South Korea, October 14, 2006

203. *Cheon Seong Gyeong*, 2nd Edition, Book 11, Chpt. 3, Sec. 1, Verse 19, p. 1179-1180

Crossroads of Heaven or Hell

204. Reverend Sun Myung Moon, "In Search of the Origin of the Universe," speech given in Seoul, South Korea, September 15, 1996

205. *Cheon Seong Gyeong*, Book 11, Chpt. 2, Sec. 5, p. 1763

206. *Cheon Seong Gyeong*, Book 11, Chpt. 2, Sec. 5, p. 1763

207. *Cheon Seong Gyeong*, Book 11, Chpt. 2, Sec. 5, p. 1764

208. *Cheon Seong Gyeong*, Book 11, Chpt. 2, Sec. 5, p. 1765

209. *Cheon Seong Gyeong*, Book 11, Chpt. 2, Sec. 5, p. 1764

210. *Cheon Seong Gyeong*, Book 11, Chpt. 3, Sec. 1, p. 1776

211. *Cheon Seong Gyeong*, Book 11, Chpt. 2, Sec. 4, p. 1759

212. *Cheon Seong Gyeong*, Book 6, Chpt. 2, Sec. 2, p. 892

213. *Cheon Seong Gyeong*, 2nd Edition, Book 13, Chpt. 2, Sec. 1, Verse 23, p. 1393

214. Reverend Sun Myung Moon, "At the Crossroads of Good and Evil," sermon given in Seoul, South Korea, July 16, 1972

215. Reverend Sun Myung Moon, "The Harmonization of Values, and the Liberation and Complete Settlement of the Realm Transcending Religions and Nations from the Providential Perspective," speech given in Rye Brook, NY, October 26, 2004

The Odyssey

216. *Cheon Seong Gyeong*, Book 8, Chpt. 2, Sec. 1, p. 1134
217. *Cheon Seong Gyeong*, Book 11, Chpt. 2, Sec. 3, p. 1745
218. *Cheon Seong Gyeong*, 2nd Edition, Book 4, Chpt. 2, Sec. 2, Verse 29, p. 410
219. Reverend Sun Myung Moon, "The Harmonization of Values, and the Liberation and Complete Settlement of the Realm Transcending Religions and Nations from the Providential Perspective," speech given in Rye Brook, NY, October 26, 2004
220. Reverend Sun Myung Moon, "Mission and Prayer," speech given in World Mission Center, New York City, NY, June 12, 1983
221. Reverend Sun Myung Moon, "Establishment of the Royal Palace," sermon given in Cheongpyeong, South Korea, December 28, 2007
222. Reverend Sun Myung Moon, "Purity, Blood Lineage, Device Which Creates Life (sexual organ)," sermon given in Belvedere Estate, Tarrytown, NY, February 2, 2001
223. Reverend Sun Myung Moon, "The Central Leader," sermon given in Belvedere Estate, Tarrytown, NY, February 13, 1974
224. Reverend Sun Myung Moon, "The Central Leader," sermon given in Belvedere Estate, Tarrytown, NY, February 13, 1974

Immorality and Youth

225. Reverend Sun Myung Moon, "In Search of the Origin of the Universe," speech given in Washington, D.C., August 1, 1996
226. Reverend Sun Myung Moon, "In Search of the Origin of the Universe," speech given in Seoul, South Korea, September 15, 1996

227. Reverend Sun Myung Moon, "The Master Speaks on Satan, the Fall, and Evil (Question and Answer Sessions)," talks given in various centers throughout the United States, March-April, 1965

228. *Cham Bumo Gyeong*, Book 4, Chpt. 3, Sec. 1, Verse 20, p. 379

229. Reverend Sun Myung Moon, "Twenty-sixth Day of Victory of Love," sermon given at Cheon Jeong Peace Museum, January 2, 2009

230. Blessing and Ideal Family, Volume I, Part I, FFWPU International, 1998, p. 99

231. Reverend Sun Myung Moon, "Building a World of the Culture of Heart Based on True Love," speech given in Seoul, South Korea, July 10, 2003

Immorality in the Family and World

232. *Cham Bumo Gyeong*, Book 4, Chpt. 3, Sec. 1, Verse 1, p. 373

233. *Cham Bumo Gyeong*, Book 4, Chpt. 3, Sec. 1, Verse 1, p. 374

234. Dr. Hak Ja Han Moon, "The Ideal Home and World Peace," speech given in Seoul, South Korea, August 23, 1995

235. *Pyeong Hwa Gyeong*, Book 10, Speech 2, p. 1473

236. Reverend Sun Myung Moon, "The Harmonization of Values, and the Liberation and Complete Settlement of the Realm Transcending Religions and Nations from the Providential Perspective," speech given in Rye Brook, NY, October 26, 2004

237. *Cheon Seong Gyeong*, 2nd Edition, Book 13, Chpt. 2, Sec. 1, Verse 14, p. 1391

238. Reverend Sun Myung Moon, "The Harmonization of Values, and the Liberation and Complete Settlement of the Realm Transcending Religions and Nations from the Providential Perspective," speech given in Rye Brook, NY, October 26, 2004

Section VI. Restoration

Learning About Sex from our Parents

239. *Cheon Seong Gyeong*, Book 11, Chpt. 2, Sec.1, p. 1707

240. Yoshihiko Masuda, *True Love, Sex, and Health: As Guided by the Words of True Parents* (Gapyeong: CheongShim GTS University Press, 2009), p. 209

241. Reverend Sun Myung Moon, "True Day of All Things and Initiator of Harmony," sermon given at Belvedere Estate, Tarrytown, NY, June 5, 1997

242. *Cheon Seong Gyeong*, Book 11, Chpt. 2, Sec. 2, p. 1725

Why Does the Messiah Come?

243. *Cheon Seong Gyeong*, Book 11, Chpt. 2, Sec. 2, p. 1725

244. Reverend Sun Myung Moon, "In Search of the Origin of the Universe," speech given in Washington, D.C., August 1, 1996

245. *Cham Bumo Gyeong*, Book 13, Chpt. 2, Sec. 1, Verse 17, p. 1486

246. Reverend Sun Myung Moon, "In Search of the Origin of the Universe," speech given in Washington, D.C., August 1, 1996

247. Reverend Sun Myung Moon, "In Search of the Origin of the Universe," speech given in Washington, D.C., August 1, 1996

248. Reverend Sun Myung Moon, "Twenty-sixth Day of Victory of Love: In the Realm of the Cosmic Sabbath There is Absolute Sex," sermon given at Cheon Jeong Peace Museum, Cheongpyeong, South Korea, January 2, 2009

249. Reverend Sun Myung Moon, "Establishment of the Royal Palace," sermon given at Cheongpyeong, South Korea, December 28, 2007

250. *Cheon Seong Gyeong*, Book 11, Chpt. 2, Sec. 5, p. 1764

251. Dr. Michael Mickler, *40 Years in America*, (HSA-UWC, 2000), p. 6

252. Reverend Sun Myung Moon, "True Parents' Final Prayer at the Coronation for the Authority of the Liberation of God the King of

Kings," prayer given at Cheon Jeong Peace Museum, January 15, 2009

253. Reverend Sun Myung Moon, "In Search of the Origin of the Universe," speech given in Washington, D.C., August 1, 1996

254. *Cheon Seong Gyeong*, 2nd Edition, Book 1, Chpt. 4, Sec. 1, Verse 77, p. 116

Midway Position

255. *Cheon Seong Gyeong*, Book 10, Chpt. 1, Sec. 4, p. 1483

256. *Cheon Seong Gyeong*, 2nd Edition, Book 8, Chpt. 2, Sec. 2, Verse 12, p. 837

257. *Cheon Seong Gyeong*, 2nd Edition, Book 13, Chpt. 2, Sec. 1, Verse 9, p. 1390

258. Reverend Sun Myung Moon, "Home Church and the Completion of the Kingdom of Heaven," speech given at the World Mission Center, New York City, NY, January 1, 1979

259. Reverend Sun Myung Moon, *Blessing and Ideal Family, Volume I*, Part I, (Washington D.C.: FFWPU International, 1998), p. 95

260. Reverend Sun Myung Moon, *Exposition of the Divine Principle*, (HSA-UWC, 1996), Introduction to Restoration, Sec. 1, p. 176

261. Reverend Sun Myung Moon, *Exposition of the Divine Principle*, (HSA-UWC, 1996), Introduction to Restoration, Sec. 1, p. 176

262. *Cheon Seong Gyeong*, Book 11, Chpt. 2, Sec. 5, p. 1763

263. Reverend Sun Myung Moon, "The True Owners in Establishing the Kingdom of Peace and Unity in Heaven and on Earth," speech given in Seoul, South Korea, April 10, 2006

Ending Shame

264. *Cheon Seong Gyeong*, Book 1, Chpt. 2, Sec. 3, p. 100

265. *Cheon Seong Gyeong*, Book 4, Chpt. 7, Sec. 6, p. 486

266. *Cheon Seong Gyeong*, Book 8, Chpt. 2, Sec. 1, p. 1132

267. *Cheon Seong Gyeong*, Book 8, Chpt. 2, Sec. 4, p. 1145

268. *Cheon Seong Gyeong*, Book 11, Chpt. 2, Sec. 3, p. 1746-1747

269. *Cheon Seong Gyeong*, Book 3, Chpt. 2, Sec. 5, p. 366

270. *Cheon Seong Gyeong*, Book 11, Chpt. 2, Sec. 2, p. 1720

271. *Cheon Seong Gyeong*, Book 11, Chpt. 2, Sec. 2, p. 1719

272. *Cheon Seong Gyeong*, Book 3, Chpt. 2, Sec. 4, p. 359

273. Yoshihiko Masuda, *True Love, Sex, and Health: As Guided by the Words of True Parents* (Gapyeong: CheongShim GTS University Press, 2009), p. 183

Life Without Shadows

274. Reverend Sun Myung Moon, "Let This Be A Good Year," speech given at the World Mission Center, New York City, NY, January 2, 1983

275. *Cheon Seong Gyeong*, 2nd Edition, Book 12, Chpt. 3, Sec. 2, Verse 3, p. 1311

276. *Cheon Seong Gyeong*, 2nd Edition, Book 12, Chpt. 3, Sec. 2, Verse 1, p. 1310-1311

277. *Cheon Seong Gyeong*, 2nd Edition, Book 12, Chpt. 3, Sec. 2, Verse 2, p. 1311

278. *Cheon Seong Gyeong*, 2nd Edition, Book 4, Chpt. 3, Sec. 3, Verse 28, p. 446

279. *Cheon Seong Gyeong*, 2nd Edition, Book 4, Chpt. 3, Sec. 3, Verse 26, p. 445

280. Reverend Sun Myung Moon, "The Providential Meaning of the 44th True Children's Day," sermon given in Cheongpyeong, South Korea, October 25, 2003

281. Reverend Sun Myung Moon, "The Harmonization of Values, and the Liberation and Complete Settlement of the Realm Transcending Religions and Nations from the Providential Perspective," speech given in Rye Brook, NY, October 26, 2004

282. Dr. Andrew Wilson, *World Scripture and the Teachings of Sun Myung Moon*, (New York: Universal Peace Federation, 2007), p. 627

283. *The Way of Tradition, Volume III*, (HSA-UWC, 1980), p. 87

284. *The Way of God's Will*, (HSA-UWC, 1980), p. 199

285. *Cheon Seong Gyeong*, 2nd Edition, Book 8, Chpt. 1, Sec. 2, Verse 5, p. 803

286. *The Way of Tradition, Volume II*, (HSA-UWC, 1980), p. 100

The Pure Love Movement

287. *Cham Bumo Gyeong*, Book 4, Chpt. 3, Sec. 1, Verse 16, p. 378

288. *Cheon Seong Gyeong*, 2nd Edition, Book 13, Chpt. 2, Sec. 2, Verse 27, p. 1400

289. *Cham Bumo Gyeong*, Book 4, Chpt. 3, Sec. 1, Verse 12, p. 377

290. Reverend Sun Myung Moon, "The Harmonization of Values, and the Liberation and Complete Settlement of the Realm Transcending Religions and Nations from the Providential Perspective," speech given in Rye Brook, NY, October 26, 2004

291. *Cham Bumo Gyeong*, Book 4, Chpt. 3, Sec. 1, Verse 11, p. 376-377

292. *Cham Bumo Gyeong*, Book 4, Chpt. 3, Sec. 1, Verse 15, p. 378

293. Reverend Sun Myung Moon, "The Youth Culture Must Become a Pure Love Movement," speech given at the Third World Culture and Sports Festival, Washington, D.C., November 30, 1997

294. Reverend Sun Myung Moon, "The Youth Culture Must Become a Pure Love Movement," speech given at the Third World Culture and Sports Festival, Washington, D.C., November 30, 1997

295. Reverend Sun Myung Moon, "The Youth Culture Must Become a Pure Love Movement," speech given at the Third World Culture and Sports Festival, Washington, D.C., November 30, 1997

296. Reverend Sun Myung Moon, "The Youth Culture Must Become a Pure Love Movement," speech given at the Third World Culture and Sports Festival, Washington, D.C., November 30, 1997

297. Reverend Sun Myung Moon, "The Youth Culture Must Become a Pure Love Movement," speech given at the Third World Culture and Sports Festival, Washington, D.C., November 30, 1997

Bibliography

Bailey, Megan. "7 Godly Love Stories that Inspire." *Beliefnet.* 2019. https://www.beliefnet.com/love-family/relationships/marriage/7-godly-love-stories-that-inspire.aspx.

Ballard, Larry. "Multigenerational Legacies — The Story of Jonathan Edwards." July 1, 2017. https://www.ywam-fmi.org/news/multigenerational-legacies-the-story-of-jonathan-edwards/.

Bloom, Linda, and Charlie Bloom. "Want More and Better Sex? Get Married and Stay Married." *HuffPost.* July 13, 2017. https://www.huffpost.com/entry/want-more-and-better-sex-get-married-and-stay-married_b_5967b618e4b022bb9372aff2.

Librera Editrice Vaticana. *Catechism of the Catholic Church,* 2nd ed. Washington, D.C.: United States Conference of Catholic Bishops. 2019.

Gresh, Dannah. "Healthy Sexuality: Sending the Right Message to Your Kids." *Focus on the Family.* June 27, 2017. https://www.focusonthefamily.com/parenting/healthy-sexuality-sending-the-right-message-to-your-kids/.

Herbenick, Debby, Michael Reece, Vanessa Schick, Stephanie A. Sanders, Brian Dodge, and J. Dennis Fortenberry. "Sexual Behavior in the United States: Results from a National Probability Sample of Men and Women Ages 14–94." *The Journal of Sexual Medicine* 7 (October 2010): 255–65. https://doi.org/10.1111/j.1743-6109.2010.02012.x.

Homer. *The Odyssey.* Translated by Robert Fagles. New York: Penguin Group, 1996.

Izquierdo, Victoriano. "How Porn & Technology Might Be Replacing Sex for Japanese Millennials." *Fight the New Drug*. April 17, 2019. https://fightthenewdrug.org/how-porn-sex-technology-is-contributing-to-japans-sexless-population/.

Lee, Sang Hun. *Explaining Unification Thought*. Bridgeport: Unification Thought Institute, 1981.

Lee, Sang Hun. *Life in the Spirit World and on Earth: Messages from the Spirit World*. New York: Family Federation for World Peace and Unification, 1998.

Lickona, Thomas. "Ten Emotional Dangers of Premature Sexual Involvement." *Center for the 4th and 5th Rs* (2007). https://www2.cortland.edu/centers/character/images/sex_character/2007-Fall-red.pdf.

Lucado, Max. *You Are Special*. Wheaton: Crossway, 2011.

Luther, Martin. "The Estate of Marriage." Sermon, Germany, 1519.

Martelaro, Nikolas. "Turning Nuclear Weapons into Nuclear Power." Course work, Stanford University, March 23, 2017. http://large.stanford.edu/courses/2017/ph241/martelaro2/.

Masuda, Yoshihiko. *True Love, Sex, and Health: As Guided by the Words of True Parents*. Gapyeong: CheongShim GTS University Press, 2009.

McIlhaney, Joe S., and Freda McKissic Bush. *Hooked: New Science on How Casual Sex Is Affecting Our Children*. Chicago: Northfield Publishing, 2008.

Moon, Sun Myung. "In Search of the Origin of the Universe." tparents.org. HSA-UWC, August 1, 1996. http://www.tparents.org/Moon-Talks/SunMyungMoon96/SunMyungMoon-960801.pdf#search=%22in%20search%20of%20the%20origin%20of%20the%20universe%22.

Messora, Rene. "A child raised by many mothers: What we can learn about parenthood from an indigenous group in Brazil." *The Washington Post*. September 6, 2019. https://www.washingtonpost.com/lifestyle/2019/09/06/child-raised-by-many-mothers-what-we-can-learn-how-other-cultures-raise-their-children/.

Moon, Sun Myung. *As a Peace-Loving Global Citizen*. Washington D.C.: The Washington Times Foundation, 2010.

Pak, Joong Hyun. "Absolute Sex—Exploring Its Meaning." Sermon, Belvedere Estate, Tarrytown, NY, February 1, 1997. tparents.org. http://www.tparents.org/UNews/Unws9702/jpak9702.htm.

Roizen, Michael. *RealAge: Are You as Young as You Can Be?*. New York: William Morrow, 1999.

Made in the USA
Las Vegas, NV
17 May 2021

23235005R00160